EIGHT NATION MAKERS

Willard A. Hanna

Of the two hundred million people who populate the political jungles of Southeast Asia, some two hundred have contrived, for good or for ill, to create about ninety per cent of the uproar. Of these two hundred, twenty or so have managed to stand out for prolonged periods in the full heat of the midday sun. Eight of them, key figures, and generally the architects of new nations, plus some two score of their best friends and worst enemies are the subjects of this book. Since the architect is often the archetype of his nation, the lives of these eight and two score tropical politicians point the course of modern Southeast Asian society as well as its political history.

Indonesia's flamboyant President Sukarno dominates a cast which includes the Philippines' President Macapagal, Thailand's King Bhumibol, Burma's General Ne Win, Kong Le of Laos, Malaysia's Tengku Abdul Rahman, Cambodia's colorful Prince Sihanouk, and South Vietnam's late President Ngo Dinh Diem.

(Continued on back flap)

Eight Nation Makers

Southeast Asia's Charismatic Statesmen

by Willard A. Hanna

ST. MARTIN'S PRESS | NEW YORK

Acknowledgment is made to the American Universities Field Staff, Inc., New York, for permission to republish certain sections of this book which have already appeared in AUFS Reports.

Preface: Eight Out of Two Hundred Million

Of the two hundred million people who populate the political
jungles of Southeast Asia, some two hundred have contrived, for
good or for ill, to create about 90 per cent of the uproar. Of these
two hundred, twenty or so have managed to stand out for prolonged periods in the full heat of the midday political sun. Eight
of them, key figures, and generally the architects of new nations,
plus some twoscore of their best friends and worst enemies, are
the subjects of this book. Since the architect is often the archetype
of his nation, the lives of these eight and twoscore tropical politicians point the course of modern Southeast Asian society as well
as of its political history.

The cast of characters for this kaleidoscopic tableau coincides
approximately but not exactly with the list of principals at any
Southeast Asian summit meeting which might have been convened
about January 1, 1964. South Vietnam's late President Ngo Dinh
Diem, however, still receives feature billing, although he has
recently and tragically departed the scene, as may others before
this book is published. President Ho Chi Minh of North Vietnam
appears only in one walk-on bit. I myself have never been within
seeing or listening distance of Ho Chi Minh and I hesitate therefore even to introduce him. Indonesia's President Sukarno dominates the stage, but then Sukarno is by far the most flamboyant
figure of the lot, the head of the biggest, most important nation,
and I myself know him best—although neither he nor I would
suggest that the acquaintance is intimate. The Filipinos and the
Thais have produced so many matinee idols that most of them

have to be relegated to the wings in order to make space for the stage-struck President Macapagal and the stage-frightened King Bhumibol. Burma's testy dictator, General Ne Win, who shuns the footlights, is in any case up-staged by the jailed U Nu and the murdered Aung Sang, and the antic Laotian princelings yield precedence to the brash young commoner, Captain Kong Lê. Malaya's Tengku Abdul Rahman and Cambodia's Prince Sihanouk each, I trust, receives his deserts, the one as the region's most imperturbable, the other as its most frenetic prime minister.

These are the bold new leaders of a brave new-old world, but most of them are aging fast and their experiences have made others and sometimes even themselves sadder and possibly wiser. They are men of extraordinary personal attainment and versatility, quite self-assured in at least two languages, two cultures, and two world blocs, acting and reacting sometimes within one frame of reference, sometimes within another. What each of them thinks, says, or does gives the cue to what some two million to one hundred million people are going to think, say, or do, but the cues are quickly reversible. Enigmas to the outside world, these men are enigmas also to each other, for most of them know Washington, Moscow, and Peking better than the capital cities of their neighbors, and state visits notwithstanding, they still mistake the official communiqué for communication. It is time they were brought publicly together, with dossiers replacing protocol.

I wish to express to my involuntary subjects my appreciation of the fact that they have generously provided material far beyond any biographer's ability to sort out unless they themselves can be provoked by essays such as mine to the labors of autobiography. While acknowledging debts of gratitude, let me also mention: the American Universities Field Staff, which places a liberal construction upon my peripatetic employment; the General Service Foundation, which has made extra funds available without bureaucratic entanglement; the hundreds of persons who contributed, through their writings or their conversations, knowingly or unknowingly, to the bulk of my files; and finally, my wife, whose sure instinct for style and error has made my rewriting job more than doubly difficult. No small degree of censure or credit, however, attaches to myself. For many years in many lands

I have diligently peered, pried, and prodded into private and public lives, impelled by the notion that politics is people, the politics of underdeveloped areas is people of overdeveloped politics, and Southeast Asian politicians, as people, are extra-special specimens.

Sedona, Arizona
January 2, 1964

Contents

Eight Nation Makers

Sukarno: The Devolution of a Revolutionary

Indonesia's President Sukarno, known to himself, his admirers, and his detractors alike as Bung Karno, is the prototype of the contemporary Indonesian at his best and at his worst. Brilliant, ebullient, handsome, mellifluous, dynamic, magnetic—pick any adjective signifying an extraordinarily attractive personality and it applies, or it once applied to Bung Karno. But so too do the adjectives reckless, profligate, and paranoiac. Those which do not fit Bung Karno are any which signify moderation. Bung Karno is an exhibitionistic extremist who cultivates contradiction and controversy in the full realization that they make him a man whom it is impossible to ignore.

For many people—a fast dwindling number in the Western world—Bung Karno symbolizes the new Indonesia, driving, leaping, and surging ahead to achieve its manifest destiny as the world's fifth most populous nation and one of those in all respects most richly endowed by nature. For many others, including many more Indonesians than dare to say so, Bung Karno personifies the tragic betrayal of a nationalist revolution into the grasp of as unscrupulous a lot of opportunists as Southeast Asia has produced in modern times, a clique of ofttimes plausible and almost always personable rogues who model their conduct upon Bung Karno's own. For others, the inevitable focus of attention on Bung Karno illustrates the fallacy of attributing to one man primary responsibility for the immensely complicated affairs of a new nation-state. Bung Karno, nevertheless, has certainly been the kinetic and the catalytic agent in Indonesian national development ever since

1927, and his role since 1957 has been climacteric. As Bung Karno now whirls about the Indonesian archipelago and the rest of the globe, "easing" the tensions which he himself creates, his political gyrations are explainable only on the basis of his personal evolution and devolution as a revolutionary.

Bung Karno, then, absolutely commands attention and, as a strict matter of record, he has come to rely upon attention-commanding devices which vitiate his own better nature. To resort to rhetorical summation such as appeals to Bung Karno himself, he is the demagogue-demigod, the philosopher-philanderer, the miracle man-medicine man, the hero-villain of the melodramatic Indonesian revolution which he keeps revving up to a higher and higher pitch of emotional fervor. He is also the ordinary Indonesian magnified to quite extraordinary proportions, at his best a sparkling human individual, at his worst deliberately impervious to anyone else's concept of organization, rationality, responsibility, or indeed, to introduce an even more tendentious element, of political or personal morality. The Bung Karno of a few years ago was a national and an international speculation on whom a very great many people placed heavy stakes. Today Bung Karno's stock has depreciated to the point where Americans, Russians, Chinese, Japanese, Australians, British and others, including his closest Indonesian associates, are ready to sell short the moment they can see any alternative investment, their calculation being complicated, to be sure, by the unhappy fact that if they have been dealing in Bung Karno's own Indonesian *rupiahs,* their money is already virtually worthless.

PUPIL AND PRODIGY

About Sukarno's childhood and youth the nationalist myth has long since crystallized. Until his familiars write and publish their unvarnished memoirs, as none of them seems at all disposed to do, there is no alternative save to report the legend, which, to be sure, embodies important elements of fact. The story of Sukarno's early years, as it is now told in Indonesia, is not that of the enslaved peasant boy emancipating himself from evil feudal or foreign masters, as it might have been had the telling been delayed until recent years. Rather it is something akin to a tropical idyll of the Java highlands, close to regions favored by the small, clever *kantjil* (mouse deer) and of the huge, fierce *banteng* (wild buffalo), both of which are featured in the Javanese folklore which the young Sukarno knew long before he began hearing about the crocodilelike colonial exploiters.

Sukarno was born on June 6, 1901, in Surabaja, the first son of a minor Javanese aristocrat, Raden Sukemi, and his beautiful Balinese commoner wife, Ida Njoman Rai. Raden Sukemi, a young schoolteacher, had been assigned to the island of Bali where he fell in love and married. Local opposition to the union of a Javanese and a Balinese proved to be so great, however, that the couple moved to Java and never returned. By birth, then, Sukarno combined the Javanese Muslim and the Balinese Hindu influences. From his father's line he inherited the affinity of the Javanese for mysticism and intrigue, from his mother's the glowing mental and physical vigor and the artistic instinct of the Balinese. Sukarno, who was destined to become the architect of an independent nation uniting a dozen mutually suspicious ethnic and dozens of linguistic groups, is himself a living witness that such a union can be fruitful but also that conflict is real. He has achieved national unity by arbitrarily imposing Javanese domination over semiresentful regions. Bali, the "paradise" and "temple" island of an astoundingly artistic and anachronistic Hindu people, has been especially loath to be Indonesianized and hence "exploited." Bali today is Sukarno's favorite retreat, but at Tampaksiring where he has pre-empted a hilltop overlooking a sacred spring and bathing pool as the site of one of his most stately pleasure domes, Sukarno is not a truly welcome guest.

Sukarno's parents gave him the name Kusnasosrosukarno, from which he himself early on dropped the "Kusnasosro." He never adopted the "Achmad" which foreign newspapers, encyclopedias, even some Indonesian sources sometimes attribute to him, misled by foreign correspondents who assumed back in 1945, when they first encountered him, that he must have a second name and that it might be Achmad. Neither did he ever adopt his father's name as a family name, a recent Indonesian innovation which Sukarno does not follow. He signs himself "Soekarno," retaining the Dutchified spelling, but the modern Indonesian usage and the official version is "Sukarno." Two further technicalities: the resonant redundancy of the name Kusnasosrosukarno proclaims at once to the initiate that its bearer belongs to the Javanese ruler class, a fact which Sukarno has never been eager to underscore, even in recent years since his pretensions have become regal; the attribution to his birth of a specific day, month, and year implies that he was no ordinary child, for birth dates, like business, social, and political commitments, are left casually imprecise by the vast majority of Indonesians.

Sukarno's father earned a schoolteacher's salary, that is to say, about 27.50 florins per month, or the equivalent of U.S. $11.00. He followed the not unusual Indonesian practice, therefore, of letting his son live with those who could and would give him better opportunity. The young Kusnasosrosukarno, being a remarkably handsome and precociously intelligent child, was not difficult to place. During his early youth he spent most of his time with his paternal grandparents in the village of Tulungagung, and in his mid-teens he entered the home of a foster parent in Surabaja. Despite prolonged periods of separation from his parents, he maintained a deep attachment for them. His father died in Djakarta during the Japanese occupation, but his mother survived until recent years, living very simply and quietly with his sister in the town of Blitar, not far from Surabaja. There Sukarno paid occasional visits, during which he displayed all the traditional marks of filial piety, his visits corresponding, his intimates point out, to periods of special crisis in his own personal or political career.

Sukarno's extraordinary gifts were recognized and applauded almost from the time he was born. His grandparents, naturally, spoiled him badly, his foster parents indulged him, and nobody ever entertained any doubt that he was a prodigy. His youthful nickname, "Djago," meaning "champion" but also "rooster," signified the strut, plumage, and courage of a prized fighting cock. Young Djago, according to the Sukarno apocrypha, dared to climb the tallest trees when his more timid companions held back. His kite flew highest. His crickets chirped loudest and kicked hardest. He caught the biggest fish, won the most and best marbles, and most consistently picked the winners in the pigeon races. Of all the village boys, he was the most dexterous in keeping the *ragam,* or wicker ball, in the air, flicking it not just with toe or heel, but with instep, ankle, wrist, elbow, shoulder, and head. He could dance and sing. He was a good student, but not too good; in fact, said his proud elders, he was a bit *"nakal"* (naughty), preferring daydreams to the droning recitation, using his slate less skillfully for sums than for drawing the *wajang* (Javanese puppet) figures he dreamed about. Even more than most of the village boys, young Djago was an amateur of the *wajang* shows. At village celebrations he would watch from dusk to dawn the glorious romances and adventures of the *wajang* representation of the *Ramayana*. He knew every story and every character. He could imitate the *dalang,* the puppeteer-narrator, in giving for every puppet, whether god, hero, ogre, or clown, the precise dramatic intonations. He could imitate the conventionalized gestures, postures, and movements of the puppets. He also knew the music which accompanied the performances.

To this day *wajang* remains Sukarno's passion. The profession of the *dalang*—one of the highly skilled, highly paid, highly respected traditional callings of Indonesia even today—lost a superb practitioner when Sukarno was diverted to other endeavors. Sukarno's addiction to *wajang* has resulted in recent years in summonses to the Djakarta diplomatic corps on very short notice to turn out for almost night-long performances. Some of the less culture-conscious diplomats enjoy the *wajang* shows even less than they enjoy other palace parties at which all guests are commonly required to sing and dance with gay abandon, but only until about one o'clock in the morning. Any diplomat who really observes and listens to the palace *dalang,* however, can be improving his time by learning to understand Sukarno. The *dalang* animates the delicately incised leather *wajang* figures, flashing them between the flickering oil lamp and the shadow screen, creating the illusion that gods and demons, princes and ordinary mortals all interact daily upon each other under the most implausible circumstances. The action is headlong; the heroes are reckless; yet intervals of abstruse moralizing monologue serve to hold even the most frenetic action in apparently interminable suspense. The motivations are as obscure as the plots are intricate, save that, whatever the appearance of mere violence or lust or vengeance as the theme, the leading characters represent the forces of virtue, or at any rate of valor, and almost always they emerge triumphant, even though they must rely upon supernatural intervention. Sukarno's own favorite *wajang* character is Bima, whose name he later adopted as a nom de plume and into whose image he projects himself. Of all the *wajang* heroes, Bima is one of the most rash and arrogant, and also, of course, one of the most valorous.

The young Sukarno daydreamed of *wajang* when he was presumably at work on his lessons; he understudied the *dalang* when he crowded in with the other small boys as close to the screen as their elders would tolerate. By living vicariously the involved epics of the heroes, he absorbed something of their conflicting values. Today Sukarno believes that he himself and the Indonesian nation can disregard ordinary cause-consequence relationships as the Western world knows them. In doing so, he believes, they can sustain a vastly bewildering lot of nonconsecutive, nonresolving complications which will command the world's startled attention, as indeed they do. Anyone who seeks to impose upon Sukarno's personal development or upon that of the independent Indonesia over which he presides any pattern comprehensible to the Western mind would do well first to analyze in Western terms the plots of the Indian epics, then to define the precise nature and extent of Indonesian adaptations, then to psychoanalyze Ardjuna, Petrok, and Bima. To do so, however, is to risk coming to the conclusion that modern Indonesian history defeats the standard Western historiographic approach.

Sukarno, for all his outside interests, progressed nicely through village primary school and moved on to Europse Lagere School in the East Java mountain town of Modjokerto. There, under the moderately watchful eye and stern hand of his father, at that time a teacher in the same school, he began to excel as a student. He acquired a fluent command of Dutch, and, studying with a tutor, he began to learn French as well. At this point he attracted the favorable attention of a well-to-do patron. Soon he left Modjokerto to enter his patron's home and to study in a Dutch secondary school in Surabaja.

Sukarno's sponsor and foster parent was one H. O. S. Tjokroaminoto, an editor, businessman, teacher, and political organizer. A gentleman of such astonishingly eclectic tastes that he could reconcile in his own philosophy major elements of Islam, Marx, Shaw, and other systems as unlikely to blend, Tjokroaminoto had been instrumental in 1911 in the establishment of Indonesia's first true political party, the Serikat Islam. About Tjokroaminoto rallied at first various Indonesian businessmen—a minute class at the time—seeking to safeguard Indonesian commerce against the further inroads of the Chinese and of the Dutch, and Indonesian religious leaders seeking to sustain and quicken the Muslim faith. Whether merchants or *kiais,* Tjokroaminoto's early colleagues were also incipient nationalists. They became politically conscious and active when the Serikat Islam attracted also the leaders of Indonesia's new intellectual class—doctors, lawyers, educators, civil servants, editors, labor union organizers, some of the most conspicuous of the latter group being Eurasian or Dutch. The Serikat Islam established branches throughout the nation, and Tjokroaminoto's Surabaja home became the general clearing house also, such was the Indonesian custom of the extended family and of all-inclusive hospitality, the rooming and boarding house as well, a kind of Serikat Islam *asrama.* There might not be enough beds, but there was plenty of floor space on which one or a dozen could spread out cool pandanus sleeping mats and settle in for a night or for a long succession of nights. The kitchen was capable of keeping a big kettle of rice and various spicy side dishes always ready for anyone who cared at any time of day to make a meal. On the spacious, shaded veranda visitors could settle in for hours on end while relays of callers casually came and went. Glasses and cups were kept replenished with heavily sweetened coffee or tea, packages of funnel-shaped clove-flavored cigarettes seemed inexhaustible, and under the circumstances, relaxed conversation knew no let or hindrance. Into this home and into this company, H. O. S. Tjokroaminoto introduced the young Sukarno as his special protégé.

Sukarno then, at the age of fourteen, made his appearance at the control center of the new nationalist movement. He enrolled as a student in the Dutch secondary school and in 1920 he was graduated. His real education, however, was his life in the politically macaronic Tjokroaminoto household. In it he met and generally grew to know, to admire, and to emulate the new Indonesian nationalist leaders, men who themselves spanned the political spectrum from Muslim theocrat to Marxist theorist. Sneevleet, the Dutch founder of the Indonesian Communist Party (the PKI), was an intimate of Tjokroaminoto's, and to Sneevleet even today Sukarno pays the most glowing tribute. Alimin and Semaun and Tan Malaka, who picked up the Marxist torch when Sneevleet was exiled, were also among Tjokroaminoto's associates, although only Alimin seems to have been an intimate. About Alimin, who triggered a bloody little pro-Communist anti-Sukarno insurrection in 1948, Sukarno has since been silent. About Tan Malaka, who conspired against him in 1946 but joined him in 1948, his feelings are mixed. Since 1956, when he brought him home from exile in Moscow, Sukarno has had second thoughts about Semaun, who has proved embarrassingly full of suggestions, some of them far to the right of the Sukarno line.

If the Communists were conspicuous at Tjokroaminoto's, so too was Hadji Agus Salim, who stood for Muslim religious modernism and Western democratic progress and constituted himself so effective a gadfly of the Communists that they were almost relieved when the Serikat Islam in 1921 expelled them. Hadji Agus Salim many years later and much more quietly opposed Sukarno and thereupon passed into political eclipse even before his death in 1954. Among others who frequented the Tjokroaminoto ménage were Hamka, the inspiration of the religiously-minded youth; Ki Hadjar Dewantoro, founder of a nationwide system of private schools of high nationalistic voltage; Kartosuwirjo, a mystic who later became leader of the fanatical and militant Darul Islam movement and in 1963 was finally captured and executed.

From the Serikat Islam Sukarno inherited no systematic philosophy; rather, he inherited an eclecticism so comprehensive that even today, after he has spent over four decades defining his own beliefs, he yearns to gather around himself all those who hold to any other, however divergent, provided only they do not personally oppose him. The Tjokroaminoto home is the model, obviously, for the "family board" around which Sukarno of late has urged all Indonesian political factions of whatever hue peacefully and happily to reunite, with him, *Papak Indonesia,* as paterfamilias.

Back in 1920, under Tjokroaminoto, the system—or rather, the systemlessness—worked out remarkably well. Most of the members of the clique were just then in process of formulating their own political, economic, and social beliefs. They were eager for discussion and debate. Most of them, furthermore, were men of great personal appeal and of astounding intellectual attainment. Thanks to a Dutch-style education, they were frequently fluent in Dutch, German, French, and English, and were sometimes equipped with considerable Latin, Greek, or Sanskrit as well. Since they needed it to study the Koran, many of them had learned Arabic. They were always proficient besides in at least two Indonesian languages and commonly more. They read and discussed Kant, Hegel, and Schopenhauer, Rousseau, Voltaire, and Renan, Abraham Lincoln and Thomas Jefferson, Sun Yat-sen and the Emperor Meiji, Rizal and Ataturk, also, when Sneevleet bootlegged it to them, the doctrine of Karl Marx. They were avid to know more about the Japanese, the Chinese, the Turkish, the Russian, as well as the French, the American, and for that matter, the Dutch revolutions. If this sounds rather too intense, they were not, it should at once be acknowledged, assembled in continuous intellectual séance in Tjokroaminoto's home. Many of them had plenty of leisure for the more relaxed pleasures of indolence, contemplation, and polygamy.

The young Sukarno, who had already acquired a knowledge of Dutch and French and was rapidly improving his German and English, proved a worthy disciple, one who was almost overendowed with a near photographic memory and total recall. Naturally he became the favorite of the group. Under the special guidance of Tjokroaminoto, who was himself a spellbinding orator and a brilliant writer, Sukarno learned to speak and to write with an effectiveness far beyond his years. He became a frequent editorial contributor, for instance, under the pen-name of Bima, to Tjokroaminoto's newspaper, *Utusan Hindia*. As an extra dash of versatility, he contributed cartoons as well as articles. He became a popular speaker of the Tri Koro Darmo, a youth group closely associated with the Serikat Islam. In Tjokroaminoto's home, he was a constant auditor and increasingly a participant in discussions which went on and on about any subject which might be raised by a group of men who were virtually all of them exceptionally skilled raconteurs and dialecticians.

Tjokroaminoto himself thought so highly of Sukarno's abilities and promise that he decided upon a relationship more binding than that of foster parent and announced Sukarno's engagement to his own daughter. Soon afterward, although the girl, Sitti Utari, was still too young to become a wife, Tjokroaminoto caused to be performed what is called in Indonesia a "suspended marriage." Tjokroaminoto was determined also to make it possible for Sukarno to continue his education and entered him in the newly established Dutch technical school in Bandung. Sukarno, it seems, preferred engineering to medicine, the other possible alternative in Indonesian higher education in those days, one which was then attracting considerable numbers of Indonesia's future leaders to the Medical Faculty in Batavia.

In Bandung, Sukarno was one of eleven Indonesian students who enrolled along with many more Chinese, Eurasians, and Dutch in the new technical school. There he proved himself a good but rather casual student, interested primarily in extracurricular rather than academic activities. Soon after arriving in Bandung he fell in with a small group of bright young men recently returned from university studies in Holland, where they had been inspired with liberal democratic—and in some cases extreme Marxist—principles, which they found difficult to reconcile with the colonial climate of Indonesia. He came under the influence also of three older men whose names were then becoming at least as significant as Tjokroaminoto's. One was Eduard F. E. Douwes Decker, the Dutch-Eurasian relative of the author of a sensational novel, *Max Havelaar,* a nineteenth-century exposé of the evils of colonialism. The second was Tan Malaka, the top Indonesian Communist, then an exile and a fugitive abroad, whose writings were being circulated clandestinely inside Indonesia by his friends. The third was Dr. Tjipto Mangunkusumo, a medical doctor and one of the most outspoken of the early nationalists. At the same time that he was breaking into the more mature intellectual set—more by indirect than by direct association, since Tan Malaka was absent and the others were never as accessible to him as had been the Tjokroaminoto group—Sukarno took up with what was for those days a fast-moving set of bold young blades. His quick intelligence, his good looks, his personal charm, and his precocious assumption of leadership all served to mark him out quickly as the most debonair and, from the point of view of the Dutch, the most dangerous young Indonesian in Bandung. In that beautiful mountain city, good climate, good food, and good educational facilities all served to quicken the pace and the pulse of life which elsewhere in Indonesia was still sleepy.

In Bandung, as he began to move in new company, Sukarno cut loose from the Tjokroaminoto ties. For a brief period, however, it seemed that the old relationship would be strengthened rather than weakened. Tjokroaminoto himself was arrested by the Dutch on suspicion of implication in some labor disorders. Sukarno, on hearing the news, returned to Surabaja to help the family and remained there for the full six-month term of Tjokroaminoto's detention. During this period Sukarno took the one and only nonpolitical job he was ever to hold. He worked with the state railway administration for about fl. 100 per month, the only regular salary he drew until many years later. On Tjokroaminoto's release from jail, Sukarno resigned from his job and returned to Bandung, this time accompanied by his young wife, Sitti Utari. From all reports, the marriage never had a chance of success. Sukarno was already involved with other women, and after a few months of uneasy wedded life he sent Sitti Utari back to her parents. He later intimated to his friends that growing political differences between himself and his father-in-law were a major cause of the failure of the marriage. Whatever the facts of the case, Sukarno broke with the Tjokroaminoto family and divorced Sitti Utari, who later remarried and now lives in Surabaja. Sukarno himself presently married his landlady, Inggit Garnisih, then newly divorced from a well-to-do and highly respected elderly gentleman, by name of Hadji Sanusi.

Sukarno's friends had grave misgivings about this new match. Inggit Garnisih was considerably older than he, and being a woman of no great educational attainment, she seemed unlikely to fit very easily into his particular circle of friends. Nevertheless, for a period of fifteen years the marriage proved reasonably happy, even though to Sukarno's great disappointment his new wife bore him no children. Inggit Garnisih, to anticipate the chronology of the narrative a bit, remained Sukarno's wife during his imprisonment and exile, and to her patience, encouragement, and inspiration he paid frequent tribute. He divorced her, however, during the Japanese occupation, whether before or after marrying his third wife, Fatmawati, is not quite clear, although from the Muslim point of view it does not greatly matter. Today Inggit Garnisih lives obscurely but comfortably in Bandung, where Sukarno occasionally pays her a call, and Fatmawati has yielded priority to a new wife, Hartini, in the palace.

LION OF THE PODIUM, PAPAK KAUM MARHAEN, BANTENG REPOLUSI, THE BUNG AMONG BUNGS

Sukarno took his degree in engineering in 1925, or possibly in 1926, as he himself sometimes says, the exact date being one of an infinite number of details never easy to verify, with which his future biographers may have trouble. As his graduation thesis he submitted a paper on port layout, a study which the frustrated foreign expediters in Djakarta's chronically bottlenecked port of Tandjung Priok today might find interesting to read. For a few months he toyed with the idea of accepting a good paying job. He had offers from several foreign and capitalistic concerns, one of them, he intimates, the Shell Oil Company. His salary would have been fl. 480 per month (about U.S. $150), an excellent salary for that time—enough, he says, for a house, a car, and a "soft mattress"; but he declined to become an "exploited proletarian." He did consent, it seems, to take on a couple of part-time commissions. One involved work on the plans for the Dutch Protestant Church in Bandung, another the plans for Sukamiskin, a new Bandung prison in which he himself was soon to become a tenant. But this basic job decision, if it was ever in question at all, was not in doubt for long. Politics was already an avocation which excluded a profession.

Bung Karno, relying upon his wife's income and the voluntary contributions of his political associates for support, turned full-time political operator. Engineering, a profession in which opportunity was then only slightly less limited and one which is still sadly neglected in Indonesia, lost a lightning-quick computer of strains and stresses. Already, however, Sukarno had become adjusted, in fact addicted, to the role not of the professional man but of the romantic political idol. He was both the model and the envy of virtually all of Bandung's Indonesian youth and the center of a rapidly coalescing group that was then in process of designing a nationalist movement of its own. Consequently, he rated at the top of the suspect list of the Bandung Dutch police, and he already entertained intimations of persecution, prosecution, martyrdom, and canonization. He already saw himself as the great Bung Karno, the nation's hero. As a matter of strict chronological and semantic fact, he was just beginning to be called "Bung," the term—deriving from *abang* or *bang,* for "elder brother"—which had just recently been coined as a personal salutation favored among the revolutionaries. Of all the Bungs, from the very beginning Bung Karno was unquestionably The Bung, just as later he was to become Bung Besar (The Big Bung), and today, Bung Besar-Besar (The Big, Big Bung).

Bung Karno's Surabaja period as the political novice in a whole *asrama* of masters was now well behind him. His association in Bandung with the more single-mindedly purposeful proselytizers, some highly trained by the Dutch, led him to head a movement of his own. Among his close associates were men whose very names now recall to the initiate quite a good deal of Indonesian nationalist history. There was Isqak, for instance, who was later to become a cabinet minister and still later to go to jail for rather extravagantly ostentatious corruption, and later yet to be pardoned by Sukarno while lesser offenders moldered away in their cells. There was Sartono, who was later to become president of Parliament and still later, not long before his death, boldly but ineffectually to protest Sukarno's dissolution of Parliament. There was Sunarjo, who was to become Minister of Foreign Affairs, then ambassador to the Court of St. James, then to pass into an obscurity too dense to invite Sukarno's "retooling." With these men at his side, Sukarno organized what he called the Algemeene Studieclub (General Study Club) in which young men banded together to achieve "self-improvement" which the Dutch police correctly assumed to entail self-assertion. He began training cadres who were not slow to establish liaison with the numerous other Algemeene Studieclubs which suddenly became the rage among the nation's youth. As study clubs proliferated, they became rivals in influence to the Serikat Islam, also to the few little Communist cells which remained when the Dutch, after experiencing scattered Communist disorders in 1926 and 1927, conducted a nation-

wide mop-up campaign. On July 4, 1927 (no symbolical significance attaches to the date) Sukarno organized into the Perseri-
katan Nasional Indonesia (Indonesian Nationalist Union) as
many of these ofttimes ephemeral groups as he could get to send
representatives or to assign proxies. In 1928 he graduated this
rather insubstantial federation into its second and openly political
phase as the Partai Nasional Indonesia. This organization, after
passing through successive mutations too transient and complicated to trace, eventually became the giant postwar PNI which,
in the course of the last few years, Sukarno has sought quite successfully to cripple.

For Sukarno, even in the 1920's, organization as such was tedious and such organizational details as membership, program, and
financing were for lesser men. As a matter of fact, these lesser
men themselves felt indisposed for such chores and preferred instead to join Sukarno in the exciting charades of politics disguised
as enlightenment. During the late 1920's, consequently, Bandung
was the scene of a rapidly accelerating political awakening which
manifested itself not half so much as the result of consecutive organizational effort as of sudden fits and starts of quasi-cultural,
quasi-religious, quasi-educational societies which, whatever the
announced purpose and program, turned out to be political. One
group after another, and frequently the same group under a succession of different names, would hold public meetings at which
would appear well-known speakers. More and more frequently,
and more and more prominently these organizations featured
Bung Karno.

Sukarno was an accomplished orator to begin with and soon
he became a sensation. *"Berapi-api"* (fiery) was the term almost
inevitably used to describe him, and more often than not he was
incandescent. Then as now, Bung Karno was endowed with a
splendid presence and an unsurpassed delivery. He was handsome,
eloquent, impassioned, a master of all the rhetorical devices of
catchword, interruption, repetition, climax, and surprise. His eyes
"flashed," his voice "thundered." His precise diction with a beautifully rolled and trilled Javanese *r*, his mellifluous sentence
rhythm, his genius for self-dramatization—none of this was lost
upon an Indonesian audience which knew the *wajang* theater and
was delighted to discover that politics could compete. Bung

Karno even then worked his unfailing trick of urging the audience to roar out antiphonal responses to his slogans, so that even the simplest peasant—a rare creature, however, in an audience of that period—had the illusion that he understood and approved what Sukarno said. When Bung Karno was in really good voice, men shouted, women wept, youths went into near-hypnotic trances, and the effect was electric. The Dutch police, for instance, were so shocked on several occasions that they halted Bung Karno in mid-period. The Indonesian audiences, delighted that the Dutch shared their appraisal, promptly dubbed Bung Karno "The Lion of the Podium."

Bung Karno's exact message during this early period is a bit difficult to reconstruct. It has come down through Indonesian nationalist history as a combination of *Trilogi, Merdeka,* and *Marhaenisme,* all of which require some explaining. Technically speaking, the *Trilogi* was three slogans: *semangat kebangsaan* (national soul), *kemauan kebangsaan* (national will), and *bakti kebangsaan* (national service). In the course of several years of oratory, national soul, will, and service all fused into Merdeka (independence). Merdeka itself signified, of course, liberation from colonialism, capitalism, and imperialism, a repellent alien trio which profaned the sacred Indonesian Trilogi. On any of these slogans, Bung Karno could orate for hours on end, and it is perhaps fairest to leave to some future researcher any recapitulation of what, exactly, he may have said, and how it corresponds to his present message of "Indonesian Identity" vis-à-vis "neo-colonialism." Marhaenism, however, cannot be quite so casually dismissed, since it has evolved into the basic philosophy of the great PNI. Even now, although the PNI itself has been nearly razed, Marhaenism remains a major albeit movable pillar in the façade of a state philosophy which Bung Karno keeps re-embellishing.

Marhaenism, originally, was more a dodge than a dogma. At the time of his revelation of Marhaenism, Bung Karno was in serious trouble with the Dutch over a matter of political semantics. "All I said," Bung Karno reminisces today, "was that if I were a BPM [Shell Oil Company] employee, I would have been a proletarian. I was referring to the senior Indonesian official who was nevertheless a laborer since he sold his skill to the colonial government. He drove a car but he was a proletarian all the same. The Dutch Secret Police stopped me in my speech and thereafter I was forbidden to use the term 'proletarian' to describe the Indonesians, who consisted of tens of millions of impoverished people."

With the term "proletarian" interdicted, Bung Karno sought what in Indonesia is always called a "way out." He happened onto it one day as he was walking in the hills near Bandung. There, he says, he encountered a young peasant, who worked his own small plot of land with his own tools, disposed of his own rice crop, but from his land and his labor was still unable adequately to feed and clothe himself, his wife, and his four children. His name was Marhaen. In a flash of intuition, Bung Karno had the answer to his linguistic dilemma. Marhaen and Marhaenism—not exactly Marxist in derivation, but almost; these would serve to describe the Indonesian masses and his program for them, and the Dutch could not protest. He himself—*Papak Kaum Marhaen* (Father of the Marhaen) as he was soon to be called—was following his own true Indonesian inspiration, and Marhaen, rather than being a Caucasian serf, was an independent Sundanese peasant who owned his own land, tools, and crops. Today, still exploiting the Marhaen, whose despoliation since Merdeka he attributes to the "neocolonialists," Bung Karno has now relabeled the old "Message of the Marhaen" as "The Message of the People's Suffering," of which he himself has been formally designated "The Custodian."

Nobody except Bung Karno himself seems ever actually to have made the acquaintance of Marhaen, and there are some who say he was in fact a philosophical peasant with whom young Kusnasosrosukarno had consorted many years earlier. Nor does anyone except Bung Karno seem ever actually to have met another important supporting character in the cast of the Indonesian nationalist drama. Her name was Sarinah and she was a humble servant girl from whom Bung Karno learned about feminine charm, charity, and chastity, also, it seems, something about national soul, will, and service. Sarinah has starred in many a Sukarno speech; she has served as heroine in a book of Sukarno homilies, written and published in Jogjakarta during the revolution and since then translated into Russian, in which it has enjoyed a brisk sale and has earned tidy royalties. Sarinah today is also the patroness after whom is to be named a big new Japanese department store now a-building in Djakarta, with several branches already being planned for other cities. In this emporium, it is to be presumed, the ordinary Indonesian woman will find at last, among the novelties and the luxuries, the rice, textiles, cooking oil and other essentials which were in copious supply at low prices for Sarinah in 1927 but are in critically short supply at prohibitive prices today.

Sarinah and Marhaen shared one important characteristic with the vast majority of the Indonesian people: they did not understand Marhaenism. For Marhaenism, according to the 1952 *Manifesto Marhaenisme,* based, one can but assume, upon empirical investigation, is officially defined as follows:

"Marhaenism is the formulation and reflection of the ideals, ideas, thoughts, and emotions as to State and Society, that *potentially* [italics added] slumber in the minds and hearts of the Marhaen-masses, who are unable to express these things for themselves. Understanding the *unvoiced ideals* [italics added] of these masses, the Marhaenists long ago embarked upon the task of translating and formulating those ideals into Marhaenism and of guiding them and fighting alongside them for its realization."

Sukarno's "Message of the Marhaen" and his slogans of the Trilogi, inflammatory as they may have seemed at the time, were nevertheless far more an indictment of colonialism than incitement to revolution. The Marhaen were not consciously aware either of their own aspirations or of their own potential, not even of their aspiration toward independence or the possibility of achieving it. It was the duty of the Indonesian elite to extrapolate from and interpolate into the healthy but still amorphous minds of the Marhaen the dedication to Merdeka. This dedication, once formulated and accepted, would somehow lead to independence. Sukarno did not in the 1920's specify any procedure or schedule; but the assumption, perhaps a deliberately misleading assumption calculated for the benefit of the Dutch, was that it would be achieved by evolutionary rather than revolutionary stages.

In the 1920's, then, Bung Karno had not yet taken over the doctrine of violent revolution which had already been developed by the Indonesian Communists, most specifically by Tan Malaka, who was already in exile. Bung Karno and the other Indonesian nationalist leaders were well aware, however, of the Tan Malaka thesis, particularly as it was defined in two key documents written and published abroad but smuggled back into Indonesia. In the first of these, *Massa Aksi* ("Mass Action," Singapore, 1924), Tan Malaka expounded upon the theory and practice of instigating the proletariat to violent uprising; in the second, *Menudju Republik Indonesia* ("Toward the Republic of Indonesia," Singapore, 1927), he defined his revolutionary objective—Indonesian independence. Bung Karno, however, rather than devoting himself to the workers and the peasants and to revolutionary agitation, as Bung Tan Malaka would have recommended, was concentrating upon the bourgeoisie, the intellectual elite, and academic discussion. As chosen agents for revealing to the Marhaen its own as yet unfelt, unvoiced aspirations, he recruited cadres of secondary and university students. He organized these young urban sophisticates into study clubs in which they discussed the workings of the Dutch-dominated Volksraad (Parliament) in Batavia and the operation of Dutch plantations in Sumatra and tin mines on Banka. The Sukarno cadres were far less diffuse in their interests than those presently to be fathered by Sutan Sjahrir, and far less pedestrian than Mohammad Hatta's, but they were quite certainly not rice-roots, greasy-overalls types.

Hatta, Sjahrir, and Tan Malaka keep popping into and out of any account of Bung Karno's career, and all demand more formal introduction, first of all Tan Malaka, who featured the most dramatically of them all, and in the end with the greatest degree of dramatic irony. The one individual who has ever seriously challenged Sukarno's hold upon the Indonesian nation, Tan Malaka is also the only person whom Sukarno in his mature years regarded as a mentor rather than as a disciple. Sukarno, in fact, after long resisting or even opposing Tan Malaka's doctrines, eventually took them over as his own. Tan Malaka can be introduced into a Sukarno biography, however, only at the risk of diverting attention to his own autobiography, aptly entitled *Dari Pendjara ke Pendjara* ("From Jail to Jail").

Quite frankly then to digress, Tan Malaka started off life as a poor but brilliant son of the Minangkabau, the Sumatran highlands region which has produced a majority of Indonesia's top intellectual and political leaders, including Hatta, Sjahrir, and Hadji Agus Salim. The youthful Tan Malaka so impressed his Dutch teachers that they sent him to Holland on a government stipend. In Holland he ran afoul of pleurisy, Calvinism, bureaucracy, and pedagogy, also of the cold climate, Dutch food, and aloofness. He drifted, naturally, into the warmer milieu of Dutch communism. On his return to Indonesia as a teacher in a school for Indonesian workers' children on a Dutch rubber estate, he not only ran headlong into Dutch educational and social taboos but compounded his offenses against rigid supervisors and their formal and formidable wives by keeping suspicious political company. Tan Malaka did not last long in plantation society, so he removed himself to Java, where he set up his own school in Semarang for children of workers and peasants. Among other innovations, he taught the children to sing "The Internationale" and invited the parents in to listen. The Dutch, naturally, arrested him. They decided they had best exile him from Java and gave him his choice of locale. To their great gratification, Tan Malaka chose Holland. Once back in Holland he ran for the Dutch Parliament on the Communist Party ticket and almost won a seat. Finding the political climate thereafter a bit too torrid even for his tropical tastes, he vanished from Holland and rematerialized first in Berlin and then in Moscow. From Moscow, presently, as a trained agent of the Comintern, he traveled to Canton. When Canton became untenable for him after Chiang Kai-shek's defection from the Communist cause, he moved on to Hong Kong, Manila, Batavia, Singapore, Penang, Rangoon, Bangkok, Saigon, Amoy, Shanghai, and some say also Tokyo. He was rarely more than one lap ahead of the police and occasionally one lap behind them. He got himself jailed—and sprung—in both Hong Kong and Manila.

Tan Malaka could masquerade convincingly as a Chinese, a Thai, a Malay, or a Filipino. He picked up languages with the ease of a tape recorder and official papers like a pickpocket. He smuggled himself back into Indonesia on one occasion by traveling as a Filipino on an American passport. At the outset of the Pacific War he was posing as a Chinese teacher of the English language in a private school in Singapore. He then hustled over to Indonesia, where he worked incognito under the Japanese at the coal mines, and heckled Sukarno and Hatta when they came to counsel the starving miners to cherish coprosperity.

Tan Malaka's career, one which bemuses even the Communist masters of mystification, was at its peak when Sukarno's was at its start. It symbolized for Sukarno and for other Indonesians, to whom the symbol is often as vitalizing as the fact, the capacity of one lone Indonesian, a maverick and a fugitive, to baffle the West and to inspire the East by kindling the unquenchable fires of revolution. Tan Malaka's career—for his wartime incarnation as a coal miner was not his last—impinged directly upon Bung Karno's, as will presently develop, and Bung Karno, once he had actually made Tan Malaka's acquaintance, entertained recurrent misgivings about his longtime model and sometime associate.

Tan Malaka too had his rivals, both for Bung Karno's ear and for the attention of the Indonesian public. Most noteworthy among them were Hatta and Sjahrir, whose intimate association with Bung Karno serves to illuminate Sukarno's reactions to Tan Malaka and to personalize the stirring events in which all of them participated. As Tan Malaka was distinctively a revolutionary activist, so Hatta and Sjahrir were intellectual theorists. They were dismayed by Tan Malaka's reckless disregard for many predictable consequences of revolution. They were themselves given to contemplation and indeed even to unrevolutionary compromise.

Over a period of decades Hatta and Sjahrir exercised a restraining influence upon Sukarno, who was by nature disposed to the flamboyant Tan Malaka brand of revolution. When the Indonesian revolution failed to bring the progress and the plenty which Sukarno had promised the Marhaen, Hatta and Sjahrir became the scapegoats. They and their followers, the Westernized intellectual elite, came in Sukarno's mind to symbolize arid "textbook thinking"; their policies came to symbolize "reactionary," "counterrevolutionary," "betrayal," adherence to the "old established order," while the future, he decided, lay with the "new emerging forces." Sukarno turned openly antiintellectual and ultrarevolutionary. Hatta and Sjahrir, who did much to condition the transformation, now suffer the consequences: Sjahrir in detention and Hatta under constant surveillance. Hatta and Sjahrir, therefore, like Tan Malaka, demand digression.

Mohammad Hatta, also a son of the Sumatran equatorial and highland area of the Minangkabau, was born and brought up in the city of Bukittinggi, within a couple of miles of Kota Gedang, the native village of both Sjahrir and Hadji Agus Salim, not much farther from Padangpandjang, the native town of Tan Malaka. Hatta's parents being wealthy, they sent him to Holland for his university education. There as a student of economics and president of the Indonesian students association, Hatta rose to prominence in the nationalist movement abroad at the same time that Sukarno was rising to prominence in Indonesia. By getting himself arrested and imprisoned by the Dutch, Hatta provided Sukarno with a nationalist martyr to exploit at just the time that the Trilogi and Marhaen were becoming a bit worn as oratorical props.

Hatta, a scholarly, deliberate, and circumspect young man, was rather an unlikely candidate for martyrdom, one whom only the Dutch, perhaps, could have cast in the role. He and his close associates—among them, Ali Sastroamidjojo, a much more flamboyant type—were held for about six months, long enough to become a *cause célèbre*. On his return to Indonesia in 1932, Hatta became involved with Sukarno not only in nationalistic collaboration but in a debate which was characteristic both of the men and of the period. The point at issue was the *prinsip-non* versus the *taktik-non*. The first was embodied in Sukarno's argument that total noncooperation with the Dutch constituted an irreducible point of principle. Hatta proposed that tactical cooperation, like tactical noncooperation, might serve in the long run to achieve the nationalist purpose and that rigidity of dogma was to be avoided. The debate served more to bewilder than to bewitch their audiences. It bothered the literal-minded Dutch so seriously that they very soon pounced upon almost every nationalist leader in sight, *prinsip-non* or *taktik-non* men alike, Sukarno and Hatta included.

Sukarno, notwithstanding some uncharacteristically dull performances based on the *prinsip-non,* had by this time become popularly known not just as "The Lion of the Podium" and *Papak Kaum Marhaen* but also as *Banteng Repolusi,* that is, "The Wild Buffalo of the Revolution." The image was that of the fierce and splendid *banteng,* the prize of the Java big-game hunter. Hatta was not but might well have been known both then and later as the *Kerbau Repolusi,* the image being that of the sturdy, plodding water buffalo, always the reliable, indispensable draft animal, never very exciting either to the hunter or even the farmer. To Bung Karno's *banteng* and Bung Hatta's *kerbau,* Sutan Sjahrir then and later played the role of the *kantjil,* the tiny mouse deer, famous in Indonesian fable for being nimble and clever, always outwitting the elephant and the crocodile, also the *banteng* and the *kerbau.*

Small, plump, and cheerful, bouncy in mind and body, Sjahrir was a brilliant dilettante who had studied in Holland but could not be troubled actually to pass his examinations. Later he was a feckless provider, dependent upon contributions from his disciples but generous toward whole families of protégés of his own. An intellectual's intellectual, Sjahrir made of democratic socialism, which he learned in Europe, an engrossing doctrine at once so provocative and so profound that it attracted into his orbit some of the most spirited and agreeable of the young Indonesian intellectual elite, parlor sophisticates who have frequently found it difficult if not impossible to switch from debate to action. Bung Rir himself skipped about on the fringes and sometimes through the center of the Bung Karno-Bung Hatta show, putting on an agile display of political acrobatics.

Bung Ketjil (Little Bung), Sjahrir is now called by his intimates, just as Bung Hatta is *Bung Katja Mata* (Bespectacled Bung). Bung Ketjil, to anticipate the sequel, is now in prison, and Bung Katja Mata is under constant surveillance. Both await the pleasure of Bung Besar-Besar, now lifetime President of the Republic, who is more formally referred to as Savior of the Nation and State of the Republic of Indonesia, Great Leader of the Revolution, Custodian of the Message of the People's Suffering, Paramount Son of Irian Barat, and *Sesepuh Agung*—this last an especially august, indeed a regal title combining the names of two great sultans.

PRISONER, EXILE, AND PROPHET

From the time that he organized the Partai Nasional Indonesia in 1928, Sukarno's next destination was as clear as his assumption of all-Indonesian political leadership, namely, Dutch prison or exile. There were unexpected delays, but on December 29, 1929, after preliminary mumblings and rumblings, the Dutch authorities pounced. They had discovered a plot, they said, one masterminded by the PNI leaders to stage a series of uprisings patterned on widespread Communist (PKI) disorders which had occurred in late 1926 and early 1927. They found Sukarno in Jogjakarta, closeted with other PNI leaders. Sukarno and three of his chief aides spent the night in jail in Jogja (Jogjakarta), the next day in a tightly closed, swelteringly hot, heavily guarded third class railway coach, and the next stretch of their lives in prison in Bandung.

The four political jailbirds had rather a hard time during the first several months. Confined to separate cells, they were forbidden to communicate with each other and were permitted visits only twice weekly, even then only by close members of their families. They were subjected to long periods of intensive questioning and were allowed to occupy themselves in the intervals only with approved, nonpolitical reading matter. All the same, prison regulations were considerably stricter in the rule than in the enforcement. A friendly Dutch guard slipped them a Dutch-language daily; an Indonesian prison employee smuggled in a Sundanese-language paper. Each day a Chinese fellow prisoner left a copy of the Indonesian-language, Chinese-edited *Sin Po* in the communal toilet. Gradually the Dutch relaxed the regulations about personal exchanges and family visits, and before long they even permitted the prisoners almost anything they wanted in the way of books and papers. Sukarno surrounded himself with his personal library and went industriously to work extending his self-education and preparing his self-defense. For relaxation he read light literature, one noteworthy item being a collection of *wajang* librettos. He urged his companions to memorize the text so that the whole group of them, under his direction, could put on theatricals of their own.

The trial of Sukarno and his three fellow prisoners began in August and lasted until December. The four codefendants were charged with being leaders of a political party which had as its objective the overthrow by force of the Netherlands Indies government. Sukarno presented a long, prepared statement in his own defense, and in so doing he converted a criminal trial into a political forum. His statement, later published under the title *Indonesia Menggugat* ("Indonesia Accuses") is now a basic document of the Indonesian revolution. It is also popular in Russian translation in Moscow. Sukarno declared that the arrest, the charges, and the trial were not in fact directed against himself and his companions but against the whole Indonesian people. The PNI, he argued, worked not for the overthrow of law and order but for the overthrow of the "lawlessness" of colonialism, capitalism, and imperialism. He did not exactly equate colonialism, capitalism, and imperialism with the Dutch colonial or any other specific government, but he grew eloquent about the "shameful" Dutch "exploitation" of the defenseless Indonesian people. After delivering a detailed indictment of the colonial record—an indictment which included a most uncharacteristic digression into formal economics—he came to his prophetic and Marxist climax:

". . . if the Indonesian people seek to end colonialism, if the Partai Nasional Indonesia strives for independence, then indeed . . . we only fulfill historical necessity—as every people and every country fulfill historical obligation—a historical necessity which cannot but become absolutely fulfilled, absolutely realized.

"But the manner in which Indonesia becomes free, the manner in which the colonial ties are loosened, that will indeed be in accordance with the desires of the imperialists themselves, that is indeed within the hands of the imperialists themselves.

"It is not with us, it is not with the Indonesian people, but rather with imperialism and the imperialists themselves that the last word lies."

It took another twenty years for "historical necessity" to prevail, and it was the imperialists, not the Indonesians, Sukarno always argued, who chose violence. Some thirty years later, with regard to Irian Barat, Sukarno once again argued "historical necessity," and when the Dutch resisted Indonesian paratroop infiltrators, it was the Dutch, he said, who once again chose violence. Even today, having gained both Merdeka and Irian Barat, Sukarno is still arguing the "historical necessity" of revolution, unending, accelerating, universal revolution, by means of which the "new emerging forces" will overthrow the "old established order." "The people who go against the dynamics of this revolution," he said a few years ago, and events, as in the case of Irian Barat, frequently seem to prove him right, "will come to grief on 'too little and too late.' . . . Their awakening one day will be very harsh."

In 1930, Sukarno and his companions were found guilty of the "offense" of striving to fulfill their own and their nation's destiny. Sukarno was sentenced to four years' imprisonment, but as a result of a political amnesty the sentence was reduced almost at once to two years. His codefendants received lesser sentences, with similar reductions.

The prisoners served their time in the new and relatively luxurious Sukamiskin (literally, "Pleasure of the Poor") Prison, located in the scenic foothills not far from the Bandung city limits, an establishment which Sukarno, as already noted, had helped to design. There, as a special concession to their importance, they were placed in the first class, European quarters. During his imprisonment, Sukarno worked for a short time in the print shop, then shifted over to the administrative section to devote himself to "anthropological calculations." He had plenty of leisure, which he spent in reading—but not about politics, which was once again a forbidden subject. He turned, therefore, to the study of religion. In his youth, of course, he had been instructed by village teachers in the Muslim faith, and later on he had discussed it frequently with such men as Hadji Agus Salim. He had discussed Christianity with a Dutch pastor and had delved into Buddhism and Hinduism on his own. Now he became a serious student of the Koran and its commentaries.

As relaxation from his studies, Sukarno took up the hobby of painting. His output took the form of romantic landscape in watercolor. His personal taste, mainly self-cultivated, has ever since run more to calendar art than to anything less sensually representational, although his painting collection, the largest and best by far in Indonesia, includes many of the masterpieces of the finest modern Indonesian painters.

Sukarno did not take the opportunity to profit from the institutional motto, conspicuously inscribed in Latin over the main doorway: "Let this be the beginning of a new life."

"Do you agree with that sentiment?" a friend asked him.

"No," Sukarno is said to have replied. "I entered prison a leader, and I shall emerge a leader."

He did. At 5:30 A.M. on December 31, 1931, Sukarno was released, to be greeted at the prison gate by a welcoming delegation. It would have been a welcoming crowd, but at the city limits the Dutch police had stopped a parade of 98 automobiles and 320 horse carriages, permitting only eight vehicles, loaded with close relatives and friends, among them Inggit Garnisih, to proceed to the prison itself.

All that day at his home in Bandung Sukarno received his friends and well-wishers. Early the next morning he left by train for Surabaja to attend the First Indonesia Raja (Greater Indonesia) Congress. Thousands of people saw him off at the Bandung station; hundreds were waiting to greet him at each stop along the way; ten thousand were crowded about the Surabaja station when he arrived at seven that evening. "Hidup [long live] Bung Karno! Hidup! Hidup!" people shouted as they accompanied him from the train through the city streets. At eight o'clock that evening, he appeared together with his wife at the conference hall. It had long since been packed tight and big crowds were massed outside to pelt him with flowers and shout their welcome: "Hidup Bung Karno! Hidup Banteng Repolusi! Hidup Papak Kaum Marhaen!"

On being asked to speak to the crowd, Sukarno gave one of the briefest and most famous speeches of his career—five minutes of thanks for the ovation, which, he said, "was not for me as Sukarno but for my high ideal . . . of Indonesian Independence." He ended with his now classical appeal to the nation's youth: "Give me one thousand old men, and with them I shall have confidence to move Mt. Smeru. But give me ten youths who are fired with zeal and with love for our native land, and with them I shall shake the earth."

For Bung Karno, then as now, the nation's youth, the *pemuda,* or alternatively the *pemuda-pemudi* (male and female youth), include almost anyone between the ages of six and sixty-six who is endowed with reckless impetuosity. To the Surabaja *pemuda-pemudi,* many of whom stayed on all that night and the next day right there in the conference hall, Sukarno next evening brought "Mementoes from Prison." In a long and stirring speech which moved the audience to tears and laughter and antiphonal shouting of slogans, Sukarno identified himself with the Marhaen and the Marhaen with Merdeka and called upon all good nationalists to unite as Marhaenists together. In the course of his speech he paid tribute to his wife, Inggit Garnisih, almost as though she were one of the *pemudi*. "Although her body is small," he said, "nevertheless, within her heart there flowers a fiery zeal; [she is] constant, loyal, and steadfast . . . a wife who constantly bears sorrows and bitterness with a light heart and without complaint."

Despite his oratory, the public ovation, and his relish of freedom, the months following his release were not happy ones for Sukarno. His former associates had dissolved the PNI, fearing that Dutch surveillance made it futile to maintain the organization. They had split into two factions, and despite Sukarno's efforts they refused to be reconciled. Some of the more daring of them had organized a radical new party, the Partindo, which Sukarno himself presently joined and dominated. Others, more moderate in view, had formed a new PNI under Hatta's leadership. It was at this point that Sukarno and Hatta became involved in the aforementioned debate over what seemed to outsiders and insiders alike rather an extenuated point of dialectics—the *prinsip-non* versus *taktik-non* controversy. Sukarno, tiring of the debate, reverted to his more accustomed motif, which was first "Merdeka," then "Merdeka Sekarang!" ("freedom now"), then before long, "Merdeka Sekarang! Sekarang! Sekarang!" In support of his Merdeka slogan he wrote and published *Mentjapai Indonesia Merdeka* ("Achieving Indonesian Independence"). In it he openly if not altogether unequivocally espoused the strategy and tactics of mass action, which he plagiarized, if one may use that term with reference to revolutionary leaders who borrow without acknowledgment, from Tan Malaka. The Dutch confiscated, suppressed and banned the book. On August 1, 1933 they arrested Sukarno. Six months later, they arrested Hatta and Sjahrir also, and some hundreds of others. Then for almost a decade, while Sukarno, Hatta, Sjahrir and numerous of their associates were in exile, Merdeka seemed a receding nationalist objective.

On August 2, 1933, the day after his arrest in Batavia, and one year and seven months after his release from his first prison term, Sukarno again took up residence in Bandung's Sukamiskin Prison. This time there was to be no nonsense about a trial. Five months later, by executive order, the Governor General consigned Sukarno to exile. First the colonial government sent him to Endah, a little town on Flores, an island in the Lesser Sunda group famous for its arid climate, its horses, and its Roman Catholic missions. Later (February, 1938) it shifted him to Sumatra, to the town of Bengkulu, once famous (as Benkoolen) for a hugely unprofitable British East India Company experiment in spice gardening and for the brief, unhappy incumbency as Governor of Sir Stamford Raffles, after he had lost Java and before he gained Singapore. Sukarno was accompanied into exile by his wife, Inggit Garnisih, her mother, and a foster daughter. He was provided by the Dutch with a small house, a small monthly remittance, and a good deal of advice about keeping clear of politics.

In point of fact, Sukarno was very lucky to be sent first to Endah. Hatta and Sjahrir, along with numerous others, were sent to Boven Digul, a pestilential prison camp on the south coast of New Guinea at a spot infested with malaria, devoid of comforts, surrounded by all but impenetrable mountain jungle through which, occasionally, filtered a few naked Papuan aborigines. After a few months, Hatta and Sjahrir were removed to Banda Neira, one of the original "spice islands" of the Moluccas. The minute Banda group, comprising some eighteen square miles of tropical paradise, had been one of the ultimate objectives of the sixteenth-century European navigators and traders. Flores was neither as beautiful nor as comfortable as Banda Neira, where the marble-floored mansions of the nutmeg planters were still intact, and Bengkulu was certainly no luxury resort; but in time of exile, almost any South Seas island other than New Guinea has its advantages.

Sukarno devoted his exile to further study. For relaxation, he turned, Rousseau-like, to gardening, or at least such is the legend. In his studies he concentrated to a considerable extent upon Islam and maintained a correspondence with Hadji A. Hassan, a celebrated religious leader in Bandung. This correspondence, later published, is more highly thought of in nationalist than in theological circles, but Sukarno has managed, all the same, partly as a result of later contributions to a religious magazine in Medan, to earn a fairly widespread reputation as a Muslim scholar.

Gardening and religion still left Sukarno plenty of time to indulge his omnivorous taste in reading. He read almost anything and everything he could lay hands upon—everything, that is, except books on economics, the one category of literature which was and is positively distasteful to him. The Dutch made no effort to prevent him from getting almost any publication he wanted unless it was obviously Communist in content. So Bung Karno, thanks to constant resupply from friends in Batavia, where the book stores were excellent, ranged through world literature in half a dozen languages and more categories, and converted a ten-year exile into a prolonged postgraduate course of self-education. Being gifted with a memory allegedly so retentive that he can at will recall verbatim whole passages from any book which has particularly impressed him, Bung Karno managed, quite incidentally, to store up during his period of exile an inexhaustible reservoir of usable quotations. In later years, drawing extensively on the original Dutch, German, French, or English sources, he introduced them to ornament his orations. To be sure, his erudition served more to astonish his international audience than to enlighten the Indonesians, but it was an impressive performance from any point of view, including that of the language-poor British or American auditor.

His obbligato of quotations has done more, in fact, than lend a patina to Sukarno's oratorical style. It has induced at times a chain reaction whereby Sukarno, stimulated by one of his own recollections to pursue a topic thus fortuitously introduced, indulges himself in what may seem at the time like non sequiturs, contradictions, and digressions but may turn out eventually to be new policy guide lines. It has also enriched the Indonesian language, of which Sukarno is not only the most highly skilled practitioner but to a remarkable degree the creator. What is a Sukarnoism one day becomes colloquial or even standard Indonesian the next, sometimes with startling effect. One of the most extreme examples derives from Sukarno's reiterated use of late of the phrase "l'exploitation de l'homme par l'homme," which has been picked up phonetically in the *kampongs* approximately as *"lumpelum,"* signifying nobody knows or cares exactly what except that it is a signal to become incensed.

While Sukarno improved upon his time in exile, the Dutch relaxed into what appears in retrospect to have been fatuous complacency. They seemed to believe that arrest, trial, and a prison sentence, then rearrest and exile to a point distant from Batavia, would constitute a healthful warning and a deterrent to Sukarno's followers. They seemed also to believe that mild treatment in exile would soon dull the glow of martyrdom. As a matter of fact, for a period of years, it looked as though they might be right. The Indonesian nationalists who remained at large made their adjustments to calm continuation of life under the colonial regime. They did not, however, forget Sukarno, Hatta, Sjahrir, and the others. When the Pacific War began to close in on the Netherlands Indies, the leading Indonesians, a great many of whom were disposed to welcome the Japanese as liberators, began to ask each other: What would Sukarno, Hatta, and Sjahrir either say or do?

Hatta thereupon published a courageous article condemning the Japanese as fascist aggressors, just as in 1957 he published articles deploring Sukarno's "Guided Democracy." Sjahrir, although equally antifascist, adopted no open position, and neither did Sukarno. It was not long, however, before each had his opportunity by choice of action to make his position quite clear. Sukarno and Sjahrir then chose diametrically different courses, Sukarno in the wartime puppet administration, Sjahrir in the underground, and the choices inspired a mutual distrust which has persisted and in fact increased ever since.

ENTHUSIASTIC COLLABORATOR, HESITANT LIBERATOR, PRESIDENT BY DISPUTED CONSENSUS

At the outbreak of war in the Pacific, then, Sukarno was living in exile in Bengkulu, the decayed little seaport on the west coast of Sumatra, notable mainly for its historic associations with Sir Stamford Raffles. When the British, at the end of the Napoleonic Wars, determined to hand the Netherlands Indies back to the Netherlands, they required an extremely reluctant Sir Stamford, who had been largely responsible for their capture and their subsequent administration, to relinquish control to the Dutch. Sir Stamford was compensated—or more accurately speaking, he was punished—with the presidency of the little settlement of Benkoolen (Bengkulu), which the British East India Company had founded over a century earlier and mostly regretted. At Benkoolen, Sir Stamford devised the scheme, which he later carried out in 1819, despite Dutch indignation and British vacillation, of founding modern Singapore, now a "neocolonial" anathema to Sukarno. The British, who had turned Indonesia back to the Dutch in the early nineteenth century, were to do so again at the end of World War II, this time over Sukarno's protest. But Sukarno, during his Bengkulu days, at least until the time that the Japanese threatened Singapore, was little interested in the nefarious British of 1819. He was continuing the course of personal studies which he had already embarked upon in prison in Bandung and in exile in Flores. He was heading also into one of his frequent matrimonial involvements, a minor one in a Muslim context and in juxtaposition to the political problems with which his later years have been replete.

Bung Karno's second wife, Inggit Garnisih, had accompanied him from Bandung to Flores and from Flores to Bengkulu. In Bengkulu, however, Sukarno had met a Sumatran girl, Fatmawati by name, who was entrusted to him by her father, a devout *hadji,* for religious instruction. At some point a couple of years later (presumably in 1943, although the chronology is not clear) Sukarno divorced the aging, childless Inggit Garnisih and married the beautiful young Fatmawati. Not Inggit Garnisih, therefore, his wife during prison and exile, but Fatmawati, his wife during the Japanese occupation and the revolutionary fighting which followed, has been widely known as Indonesia's first First Lady. In 1944 Fatmawati gave birth to a son, Guntur, now a student at the Technical University in Bandung. In the course of the next decade she gave birth to three other children, two girls and a boy, before she herself was displaced in Sukarno's affections by a fourth wife, by name, Hartini. To all of his children, including two whom Hartini has borne him, Sukarno has been a doting parent.

The other aspects of Sukarno's matrimonial and extramarital career might best be left altogether to the tabloids save that in Djakarta at least they have a degree of political barometric value. Among the inadvertently prominent figures in Djakarta from time to time have been a certain "Miss Elena," a Russian, also numerous but nameless Japanese ladies who shuttle between Djakarta and Tokyo, and many Indonesian beauties whose friends and relations turn up, melodramatically, some with the pro-, others with the anti-Sukarno factions.

As the Japanese approached Indonesia after seizing Singapore, the Dutch removed Sukarno and his family from Bengkulu to Padang, planning, it seems, to evacuate them to Australia. At the same time they brought Hatta and Sjahrir from Banda Neira to East Java. In the confusion of the times, however, and in the congestion of their own exodus to Australia, the Dutch somehow misplaced their hostages. Sukarno made his way to Bukittinggi, the highland city near Padang, and from Bukittinggi, presently, with the Japanese laying on all facilities, to Batavia.

Sukarno, Hatta, and Sjahrir, once reassembled in Batavia (to which the Japanese soon applied the Indonesian name of Djakarta), arrived at an approximate meeting of minds as to their respective roles under the Japanese occupation. Sukarno became the leader of the pro-Japanese Indonesian puppet administration. Sjahrir became the leader of the anti-Japanese underground. Hatta became the intermediary between the two, working together with Sukarno in the administration, maintaining contact meanwhile with the Sjahrir group.

Tan Malaka, parenthetically, returned to Indonesia on his own, shipping on a leaky old junk from Singapore and arriving incognito in Bukittinggi about the time that Sukarno was departing for Djakarta. Tan Malaka assumed a variety of uncomfortable disguises during the Occupation and held a similar variety of ill-paying jobs, including one at the coal mines. Always, according to his own account, he was waiting for the opportune moment to reveal himself to the nationalists and to rally sentiment against the Japanese, holding suspiciously aloof from Sukarno and Hatta and never establishing contact even with Sjahrir.

Each of these roles seems to have appealed well enough to the man who played it. Sukarno, in fact, played his part so enthusiastically that he created the distinct impression in the minds not only of the Japanese but of the Indonesian nationalists, a great many of whom joined him in the administration, that he found it completely congenial. The unpleasant words "collaborator," "tool," and "opportunist," in fact, became indelibly associated with Sukarno's name in the immediate postwar period. Sjahrir himself in 1945 published a thinly veiled denunciation of

Sukarno as a puppet. The indelibility of the appellation faded perceptibly after about 1947, but such terms as "demagogue" and "dictator" became current about 1957. The decade 1947 to 1957 thus constitutes the approximate span of Sukarno's greatest nationwide and international prestige on the basis of genuine admiration.

For Sukarno and for Indonesian nationalists and Indonesians in general, the Japanese occupation is not a happy memory. Nevertheless, in many respects it was a period both critical and advantageous to their personal and national development. The Dutch had collapsed after what even they admit was a poor show of defending themselves, let alone protecting the interests of their subjects. The Japanese relied for a while mainly upon the Dutch to keep the administration and the public services functioning. There were plenty of Dutchmen who preferred the humiliation of service under the Japanese to internment in wretched prison camps, and it can reasonably be argued that maintenance of essential services was a responsibility of which defeat in war did not automatically relieve them.

The Japanese dispensed progressively with the services of the Dutch and put into their places the Indonesians who had understudied and backstopped them. For these Indonesians, who included the great majority of the postwar leaders, it was a heady experience to discover that trains ran, telephones operated, electricity flowed, regional and even central government offices did not close down if Indonesian rather than Dutchmen gave the orders—or, as was sometimes the case, if nobody at all gave the orders but mere momentum carried things along. Indonesia did not then and did not later experience the paralyzing effects of widespread devastation and loss of life. Indonesians did experience the exhilarating effects of accepting and to an appreciable extent discharging responsibility for running the nation. They did so under Japanese military orders, to be sure, but under individual Japanese who did not know the procedures and were only too willing to rely upon Indonesians rather than the Dutch to keep things running. When Japan itself collapsed, Indonesians were ready to dispute the thesis that anyone other than an Indonesian was needed even for the most specialized technical jobs. They had not heretofore occupied such jobs, but saw no compelling reason why they should not.

Sukarno's special role under the Japanese was in itself a vindication of the general Indonesian nationalist point of view. Sukarno was the top figure in the Indonesian administration. His responsibilities and his achievements, however, were almost exclusively nonadministrative. They lay, rather, in areas in which Indonesian competence, pride, and interest were far more profound, areas which then and later Indonesians came to regard as much more significant to their own development than either administration or technology. Sukarno did very little governing, and times being what they were, he had no occasion even to consider economics, a subject which in any case he relegated to Hatta even for general thinking purposes. Sukarno concentrated largely upon dissemination of propaganda among the masses and recruitment of soldiers and laborers to backstop the Japanese war effort. He engaged also in a highly complex lot of political maneuvers calculated on the one hand to bring pressure to bear upon the Japanese for independence and on the other to rally the Indonesian nationalists to a united stand. Sukarno's own position combined the contradictory features of being at once pro-Japanese and pro-Merdeka. His achievement, however, almost matched his objectives and at the very end of the Japanese period, when his objectives proved no longer quite appropriate, he did not long delay in revising them.

Of Sukarno's major objectives and achievements, the one which was by far the most controversial within Indonesia itself was the recruitment of a labor corps. Sukarno bears primary responsibility, as his critics have never been slow to point out, for persuading tens of thousands of laborers to "volunteer" as Japanese *rōmusha* (labor corps members) to be shipped off to Burma, Thailand, and the Pacific islands. Only a relatively few ever returned to Indonesia, although some thousands of others managed somehow to survive and to adopt the nationality of the country in which they found themselves at war's end.

Sukarno was also largely responsible for the recruitment of tens of thousands of young Indonesians whom the Japanese trained for military service to "defend" Indonesia in case of Allied attack, an army for which Sukarno himself later and quite unexpectedly found good use. This army, augmented by a wildly heterogeneous lot of guerrillas, volunteers, students, and *kampong* guards, rose up against the Japanese in 1945 to seize the arms and equipment with which they resisted British and Dutch reoccupation. They fought for—but also sometimes against—the Sukarno revolutionary government. The nucleus of the present Indonesian officer corps, as well as some of the best if also some of the oldest fighting troops, consists of veterans of Japanese training and of revolutionary warfare. So too, however, are some of the worst trained, most demanding, undisciplined and indisciplinary troops which make the Indonesian Army even today a menace to itself.

Sukarno recruited not only laborers and soldiers; he recruited also major segments of the Indonesian public which came within range of the podium, radio, and printing facilities with which the Japanese gladly provided him. Sukarno carried to the *kampongs* and to the provinces the message of Japan's Greater East Asia Co-Prosperity Sphere. "Japan the Light of Asia, Japan the Leader of Asia, Japan the Protector of Asia," was a theme upon which he orated with great fervor, clouding his prophetic record, however, by hailing a not distant day when the Chinese dragon, the Indian peacock, the Thai elephant, and the Indonesian *garuda* (mythical bird) would all lie down together, basking in the warm glow of Japan's rising sun. To this "Triple A" slogan of the Japanese, he added his own Bung Karno "Double Kita" coinage: "Inggris kita linggis dan Amerika kita seterika" (We'll clobber the English and iron out the Americans). Some of the other Indonesian leaders, and some of the Indonesian public, upon becoming disaffected with the Japanese and for that matter with Sukarno, impudently revamped and telescoped the "Triple A" and the "Double Kita" slogans to read, "Awas! Ada Amerika!" (Look out for America.)

This protean Indonesian capacity for accepting and at the same time parodying a slogan or a policy has reasserted itself frequently over the years, particularly since the 1959 advent of USDEK, an oratorical cryptogram of Bung Karno's, denoting political and economic policy. The cynics, of whom there are many, read it as "Uang Sudah Dipotong, Ekonomi Katjau." (Our money's devalued and our economy's a mess.)

Well before Japan's collapse in 1945, many Indonesians had

begun to entertain not always unvoiced misgivings about Sukarno's main thesis regarding Indonesian-Japanese collaboration. Indonesia, Sukarno kept reiterating, had to "earn" its independence by helping Japan to win the Pacific war; it was not appropriate to Indonesia's national dignity either to ask for or to receive independence as a gift. Tan Malaka, speaking incognito but in public, once asked, "Would not Indonesians fight more bravely alongside Japan if they had already been given their independence and were fighting to maintain it?" It was a question, says Tan Malaka, whose reporting is not always unimpeachable, to which Sukarno had no reply.

When the defeat of Japan became an imminent probability, Bung Karno ceased to talk about "earning" Indonesian independence and concentrated rather upon maneuvering for it. The time had come, he said, for the Japanese to fulfill their promise. The Japanese, whose position was already shakier by far than the Indonesians suspected, still delayed and hedged. All the same, they set in motion machinery which Sukarno thereafter concentrated upon speeding up. In late April of 1945 they designated the members of an Indonesian "Investigating Committee for Preparation for Independence" which in early August they promoted into a "Committee for Preparation for Independence." The Investigating Committee, in point of fact, was slow in getting under way. Once it did get started it showed immediate signs of bogging down in abstruse debate over the precise provisions of a constitution, a debate which some of the Japanese seemed happy to keep well fueled. Before this committee, however, on June 1, 1945, Bung Karno delivered the most famous of many famous speeches in his career. Dramatically he called for an end to "hairsplitting" debate and for a speedy conclusion to independence preparations. Then, interrupted again and again by applause from the floor, he defined the *Pantjasila,* the "Five Principles" which at once became the official state ideology: Nationalism, Internationalism, Democracy, Social Prosperity, and Belief in God.

Sukarno's speech was lengthy, sometimes erudite and abstruse, sometimes colloquial and facetious. It was punctuated with references to such assorted nationalists as Ibn Saud, Stalin, Lenin, Hitler, Sun Yat-sen, and Gandhi. It included quotations in the original languages from Ernest Renan, Otto Bauer, John Reed, and others, East and West. Before a strongly Muslim assembly, Sukarno dared to substitute nationalism for Islam as the first principle of state, and belief in God rather than specific belief in Islam as the fifth. If devout Indonesian Muslims found sections in the speech that jolted them, so too, when and if they later studied it, did devout Western democrats. In the section on "social prosperity" (later redesignated "social justice," and now supplanted in Sukarno idiom by "a just and prosperous society"), Bung Karno referred to the "failure of the American Revolution" to achieve either "social justice or economic democracy," and to the "supremacy" in the United States and Western Europe of "capitalistic bosses."

The Pantjasila, like many other state doctrines, has become for the insider a symbol so sacroscanct, subject to interpretations so pious as to obscure rather than to reveal meaning. For the outsider, it is best studied in context, with historical, social, biographic, and literary exegesis, not as a repository of wisdom but as a revelation of national aspiration. The Pantjasila means precisely what Sukarno, in his various periods, has said that it means. It meant "constitutional democracy," for instance, when the Allies arrived in late 1945. It has meant "Guided Democracy" ever since Bung Karno in 1957 rejected and reviled "Western," "liberal," "vote-counting" democratic theory and practice. Even more recently it has also come to mean "NASAKOMIL," i.e., coalition of nationalist, religious, communist, and military elements in an authoritarian regime.

For Indonesians, nevertheless, the Pantjasila has taken on and retained the magical quality traditionally attributed to an item of royal regalia—in the old days the *kris,* the betel jar, the amulet or other treasure without actual physical possession of which no sultan could legitimatize his rule. These same qualities attach today to other emblems of state: "Indonesia Raja," the national anthem; *Sang Merah Putih,* the "Sacred Red and White" national flag; *Politik Bebas,* Independent Policy; the Marhaen and Marhaenism, Nonalignment, Afro-Asian Solidarity, Irian Barat, Merdeka, and the Revolution (or *Repolusi*). When and if Sukarno wills it, the Pantjasila means also *"konfrontasi,"* or total, uncompromising, noisily propagandistic opposition to any officially designated enemy, for many years the Dutch, more recently the

British "neocolonialists" and their "Malay puppets" who "plotted" to form Malaysia. Bung Karno possessed himself of the Pantjasila and the *Repolusi,* just as he possessed himself earlier of Merdeka and the Marhaen and more recently of USDEK. As proprietor of the Pantjasila and USDEK, as Papak Merdeka and Papak Kaum Marhaen, and more recently as Custodian of the Message of the People's Suffering, Great Leader of the Revolution, and *Sesepuh Agung,* Bung Karno becomes in fact not just a modern sultan but a dealer in a highly potent line of nationalistic magic and spells.

Sukarno's June 1, 1945 performance—and American bombings of Japan—induced the Japanese to make more explicit commitments than before regarding Indonesian independence. Whether motivated by realism, idealism, despair, indifference, or calculated intent to block the restoration of Western authority in the archipelago, or a combination of all these considerations and more besides, the Japanese moved fast. On August 8 they flew Sukarno and Hatta to Dalat in French Indochina, there to confer with Field Marshal Terauchi, who had authorization to act for Tokyo. From Marshal Terauchi, the Indonesians received absolute assurance that they would be granted independence in the very near future, possibly on August 24, possibly on September 24, although the Japanese may not actually have designated any specific date. On August 14 the Japanese flew them back to Djakarta, via stops in Taiping, Malaya, where Malayan nationalists were tentatively introduced into the proceedings, and in Singapore, where news of the dropping of the atom bombs and of Russian entry into the Pacific war filtered through the censorship.

Sukarno and Hatta thereupon made their own evaluation of the situation: Japan probably could not last another month. On his arrival in Djakarta, therefore, Sukarno greeted the waiting crowd with an oracular pronouncement: "If I said before that Indonesia shall be free before the corn matures, I tell you now with certainty that Indonesia shall be free before the corn flowers."

Indonesia was destined in fact to be free even sooner than Sukarno anticipated. On the evening of their return to Djakarta, Sukarno and Hatta were visited by Sjahrir, who gave them the news, picked up by his clandestine radio monitors, that Japan had already sued for peace. Notwithstanding their own estimate of

Japan's chances, Sukarno and Hatta thought that the report of surrender overtures was premature. Nevertheless, they set themselves to analyze their own situation and their extremely delicate dilemma.

Japan had now not only promised independence but had set up a procedure, and if not a date, then virtually a deadline of late September. If Japan actually surrendered before Indonesian independence was an accomplished fact, would the victorious Allies, they asked each other, permit the plan and the timetable to be carried out? Was it not altogether likely, rather, that the Allies would insist upon restoration of Dutch authority? Even if Indonesia did gain its independence under Japanese auspices, would the Allies not argue that the whole procedure was without validity, that Indonesian Merdeka was a "Made in Japan" imitation to be treated with contempt? On the other hand, if the Indonesian leaders now ignored or defied Japan and declared independence on their own authority, what would be the justification under international law for such an action? What would be the consequences should Japan oppose them with force? What would be the assurance that the Allies would not in any event treat them as discredited Japanese collaborators rather than as authentic Indonesian patriots?

Sukarno and Hatta arrived at a difficult decision. They would proceed with the agenda much as it had already been drawn up. They would work with the Japanese through the Japanese-appointed Preparations Committee, which, they thought, might now be enlarged to include representatives of special regions. It would be advisable, they thought, to advance the date of independence, but not to take precipitate action in anticipation of swift Japanese surrender which might even yet be delayed. The Allies might indeed regard them as Japanese collaborators and Indonesian independence as a "Made in Japan" product; certainly the Dutch would adopt this position. Nevertheless, the procedure already determined upon had validity under international law. They could not devise a new procedure which would be equally valid. To adhere to plan, they believed, would be to avoid a needless blood bath such as defiance of the Japanese would almost certainly provoke. The risk of facing Allied charges that they were mere puppets of Japan was a risk they would have to accept. It was preferable to the risk of illegality or of violence.

Sjahrir disagreed. Sukarno, he said, should by-pass both the Japanese and the Preparations Committee and immediately, on his own authority and in the name of the Indonesian people, make an international broadcast in which he would read a declaration of Indonesian independence. The new Indonesian nation, he said, could not risk sponsorship by an already defeated Japan or contamination from the Japanese-appointed Preparations Committee. Nor could it risk procrastination, for Japan might already be preparing on Allied orders to block any move toward independence.

For several days, while Djakarta throbbed with news of the A-bomb, rumors of Japanese collapse, and speculation about Indonesia's future, the nationalist leaders debated. Ever since then, when they have been disposed to think back on this particular period, they have redebated their own stands and those of their associates. Some of them point out that in this particular circumstance, the roles of Sukarno, Hatta, and Sjahrir were curiously revealing. Sukarno, who has almost always since then stood for impetuosity, stood for indecision and circumspection. Sukarno's role throughout this whole period is described even by his admirers as unheroic and by his detractors as craven—a factor, no doubt, in determining his later attitudes. Sjahrir, who came later to represent caution and circumspection, advocated swift, bold action. He associated himself with the youths who, as will presently develop, forced that action. These same youths, it should be noted, soon shifted their support to the Communists and later (after 1956) back to Sukarno. Hatta held out for legality, as he always did before and as he always has since, for scrupulous adherence, whatever the apparent arguments against it, to the letter of the law. It was this same attitude which led him in 1956 to break with Sukarno when Sukarno disregarded the law, but in 1958 to withhold his support from the rebels, who turned to armed insurrection in an attempt to force Sukarno to take cognizance of the law.

While Sukarno, Hatta, Sjahrir, and various others of the top echelon temporized and debated, the *pemuda*—that is to say, the activist youth, a critical element in the Indonesian nationalist and revolutionary scene—resorted to action. Chaerul Saleh, a young university law student, one of the boldest and brashest of the new *pemuda* leaders, masterminded and led an escapade which Sukarno and many other Indonesians now prefer to forget. The episode is mentioned in the history books, if at all, only by cryptic indirection. Nevertheless, it is almost uniquely revealing of the times, the people, and the future. Chaerul Saleh, then a protégé of Sjahrir, later a Communist-line conspirator, jailbird, and exile, today one of Sukarno's right-hand men and possibly his political heir, kidnaped Sukarno and Hatta. He "persuaded" them to declare Indonesia's independence and posted a *pemuda* vigilante corps to make sure that they did so and to spread the news. Subsequently, to anticipate the narrative, Chaerul Saleh joined Tan Malaka and repudiated Sukarno together with the Declaration of Independence. He was implicated in the kidnapping of Sjahrir in 1946, and in the Communist insurrection at Madiun in 1948, and in 1950 he headed a little "people's army" which defied the newly independent republic.

The 1945 kidnapping, like many other episodes in Sukarno's life, seems even less credible if expanded upon. Chaerul Saleh in 1945 was leader of a Djakarta *pemuda* group composed of students, army officers, and civil servants. This group had constituted itself—or had been so constituted by the Japanese—coordinating body for a nationwide but highly diffuse and disputatious youth movement, one which was in general anti-Japanese and pro-Sukarno. In August 1945 the chief Djakarta cell of the *pemuda* was a university hostel at Djalan Menteng 31, very close to the colonial mansions which the Japanese had put at the disposal of Sukarno and Hatta. The Chaerul Saleh group took its arguments from Sjahrir, but took its cue, possibly, from Tan Malaka, who materialized at just this moment in Djakarta, a self-styled "youth leader," age 49, going by the name of Hassan and hailing from Bantam. The *pemuda* first sent emissaries whom Sukarno and Hatta brushed aside. They then devised the logistics of abduction and the dialectics of persuasion.

On the night of August 15, Chaerul Saleh and one companion provided themselves with a motorcar—cars were to be come by in Djakarta during this period by anyone with a gun. They drove to Sukarno's home in the middle of the night, routed him out of bed, and trundled him off, together with Ibu Fatmawati and little Guntur, into the waiting car. Another pair of *pemuda* with another vehicle hustled Hatta over to the Sukarno home. A few other conspirators joined in and a small caravan of cars and trucks proceeded without obstruction from the Japanese sentries through the silent city. They traveled out into the countryside to the Indonesian military barracks at Rengas Dengklok, forty miles from Djakarta, where military confederates awaited them.

Next day the *pemuda* solemnly declared independent Indonesian sovereignty over the Rengas Dengklok Barracks area and set up a little self-government which occupied itself, *inter alia,* with detention of a couple of local administrative officials who happened by. They then devoted themselves mainly to "persuasion" of Sukarno and Hatta. Their major argument was that if Sukarno and Hatta did not declare independence at once, they, the *pemuda,* would stage an armed uprising to which who could foresee the consequences to the nation or to himself? The Djakarta *pemuda,* they said, were merely awaiting the signal. For the better part of a day Sukarno and Hatta listened, but did not commit themselves.

That afternoon, having failed as yet to "persuade" their hostages, the *pemuda* dispatched a reconnoitering party to Djakarta. In the evening the emissaries returned, in company with Dr. Subardjo, chief Indonesian official working with the Japanese Naval Liaison (Intelligence) Office which, under Admiral Maeda, was the most favorably disposed of all Japanese military groups to Indonesian aspirations. Dr. Subardjo, who was widely believed then and later to be in league with the Communists but in 1952, as Foreign Minister, was to be completely discredited for entering secretly into an aid agreement with the United States, apparently brought acceptable evidence that the Japanese had indeed surrendered. Whether it was conviction that the Japanese were finished or conversion by the *pemuda* which made the difference, or perhaps even an assurance from Admiral Maeda that the Japanese would lend support, Sukarno and Hatta agreed to declare Indonesia's independence without delay. At 10:00 P.M. the whole party set out on the return trip to Djakarta.

Once back in the city, the Sukarno-Hatta-Subardjo-*pemuda* party met with hastily summoned representatives of virtually all nationalist groups which could be reached on such short notice. Only Sjahrir was conspicuously absent. At this point he trusted neither Sukarno nor the *pemuda* and he declined to come. The place of the rendezvous was the official residence of Admiral Maeda (now the British Ambassador's residence), one of the few really safe spots in a city where street fighting was to be expected almost momentarily. Admiral Maeda discreetly absented himself from the discussions, which lasted until about 1:30 A.M. After long debate, Bung Karno then wrote out in his own hand the brief text of the Declaration of Independence which all could agree upon. Bung Karno and Bung Hatta both signed it. There had been vigorous debate, however, whether many or few should sign, and some of the many later repudiated the document. Bung Karno promised to read the declaration in public at a ceremony scheduled for the following morning at his residence. The assembly then broke up, the *pemuda* to rush off to the radio station, the newspaper offices, and various other strategic spots, in all of which they had alerted their friends and relations.

At 10:00 A.M. on August 17, in the presence of a small crowd assembled in front of his house at Pegansaan Timur 56, thereafter to be known as Gedung Proklamasi (Proclamation Hall), Sukarno made a brief preliminary speech and read the statement:

PROCLAMATION

We the people of Indonesia hereby declare Indonesian independence. Circumstances pertaining to transfer of authority and the like will be properly arranged in the shortest possible time.

Djakarta, 17 August 1945

In the name of the Indonesian People

(signed) SUKARNO   HATTA

Sukarno then raised the red-and-white flag which, according to the legend, Fatmawati had sewn together the night before, and delivered his brief peroration:

"Thus, brothers, we are now free! There is not now one more fetter that binds our native land or our people! Beginning at this moment, we form our nation. A free nation. The Republic of

Indonesia. Free, completely and forever. May God bless this freedom of ours."

Sukarno and the Indonesian nation thus launched themselves into an immensely complicated and troubled world, one in which, ever since, they have been recurrently dismayed, in fact outraged, to discover that they are not completely free, that there are still fetters which bind, that "circumstances" can rarely if ever be "properly arranged" and certainly not in what they conceive of as "the shortest possible time." In the days and weeks immediately following the Declaration of Independence, however, and even in the subsequent period of fighting, despite obstacles which might have looked insuperable to men of lesser faith or greater experience, Sukarno and his associates accomplished—or at least they experienced—miracles enough to give them confidence that the supply was virtually inexhaustible.

The Japanese did not choose strenuously to obstruct. The Indonesian politicians, *pemuda,* and public did not immediately obscure the national destiny by disputing too violently among themselves what needed to be done next. Everything needed to be done next. Virtually everybody who counted set about doing it exactly as he saw fit, without direction or coordination, to be sure, but also without the disruptive acrimony which set in later whenever anyone tried to impose direction or coordination. Sukarno, it was first presumed, then officially affirmed, was President, and Hatta was Vice-President. A democratic constitutional government was proclaimed. An administration began coalescing about the leaders, to whom flocked volunteer followers of every description from every direction. In the course of the next few days and weeks, the formalities of legalizing the new regime were more or less devised and adhered to. But to the consensus that the Sukarno-Hatta declaration and government were in keeping with the true ideals of Merdeka, important political elements, most specifically the Chaerul Saleh *pemuda* group which now aligned itself openly with Tan Malaka, withheld their private and occasionally even their public consent.

FREEDOM FIGHTER,
LEASHED AND UNLEASHED

Notwithstanding the achievements which the dates June 1 (Pantjasila) and August 17, 1945 (Merdeka) now signify in Indonesian history, for Bung Karno the year as a whole was one of irresolution and several times of nearly disastrous procrastination. His failure swiftly and accurately to gauge the temper of the Japanese, the *pemuda,* and the Allies, and also, save on June 1, of the politicians, almost forfeited for him the leadership of the nation. It almost forfeited for the nation itself the immense advantage of the days and weeks of reprieve between mid-August and late September. During that interval, before the British occupation contingents had begun to arrive in any strength, the Indonesian nationalists enjoyed the priceless opportunity to entrench themselves.

The events of August 15–17 seem to have upset Bung Karno's usual perceptivity. Shortly after August 17 he erred seriously in judging both the Japanese and the *pemuda.* The *pemuda* demanded that he call a monster public demonstration in defiance of the Japanese military authorities. Bung Karno exhibited near panic at the thought of Japanese reprisals, but the *pemuda* forced his hand. The demonstration was held on September 17, and even though the *pemuda* and the Japanese both fingered their triggers, it led to no violence and was in fact a nationalist triumph.

Bung Karno yet once again misjudged practically everybody when street fighting broke out in Surabaja in late September. Local Indonesian army and *pemuda* forces, led by a fiery young demagogue, Bung Tomo by name, today a disaffected parliamentarian, resisted the incoming British occupation troops. Bung Karno decided, apparently, that the Allies would more willingly accept him if he stopped the fighting, that his personal prestige was sufficient for him to risk intervention, and that "historic necessity" did not dictate a bloody conflict. In each of these appraisals, he was perhaps 49 per cent right, but his score in political judgment tests is normally much higher. The Allies were not yet about to have the "Japanese collaborator" Bung Karno on any terms; his prestige was sufficient only to get the fighting uneasily suspended; and the renewal of much more widespread disorders a few days later precipitated the Indonesian revolution into one of its most futile, most blood-soiled phases. In Surabaja everybody felt himself betrayed, although the Indonesians, who lost the battle, now treat it as their Bunker Hill.

These episodes—to which, of course, there are other interpretations—illustrate one basic point about which there can be little dispute. Bung Karno in August, 1945, found himself thrust into a position of such extreme hazard that his survival and that of his nation constitute a major miracle. In mid-1945, furthermore, and for a considerable time thereafter, it was a case not so much of Bung Karno precipitating as of Bung Karno himself being precipitated and somehow prevailing. Bung Karno's aggressive recklessness in later years may perhaps trace back to a decision, made on the basis of long experience through which, always, his luck or his *karma* has sustained him, in dangerous times deliberately to live dangerously.

Bung Karno was living during the latter part of the year 1945 under circumstances which impressed upon him daily, indeed almost hourly, that he still had far more to win than to lose in international blackjack and that the gamble was forced upon him. As President of the Republic of Indonesia, he exercised only the most shadowy authority over a government which rocked along on diminishing momentum even within the limits of his capital city, which he called Djakarta and the Allies Batavia. The state of affairs outside the capital was a matter only of badly informed conjecture save that certainly it was even worse. In Djakarta-Batavia, Bung Karno himself did not even occupy the governmental palace, and symbols of authority such as tenancy of the palace can assume really critical importance among the feudally conditioned Indonesian revolutionaries. The Japanese and presently the British and still later, of course, the Dutch occupied the palace. Bung Karno, together with his wife and son and quite a retinue of retainers, continued to occupy the Dutch-owned mansion at Pegansaan Timur 56, which after August 17 had become known as the sacred Gedung Proklamasi. To this presidential seat, therefore, he had only squatter's rights, and with it his personal associations—the August 15 kidnapping, for instance—were not nostalgic. It is perhaps revealing to note that Bung Karno never shared the enthusiasm which many of the other nationalists later entertained for preserving the Gedung Proklamasi as a national shrine. He never liked the ten-foot memorial obelisk which they erected in the front garden, and anyway, he thought, it was much too modest. Several years ago he gave orders for the demolition of both memorial and mansion and for the construction in downtown Djakarta of a vast and costly new monument to the revolution, one which will not automatically call to mind the critical but unhappy August-December, 1945, period.

Anomalous housing arrangements, involving not only Sukarno but also other Indonesian nationalists who settled as squatters into any house that was without a legitimate caretaker, signified a totally anomalous situation. The Indonesian nationalists assumed control over government offices and other installations, relieving their Japanese colleagues of facilities and perquisites, posting armed *pemuda* with instructions to exclude all intruders, including any British who might turn up with ideas about running a military government. The Indonesian nationalists thus took over control also of Batavia-Djakarta's telephone system, the electric power plant, the water works, the tramways, the railways, the hospital, the university—all of which continued to function, if rather sketchily, with nobody in particular clearly responsible for giving the orders, collecting the bills, taking the tickets, or checking the maintenance. Indonesian army units, to which bands of *pemuda* half attached themselves, assumed custody of Japanese military installations, arms, and equipment, sometimes by force, sometimes by wile. They organized vigilante squadrons, uniformed in Japanese hand-me-downs supplemented by Australian hats, Texas boots, and whatever additional items sartorial whim might dictate. Armed generally with at least two lethal weapons per *pemuda,* equipped also with flags, placards, musical instruments, and a generous supply of paint for slapping up slogans on any white wall space, these Merdeka-intoxicated *pemuda* roamed the streets by night and by day, converting *Repolusi* into a fiesta and, if they met with any challenge, into a riot. In the suburbs there were bloody little massacres of Chinese and Eurasians, and in the prison camps where the Dutch were still concentrated, there occurred a variety of outrages to which nobody could or would affix the responsibility.

Bung Karno's government, meanwhile, was an accidental agglomerate of politicians who formed themselves into a "Parliament," devised a stop-gap "Constitution," parceled out some "ministries" among themselves, and alternated between moments of historic glory and intervals of scrounging food, clothing, transport, housing, and any available privilege. In theory, the Republic of Indonesia was a constitutional democracy administered by a presidential cabinet. In practice things were pretty haphazard. It was evident to everyone that if the Indonesian nationalists themselves did not somehow get things better under control, the incoming British or even more probably the Dutch would have a go at it. Two of the more organization-minded of the leaders, Sjahrir and Tan Malaka, set out each in his own way to do something about it, which meant, of course, then as always, doing something first about Bung Karno.

Tan Malaka's device was conspiracy, Sjahrir's was argument, and neither achieved much success. Sjahrir did persuade enough of the politicians and the *pemuda* to convince Sukarno that he must appoint a cabinet responsible to parliament rather than to himself—one, incidentally, which could not only do some administering but also negotiate with the Allies. Sjahrir, naturally, became the new Prime Minister, and since he enjoyed the confidence of the Allies, which Sukarno did not, meaningful negotiations became a possibility. Tan Malaka rallied other politicians and *pemuda* to support a clandestine Tan Malaka for President movement. When that failed to make much headway, he played upon Sukarno's own fears that he would be cashiered by the Allies. Presently, in early 1946, Tan Malaka extracted some sort of document from Bung Karno, a "political testament," it is said, naming himself as legitimate political heir. Armed with this document—whether genuine, forged, or imaginary is still a matter of debate—Tan Malaka stumped the provinces on his own behalf, conceding to Sjahrir the bustle of Batavia. Sjahrir, learning of the Tan Malaka strategy, persuaded Sukarno himself, who had by this time moved to Central Java, to tour the hinterland. The Sukarno tour turned into a triumph, one which demonstrated quite clearly, however, that the real strength of the revolutionary movement lay not in any political clique or program but in Sukarno's hypnotic hold over the awakening Indonesian masses.

Sukarno thus asserted his own authority over Tan Malaka and Sjahrir and many others besides, and demonstrated that oratory was immeasurably more potent than organization in the Indonesian revolution. Between the republican leaders and the Western world, meanwhile, conflict was proving to be much more significant than cooperation. The British had discovered in Surabaja, and they confirmed their findings in almost equally violent experiences elsewhere, that fighting was likely to be more decisive than negotiations. Nevertheless, they were eager to negotiate, and even more eager to withdraw. They worked out a very shaky compromise agreement between the Indonesian Republicans and the Dutch. Meanwhile, they admitted more and more Dutch troops and administrators to whom, presently, they hastily relinquished control with an unmistakable air of relief.

Long before the British decamped, the Sukarno government itself had made a stealthy and strategic shift of locale. From its Central Java stronghold in Jogjakarta, the republican railway administration had dispatched a special train to Batavia, a train to which there was attached an air-conditioned red plush parlor car which had been the pride of the prewar Dutch officialdom. Onto this train, drawn up to a siding near Pegansaan Timur on the night of January 4, 1946, while the Dutch were patrolling the motor roads, were loaded Sukarno, Fatmawati, Guntur, and a quite astonishing number of other republican officials, their families, and their chattels. Also, according to the "malicious" later report of the Dutch, there was loaded into a baggage car the total stock of the official opium monopoly which was later marketed "illicitly" overseas to pay the expenses of the first republican representatives dispatched to the United Nations and elsewhere abroad. Comfortably established in the special carriage of the getaway train rode Sukarno and Hatta and most of the cabinet, except for Sjahrir, who remained behind to handle republican affairs in Batavia and moved, incidentally, into the Gedung Proklamasi which Sukarno now happily and permanently vacated.

The government-in-voluntary-exile from Batavia proceeded via the coastal route to Jogjakarta, where it found itself not so much a new home as a first home. The population of Jogjakarta, a small principality whose Sultan, Hamengku Buwono IX, had thrown in very early on with the revolutionary leaders, turned out to give the émigrés a joyful welcome. The sultan himself acknowledged the republican government's authority, and his princely neighbor, the prestigious Susuhunan of Surakarta (or Solo), if he did not exactly welcome it, did not openly dispute it either. The republic thus for the first time ruled over a fairly well defined geographic area and an acquiescent population, and began to operate something approximating an administration. There were no Europeans nearby to dispute it, except some tens of thousands of Dutch, whose miserable existence, dragged on in wartime internment camps, remained for months a matter of very delicate negotiation.

Bung Karno himself moved into what had been the seat of the Dutch Resident. It was a vast mansion in the old style, with red-tile roofs, white pillars and porticoes, marble floors, crystal chandeliers, and red plush furniture, set in shaded grounds ornamented with ancient Javanese sculptures. Bung Hatta moved into a rather less pretentious mansion nearby. The other republican émigrés distributed themselves about the city, occupying such onetime Dutch residences as were not already overpacked with official or semiofficial squatters.

The focal point of the whole city, of course, was the *kraton* (palace), and the nearby *kabupaten* (administrative office) of the Sultan. Along Malioboro Street (named for the Duke of Marlborough during the Raffles period) horse carriages and bicycle traffic made way for the official limousines, decrepit models which had somehow more or less survived the war. One of them was the "Buk Repolusi" (Revolutionary Buick) which Sukarno had levitated up from Djakarta. On Malioboro Street, as in Dutch times, pedestrian traffic was diverted from the sidewalk just in front of the residency, now the *kepresidenan* (presidency), at the gates and in the grounds of which were posted far more sentries equipped with a much bigger armory than the Dutch had ever imagined necessary. Inside the *kepresidenan,* dressed in white drill trousers and bush jacket, his balding head covered by a smart black Muslim cap, Bung Karno received relays of visitors. Politicians, *pemuda,* military officers, leading citizens from all over Indonesia who somehow managed to make their way to Jogja—everybody wanted to talk with Bung Karno and almost everybody did. Presently a trickle, then a steady stream of foreigners began to flow through or over the lawless countryside surrounding Jogja and to turn up also at Sukarno's levees. Upon all but the most tenaciously suspicious of them, Sukarno exercised the personal magnetism which had gained him acknowledgment as Papak Merdeka and Papak Indonesia. He was very soon to inspire some of his overseas agents to print up Indonesian Republican postage stamps with paired portraits of Bung Karno and George Washington. Americans, among others, happily collected these stamps until the international philatelic union rejected them as political gimmickry invalid for postage, even if presented to the post office in Jogjakarta; but by that time Bung Karno was favorably if rather vaguely known even overseas as the Father of His Country.

Bung Karno had clearly found his element. For the next four years, although crisis was as endemic to Jogja as was dysentery, and periods of excruciating seizure were frequent, Bung Karno flourished and the new Bung Karno legend flowered. Prior to 1945, Bung Karno had been successively the political prodigy, the spellbinder, the dialectician, then the martyred but still indomitable hero. Between 1942 and 1945 he remained the great Bung Karno, but his record had been tarnished in the eyes even of his close adherents by reason of collaboration, vacillation, and opportunism. Now he became the great freedom fighter. Not that he himself actually carried arms or put up any physical resistance to his enemies, although his favorite costume ever since has been a profusely beribboned military uniform. At one point, indeed, he even allowed himself to be taken prisoner by the Dutch without any show of fight, to the dismay of some of his close associates at the time but to no permanent detriment to his reputation.

Bung Karno, rather, was the freedom fighter's freedom lover. By force of an arresting personality, he imposed a centripetal control which, although it never allowed for any stabilization of the wildly heterogeneous military, political, and social forces then at work in the nation, nevertheless kept them within the orbit of one constantly shifting center—always himself. Bung Karno was the revolutionary's revolutionary, in the literal sense that he kept things revolving, or to be more precise, gyrating. He has since then become the professional revolutionary, for whom freedom-fighting has become an avocation, but for whom freedom-finding in any quiet, routine form of labor has always been a bore. The Jogja rebel, once national independence was won, continued to rebel, attempting, like the champion boxer who cannot take his mind or his eyes off his trophies, constantly to relive his own legend. Bung Karno, however, has defied the laws of chance and of obsolescence; he has continued to acquire trophy after trophy, but for victories which often seem self-defeating.

Sukarno's great triumph of the Jogja period was that he led his nation to victory over the Dutch colonial forces. It might be more accurate to say that he played a major role in sustaining the revolution in motion until the Dutch conceded defeat. This re-phrasing, which allows for the roles played by other leaders than Bung Karno, is no derogation of the accomplishments either of Bung Karno or of the nation as a whole. The extent of the accomplishment becomes the more impressive upon consideration of just how close Indonesia came to defeat. Sukarno and the insurgent republic survived by reason of ingenious improvisations and providential escapes which combined heroism, melodrama, and sheer chance in almost equal proportions. Perennial survival led to the expectation that good management would soon follow good fortune, or if it did not, it might not much matter, such was the resiliency, the resourcefulness, and the overwhelming vitality of leaders and people.

Bung Karno's career and that of the republic were so hectic during the years 1946–49 that the pattern comes out best perhaps by mere enumeration of some of the major episodes, leaving to conjecture the explanation of the many non sequiturs, which in any event no brief historical reconstruction can clarify. On June 27, 1946, for instance, Bung Karno awoke to learn that his Prime Minister, Sutan Sjahrir, had been kidnapped, together with quite a covey of other high officials, presumably by the extremist *pemuda* friends of Tan Malaka and Chaerul Saleh, both of whom were in jail. One week later, on July 3, 1946, he was visited by Professor Doctor Mohammad Yamin and his military and civilian friends, who were presumed to be Sukarno's supporters. Mo-hammad Yamin (d. 1962), to digress momentarily, was a poet, lawyer, historian, and full-time jingoist, destined in the 1950's to become repeatedly a Minister of State and in 1960 Sukarno's top

economic planner. Bung Yamin delivered to Bung Karno an ultimatum, demanding in effect, that Bung Karno hand over the government to Tan Malaka. Bung Karno ordered his guards to arrest
and detain Bung Yamin. The army command, which had been
teetering on the edge of treachery to someone, no one could be
sure to whom, decided to remain loyal to Sukarno. Yamin and
party went to jail; Sjahrir and party were set free by their kid-
nappers; Sukarno emerged from the encounter not exactly the
acknowledged master of the situation but the acknowledged master of maneuver and countermaneuver.

Sukarno and the republic survived to encounter two Dutch
military actions and in the interval between them a Communist
insurrection, any one of which had better reason to succeed than
the republican resistance. By mid-1946, the Dutch had despaired
of negotiated agreements which, to attempt historic objectivity,
not one but both parties had sabotaged. They had despaired also
of any possibility of working out a *modus vivendi* with Sukarno.
Instead, on July 21, 1946, they launched a formidable military
operation aimed at eliminating the republic. International protest,
initiated by India, stopped the Dutch in their tracks. Then, while
a United Nations Good Offices Commission attempted to patch
together a settlement, the Dutch resorted to an economic block-
ade. Sukarno and the republic hung on, substituting for food,
clothing, pharmaceuticals, and ammunition practically nothing
but zeal.

At a moment when it looked as though a few firecrackers could
topple the state, on September 18, 1948, the Communists staged
an armed uprising at Madiun. In the course of the revolt, Tan
Malaka sided with Sukarno and then for the last time vanished,
presumably killed, but whether by the Communists, the Dutch,
or the Republicans is subject to dispute. Sukarno and Hatta called
for nationwide resistance to the Communists, while the Communist Party and Radio Moscow branded them both as "Quis-
lings," "dealers in forced labor," "tools of the imperialists," and
"counterrevolutionaries." The army, especially the crack Siliwangi
Division under the command of then Colonel Abdul Haris Nasution, today General Nasution and Defense Minister, took swift,
decisive measures, and both the insurrection and the Communist
Party were crushed.

The Madiun insurrection was no sooner put down than the Dutch on December 18, 1948, began a second military action which netted them, within a matter of hours, the capital city of Jogjakarta, the person of Sukarno, most of the chief members of his government, and the outraged protests of the Indonesian and the outside world. After a few months of savoring the bitter dregs of military victory, the Dutch restored Sukarno to Jogjakarta and Jogjakarta to him. They then negotiated for transfer of sovereignty and on December 27, 1949, recognized the new Republic of the United States of Indonesia. As Sukarno immediately started pointing out, however, they reserved immense Dutch properties, powerful political and cultural influence, even a small military mission —"fetters," in other words—and Irian Barat.

The course of all these events, so far as Sukarno was concerned, was far less important apparently than the surge of emotions. Events, up until the very end, worked to Sukarno's disadvantage and the republic's. Emotions rose higher, however, as fortunes dropped, and in the end emotions overrode even military defeat. In Jogja it was always the spirit which counted and not the fact, and Sukarno himself was never much concerned, therefore, with the details of administration or even of negotiation, neither of which he found at all congenial. He left such pedestrian matters to his associates, mainly to Hatta and Sjahrir. He dissociated himself, consequently, from the drudgery of attempting to provide food, clothing, arms, medicines, housing, transport, and all material things, of which nobody ever received more than a small fraction of what he wanted or needed. He dissociated himself also to a noteworthy extent from the negotiation of a series of agreements with the Dutch, including the final transfer-of-sovereignty arrangement, all of which, being imperfect and based upon compromise, were vulnerable to attack. It was Sukarno himself, privately during the Jogja period, publicly soon thereafter, who cued the criticism. He then accepted the feedback as a mandate to redouble the attack.

Sukarno did not participate very much even in expediting the highly significant social achievements of the Jogja period, such as running the schools, establishing a university, publishing newspapers and books, operating hospitals, all at a time when personnel, equipment, supplies, buildings, money and everything else presented almost insuperable problems. Sukarno devoted himself rather to the passing show, put on by the Parliament, for instance, which, having little reason to legislate, mostly played politics; by the military services which at times fought courageously, to be sure, but mostly just survived, that in itself no small victory. Sukarno was always ready to consort with the military, about as unlikely and as resourceful an assortment of fighters as ever bore arms. The army was compounded of trainees of the Japanese, volunteer guerrillas, student patriots, anyone who could load a gun or sharpen a bamboo spear. The navy had a few *prahus* and smuggler craft. The air force pilots spliced together junked Japanese planes, got them into the air, and if they did not crack up immediately, they learned to fly. Rarely have so many made do with so little. Most of all, of course, Bung Karno associated himself with the politicians, but then, virtually anyone who could read or write was a politician and all of them seemed determined to associate themselves with Bung Karno, if only, like Tan Malaka, to undermine him.

Bung Karno's position by mid-1949 was a vast improvement over his position in mid-1945. He had met the challenge of the leftists from within and the rightists from without—specifically, the Communists and the Dutch. He had held in delicate balance the influence of the rightists within and the leftists without, namely, although the categorical description would not please the members of the first group, the Hatta-Sjahrir moderates, who could not persuade Bung Karno to orient the nation toward the Western world, and the international Communists, who could not induce him to soften toward domestic Communists, at least not when his own position was being threatened. Despite such lapses as letting himself be captured, he had neither vacillated nor compromised in what seemed in Jogja to be the major issues, such as fighting the Dutch, although he had obfuscated what seemed the lesser ones, such as the basis on which he removed and appointed the members of a presumably democratic Parliament. He had not staked his prestige on an imperfect formula for achievement of independence, a formula which every politically-minded person knew would ultimately lead to trouble. Most of all, he had restored and re-embellished the national image of Bung Karno, the compelling personality, whose magnetism not even the Communists could resist. The Communist survivors of the Madiun Revolt, in fact, were already beginning to argue that they disliked not Bung Karno but Bung Hatta.

In late 1949, then, Sukarno emerged on the international scene as the national hero who had led a once forlorn revolutionary movement to a triumphant climax, fighting in the process the first successful Southeast Asian nationalist war not only against the colonialists but against the Communists too, and, for a time, concurrently. Regardless of such details as wartime collaboration with the Japanese, Bung Karno was the sort of man whom the Western world could now accept and the Communist world might not automatically sabotage. As he moved into the international floodlights as President of the world's fifth largest nation, Sukarno had behind him widespread national and international support such as no other Southeast Asian nationalist leader has ever enjoyed. Within the next eight years, a time span which to Indonesians constitutes a mystical unit, Bung Karno's position was again to undergo drastic changes.

ALARMS, DIVERSIONS, AND EXCURSIONS

On December 28, 1949, the morning after the transfer of sovereignty from the Netherlands, President Sukarno returned to Batavia, now permanently renamed Djakarta, together with his wife Fatmawati, his children, and a retinue of officials. He flew in from Jogja by Garuda Indonesian Airways, bright new red and white paint covering the KLM markings which the plane had carried when it left the city the day before. At the airport he was greeted by an immense and hysterically happy crowd. The streets were so packed with spectators that his car could scarcely pass. For once in his career, Bung Karno was almost inarticulate. He spoke words of greeting, but he delivered no oration.

That day for the first time Bung Karno climbed the marble steps into the Istana Merdeka on Medan Merdeka; the previous day it had still been Gambier Paleis on Koningsplein. With his family he took over the private quarters while other republican officials and their families moved into the pavilions. Soon Bung Karno was to install his collection of modern Indonesian paint-

ings to cover walls from which had just been removed the drab
oil portraits of three and a half centuries of Dutch Governors
General. But already he had made the palace his home, and even
to his trained architect's eye and to his experienced politician's
mind, although he talked of renovating the colonial design, there
were few improvements which needed immediately to be made to
its classical and spacious proportions. Later he would want a palace
mosque, a guest annex, a barracks for the ever-growing security
guard, quite a lot more offices, and also more palaces. For the
time being it was sufficient to weed out the Dutch marigolds
from the gardens, to replenish the flock of peacocks, to install
projection equipment for private movie showings, to make provision for *wajang* and dance performances, and here and there
to hang a few more crystal chandeliers.

Bung Karno began at once to preside over presidential salons
at which there turned up congratulatory representatives of all
Indonesian and a great many alien interests, including the Dutch.
Foreign governments had already begun to extend recognition,
the Ceylonese jumping the gun on December 26, the Philippines
crowding the field on December 27, many other nations, including Great Britain and the United States settling for December 28.
The Russians and the Communist Chinese, however, mysteriously
held back. Ambassadors queued up to present credentials, the
American being first in line, politically a bit disheveled from having been held up by a snowstorm in Istanbul while racing his
British colleague toward the equator. The Nationalist Chinese,
incidentally, had queered themselves by being importunate. They
had flown in a planeload of dignitaries when none was expected
and hotel accommodations, as usual, were not to be had; in any
event, Indonesian nationalists were already beginning to be very
unhappy about the two Chinas.

President Sukarno enjoyed the show and savored the complications—most of the show, that is, and most of the complications.
Within a month of Sukarno's succession to his national inheritance, however, Sultan Hamid of Pontianak, a theatrically handsome and adventuresome Borneo princeling, implicated himself
with "Turk" Westerling, a swashbuckling Dutch-Armenian soldier of fortune, in an anti-Sukarno conspiracy. The pair of them
convoked an eerie coterie of Darul Islam fanatics, renegade

Dutch, Eurasian, and Ambonese soldiers, and Chinese speculators, who seized the mountain city of Bandung for a few days, fired some random shots in Djakarta, and botched an assassination plot aimed against leading members of the cabinet. Chaerul Saleh, meanwhile, was leading a little "people's" army of guerrillas who promised to fight against everybody else until independence was genuine, which Sukarno's brand of Merdeka, they said, was not. Even more troublesome and persistent rebellions were smoldering elsewhere—in Sulawesi (Celebes), Sumatra, Kalimantan (Borneo), even on idyllic little Ambon, which soon declared itself, together with Ceram, the independent Republic of the South Moluccas.

Neither the motivation nor the resolution of the rebellions was ever very clear, but what happened with regard to Chaerul Saleh, to choose one individual rebel, was typical. Saleh was successively captured, jailed, released, rejailed, exiled, pensioned, and then for a period of years almost forgotten while he "continued his studies" abroad—in Holland until the Dutch threw him out, in Switzerland and Germany until he tired of waiting for unreliable government remittances. In 1956 he made his way back to Djakarta, where he suddenly became an inseparable companion of Sukarno's and very rich and very important.

All things considered, insurrections were rather more Sukarno's cup of tea than were certain other distractions, especially those related to organizing, administering, and developing the nation. The new nation, then called the Republic of the United States of Indonesia, had started out as a montage of semifictitious Dutch-established states joined in polygamous shotgun marriage to Sukarno's phantom republic. Within six months it had become the "integrated" and "unified" Republic of Indonesia, Sukarno's republic made corporeal and all-inclusive, highly centralized in theory but centrifugal in practice. The administration was based upon the colonial civil service, by then both discredited and disrupted, and upon new political appointees charged with performing undefined functions for which they rarely had either the experience or the qualifications. As a result of almost a decade of war and revolution, the economy, like the administrative system, had dangerously deteriorated. The immediate priority in most Indonesian minds, however, was not the onerous business of administration, rehabilitation, and development, but the swift transfer to Indonesians of the positions and the profits which still accrued to the Dutch or to the Indonesian Chinese. The military establishment was more of a menace than a safeguard to national security. It was a sudden and unstable amalgamation of troops which had very recently fought each other: the regular, guerrilla, and student volunteer forces of the republic, plus the Indonesian colonial troops which had served with the Dutch. Many of the units were badly trained and badly disciplined, all of them were wretchedly paid. Many millions of the Indonesian people, meanwhile, were confidently awaiting the swift materialization of adequate food, clothing, housing, and transport facilities, the extension of educational, medical, and other social services, even the adoption of the five-day week and the seven-hour day—actually legislated in 1950. They anticipated, in short, the spontaneous emergence of the new Indonesia which would match the promises of the revolution and of its leaders. Sukarno, said his critics, failed to comprehend the dimensions of the problem. Sukarno, quite possibly, comprehended all too well.

President Sukarno elected publicly to play the role of ceremonial Chief of State, delegating to Hatta and to a succession of cabinets the responsibility for getting things done. But Sukarno could never resist, indeed he never tried to resist, the lure of excitement. Of all forms of excitement, public adulation, political manipulation, and private indulgence were those which most appealed to him. Opportunity was readily at hand, and gratification led to addiction.

Bung Karno's public ovations became Augustan, his political machinations Machiavellian, his private indulgences Cassanovan, and as time went on, they all became more and more critically important to national polity, if only because they were chronically diverting and disruptive.

By the mid-fifties, Sukarno's romances had resulted in sensational press exposés of a succession of lurid intrigues which made his round-the-world progresses as interesting to the tabloids as to the *New Statesman and Nation*. His political maneuverings had succeeded in converting almost every onetime revolutionary into a political bureaucrat, obsessed with position and privilege, usually at the cost of his rivals and the public. They had converted the foreign diplomats in Djakarta into jealous rivals competing to woo and win the Bung Besar. Sukarno's public ovations proved to be the greater the more noisily he played upon the emotional appeal of ultranationalism and xenophobia. The "liberation" of Irian Barat was his favorite theme, combined, of course, with anticolonialism, antiimperialism, and anticapitalism. His public appearances produced the repeated spectacle of Bung Karno hypnotizing not only his audiences but also himself. The years 1949–55 thus gradually revealed Sukarno not just as the nation builder, but as the nation wrecker. During the early fifties, nevertheless, although the pretense wore increasingly thin, Sukarno maintained the fiction that he was a spectator rather than ringmaster of the whirling Indonesian circus. The Sukarno chronicle seems for a time, therefore, to deal not with momentous national developments, as in previous years, but with the side shows. The major events, in fact, were often disarmingly described by Indonesians themselves as *peristiwa* (incidents), too numerous and trivial, presumably, to warrant more than passing headlines, some of them aseptically referred to only by date. The *peristiwa* seem, in retrospect, a series of national alarms which, as the years went by, began sounding with increasing frequency and urgency on every political, economic, military, and social wave length. In between the alarms were telescoped a series of minor diversions and excursions, diversions in the fashion of tawdry romantic or political assignations, excursions in the fashion of showy state-visit tourism.

The *peristiwa* may ultimately prove to have been far more significant if not more comprehensible than the comings and goings of the numerous cabinets, whose most strategic moves, although this was not generally known to the public, were schemed in Bung Karno's busy anteroom. The *Peristiwa* 5 April (1950) and the *Peristiwa* 26 April (1950), for instance, were two obscure, overlapping insurrections in the eastern islands, which Bung Karno first ordered to be negotiated, then to be suppressed by force of arms. He discovered, however, that military campaigning was as endless as negotiation, that neither led to reconciliation, and that the new Indonesia was as little susceptible to discipline, let alone to organization or administration, under Indonesian as under Dutch masters. The *Peristiwa* 6 August (1951), to pick at random again from the chronological file, was a small-scale Communist armed attack near Djakarta, and the *Peristiwa* 16 March (1953) a large-scale Communist-inspired disorder in Sumatra. Both of them demonstrated that relatively efficient countermeasures were likely to inspire the politicians to conspiracy, the Communists to resurgence, and the general public to far keener appreciation of the drama than of the danger. In the *Peristiwa* 17 October (1952), the army tried to dissolve the Parliament and to dictate to the President. At the climax, however, while field pieces pointed at him and at his palace, Bung Karno hypnotized a hostile mob with his oratory, sacked the army Chief of Staff (Colonel—now General—Nasution), and completely mystified everyone as to what else had just happened or was about to happen, save that Bung Karno had triumphed. The high political wages of obfuscation, if ever they had been in doubt in Indonesia, were in doubt no longer.

The next real *peristiwa* seemed to many observers too unimportant, to some much too important to christen by date. It was the "Hartini Affair," to which, indeed, it would be difficult to attach a precise date since it has in fact covered an era. Chronologically speaking, however, the *Peristiwa* Hartini began on September 15, 1954, when the crusading editor, Mochtar Lubis (now in jail), published in his newspaper, *Indonesia Raya,* the first of a series of especially sensational stories. He revealed successively that Bung Karno had secretly and polygamously remarried, that the new wife was a beautiful divorcee named Hartini, whose reputation did not endear her to the Djakarta matrons, and that there had been some very fancy hocus-pocus about her divorce, the wedding, and practically everything else that related to the case.

The *Peristiwa* Hartini suddenly inflated into a national and an international furore. Ibu Fatmawati left the Merdeka Palace, established a separate home of her own, and attempted unsuccessfully to get a divorce. She was urged on by wives of top officials who boycotted "that woman in Bogor." Hartini, who had moved into the Bogor palace in the cool and scenic highlands thirty miles from Djakarta awaited her time. For company she had her five children from her previous marriage and an occasional dropper-in from among the army wives. Bung Karno either brushed aside or cajoled the indignant feminists. He brought inducement to bear upon their husbands, not a few of whom have proved to be susceptible to the pleasures not only of promotion but also of polygamy. Eventually, Hartini was being invited out to dinner—first at the American Embassy; then abroad on state visits—first to Communist China. Many of the once irate ladies, prompted by curiosity and by expediency, were soon accompanying their husbands to official functions in Bogor, where Hartini was the hostess. According to an early 1963 bulletin from Djakarta, to bring the Hartini Affair precipitately up to date, Fatmawati had at last conceded defeat and returned to the Merdeka Palace, where her children had remained all along, except more recently for Guntur, now a dashing young university man with his separate establishment in Bandung. Hartini too is often in residence in the Djakarta palace. So too, as everybody now knows and feels quite free to say, are miscellaneous other ladies of assorted nationalities, on short- or long-term arrangements.

Sensationalism and scandal surrounded the *Peristiwa* Hartini, and sober, scholarly analysts of Indonesian history refer to it with only the greatest of delicacy. In Southeast Asian historical significance, it may rate, nevertheless, not on a level with the amours of Mussolini but with those of Mark Antony. It was not merely a case of Bung Karno defying the social conventions and getting away with it, for conventions, as everyone knows, are breached by lesser and greater men than Bung Karno, and Indonesian Muslim matrimonial standards are not Victorian. Rather, the Hartini Affair demonstrated, under circumstances in which obviously Bung Karno himself had misgivings since he resorted to uncharacteristically clumsy subterfuges, that so far as he himself was concerned no conventions of any kind were binding. At a time when the Western practice of monogamy, along with a great many other Western customs, was gaining acceptance by important segments of the Indonesian educated public, Bung Karno made it quite clear that for himself such self-imposed restraint was inacceptable. He reverted to the traditional Muslim practice of polygamy, as liberally interpreted to allow for the sultan's harem, and he did so in contravention even of accepted Muslim mores. The marriage itself was a distinctly minor episode. It illustrated far more dramatically than any of the other incidents, however, the fact that Bung Karno was entering a world of willful anarchy and that influential elements of the nation were ready to abet him.

The *peristiwa,* of which, to reiterate, there were far too many either to remember or to recount, introduce or reintroduce onto the scene the cast of characters who, whatever their fortunes in the period of the early 1950's, today support and rival Sukarno and each other. Each anticipates for himself the Sukarno succession; each distrusts and dislikes the other; and each finds his own following at once so fragmented and so infiltrated as the result of complex mutual animosities, that Sukarno has only to flex his own tough political muscles to signal everyone else to assume a judo stance. Among the top figures surrounding Sukarno, three stand out as most durable and redoubtable. Each of the three seems at times to be more rather than less vulnerable to his rivals by reason of long-time tenure in office and close association with Sukarno. Each, on the other hand, believes his own chances for survival improve by reason of his rivals' obsolescence.

Contestant Number One, as commonly named in order of apparent prospect of assuming eventual control, is General Abdul Haris Nasution, long-time Chief of Staff, now Minister of Defense, and reputedly Indonesia's anti-Communist "strong man." Number Two is Saudara (Brother, another favorite form of nationalist greeting) Chaerul Saleh, responsible under one title or another for economic development, the brightest scion of the "Generation of '45," apostle of the revolutionary "Spirit of '45," and inspiration of the nation's *pemuda,* both the aging and the adolescent. Number Three is Comrade Dipa Nusantara Aidit, Secretary-General of the PKI (Indonesian Communist Party).

Comrade Aidit, whom some handicappers name for Number One position, does not appear at first glance to be a particularly formidable competitor. He lacks the physical and intellectual glow which are characteristic of most of the Indonesian leaders. For a Communist he often seems more slipshod than sinister, slapdash rather than doctrinaire. Comrade Aidit, nevertheless, is not as youthfully immature or as ideologically diffuse as he seems. He managed in the course of a very few years to run up party membership from about 50,000 to about 2,500,000, to purge deviationists, and to impose both dogma and discipline. He was largely responsible for formulating an inspired Post-Madiun PKI apologia: that the rebellion was the result of "intolerable provocation" on the part of the "Hatta government," but that the party is unswervingly loyal to Sukarno and eager to cooperate with all "progressive" nationalist elements.

Comrade Aidit has displayed great style and agility in keeping everybody both at home and abroad guessing about the PKI, its affiliations and its intentions. He has done so of late, for instance, by obscuring the PKI's stand on the Moscow-Peking split. For a young man who was on the remote periphery of the Sjahrir group in 1945, close to Tan Malaka in 1946, prudently distant from the Madiun rebels of 1948, and then an obscure understudy in Moscow, Peking, and Hanoi, Comrade Aidit has moved far and fast since 1950 in establishing himself at the center of things in Djakarta. He has made himself one of the fixtures of the Sukarno entourage, featured both at home and abroad in the presidential state progresses, being one of the first whom Bung Karno introduced one day in Washington to a startled President Eisenhower. Comrade Aidit, furthermore, exhibits strange idiosyncrasies which make him perhaps, just as he claims, an Indonesian first and a Communist second. He shows a predilection, for instance, for a chauffeur-driven American Ford instead of the Skoda which the priority board tried to palm off on him. He admits to willingness to condone "a little exploitation" of laborers and peasants by strictly "national capitalists." Save for his Ford, he shows a disposition to forego the more lucrative and luxurious rewards which come from swelling the Sukarno retinue so that in comparison with other prominent Indonesian politicians, he lives in proletarian rather than capitalistic style.

General Nasution would seem at first, indeed at second, third, and later glance to have better measurements than Comrade Aidit to fit him for the Sukarno vestments. He is handsome, vigorous, articulate, popular, and what is more, he has three big powerful armed services which seem ready these days to take his orders. His career is that of the self-made man, and, as contrasted with that of Aidit, the fighting revolutionary. Starting out as a school teacher from Tapanuli, Sumatra, Nasution received military training first under the Dutch, then under the Japanese, and became one of the outstanding young officers in the Japanese-sponsored Indonesian armed services. During the revolution he rose to the rank of commander of the crack Siliwangi Division, which not only fought an effective jungle war against the Dutch but also put down the Madiun Communist insurrection. After independence, General (then Colonel) Nasution was appointed Chief of Staff, but he experienced thereafter both hard knocks and hard times. Presumably because he was the organizer of the *Peristiwa* 14 October (1952), Sukarno cashiered him and allowed him for a period of about three years merely to vegetate. On his reinstatement in 1955 he incurred such animosity on the part of his senior staff that intra- and extramural attempts at an anti-Nasution coup became a Djakarta commonplace. In 1958, when certain provincial commands went into active insurrection, they were rebelling almost as much against Nasution as against Sukarno. Once Sukarno gave the signal, Nasution put down the insurrections with such despatch and efficiency that he vastly enhanced his own prestige, re-enhanced Sukarno's, and gave rise to endless speculation as to how long the two could tolerate one another. In recent years, however, General Nasution has let pass many an opportunity to seize power. Possibly, as some suggest, he is waiting first to dispose of Comrade Aidit, in which case he would still have to deal with Saudara Chaerul Saleh.

Saudara Chaerul Saleh, like Comrade Aidit and General Nasution, has staged a sensational comeback from adversity—in fact, a whole series of dramatic adventures reminiscent of his great friend and mentor Tan Malaka. As already noted, Saudara Saleh compiled rather a remarkable record as kidnaper, conspirator, prisoner, insurrectionist, and pensioner. He rose from penury to affluence when Sukarno in 1957 suddenly again had need for a *pemuda* claque, and Chaerul Saleh, as leader of the "Generation of '45," supplied it from among his old-time companions and their younger followers. Chaerul Saleh himself is young, handsome, vigorous, articulate, and popular. He has everything that Nasution has save an army, but then he has *pemuda* to spare and the *pemuda* spirit. He has the reputation of being a smart thinker, dresser, and actor, and in fact he is known to his intimates, not altogether favorably, as "the Yankee." To quite a respectable number of visiting Yankees, who usually admire his haberdashery and his uncluttered in-basket, Saudara Saleh seemed for a year or two to be the one Indonesian cabinet official who talked "good sense" about such everyday matters as money, jobs, and contracts. Chaerul Saleh's "good sense" has been responsible, perhaps, for prompting him to deny the need, value, or even the possibility under prevailing Indonesian economic and political circumstances (an atmosphere of "revolutionary romanticism," he says) of effective foreign aid. He does, however, propose something he calls "production sharing," a device whereby foreign concerns put up the capital, forego the management, and hope for a transferable cut in some eventual profits. Whatever the shortcomings of the Indonesian economy, which has plunged further and further into chaos under Chaerul Saleh's guardianship, and whatever the excesses of the Indonesian *pemuda,* who have reverted recurrently on his prompting to the revolutionary carnival spirit of August, 1945, Saudara Saleh does undoubtedly possess something of the Sukarno genius for exercising sheer concentrated personality upon any chosen audience. He exercises it, apparently, even upon Sukarno. Saudara Saleh called upon Bung Karno not long ago and elicited a resounding commendation for presenting to him an historical document, the full symbolical significance of which only Bung Karno and Chaerul Saleh could appreciate. It was the original copy of the August 17, 1945, Declaration of Independence, which Saleh himself had in part dictated and then *in toto* denounced. Even more recently (May 20, 1963) Saudara Saleh featured conspicuously at a formal state occasion when he conferred upon Sukarno, on behalf of the People's Consultative Congress, the title "Lifelong President of the Republic," thus adding one more to Sukarno's imposing list of titles.

The *pemuda,* the PKI, and the tommy-gun chiefs and cliques did not altogether surround Bung Karno until 1958, but by that time they had elbowed out most other aspirants to influence. Specifically and successively, they had dispossessed the Socialists, Sjahrir's disciples; the Masjumi, Hatta's associates, and then Hatta himself; and the PNI (Nationalists), namely, Ali Sastroamidjojo and his coterie of mutually inimical politicos who sought to freeze the desperate status quo to their own political and financial advantage.

The gradual but conclusive squeezing out of Vice-President

Hatta was particularly significant and symbolical. Ever since 1945, Sukarno and Hatta had constituted in Indonesian political folklore the inviolate *Dwitunggal*—a Javanese word coinage for "duumvirate." The *Dwitunggal* signified to Indonesians, who delight in resonant Javanese nomenclature, the emotional flamboyance of Sukarno counterbalanced by the systematic rationality of Hatta. The *Dwitunggal,* the theory went, satisfied the spiritual craving of the Indonesian people, who would perform whatever labors were required of them so long as drudgery was always enlivened by drama.

Through the *Dwitunggal,* Indonesians said, they achieved the almost magical reconciliation of diametrically divergent forces and personalities; they achieved the complex and in the end constructive interaction of the ultranationalistic demagogue and the rationalistic administrator. But on December 1, 1956, after sounding the warning long and often, Bung Hatta resigned and retired. He did so to the accompaniment of much-publicized private and public statements of dismay at Sukarno's politics. He withdrew to play the role of secluded elder statesman, consulted mainly by those, like Sjahrir, who had preceded him into eclipse. Bung Karno presently persuaded Bung Hatta to pose with him again before the photographers and the politicians, everyone beaming happily at one another. But even Bung Karno's legerdemain could not long disguise the fact that the *Dwitunggal* was shattered and the vision of Indonesia's past, present, and future revolutionary glory was dimmed.

As he passed into retirement, Hatta spoke out bluntly about a "crisis in confidence" occasioned and characterized by "economic chaos" and "political anarchy and adventurism." The recently promising Republic of Indonesia, according to Hatta and all other relatively sober observers, was drifting toward disaster. To some it seemed to be steered toward disintegration by leaders whose follies were matched only by their fantasies of power. Bung Karno himself was very soon not just to acknowledge but actually to claim—while blaming, of course, his critics and the colonialists— that in Indonesia one could find only "excesses," "errors," "deterioration," "disintegration," in every field, also "deviations, deviations, deviations" from the "sacred principles" of the revolution. The Indonesian nation, he announced, was approaching the "abyss of annihilation." It must now be redeemed and purified, he said, and only he had the magic potion.

By 1956 the Indonesians had become so calloused to crisis and so reconciled to corruption that it took an exposé of a refusal to conspire or to embezzle to cause a sensation. High officials had already been brought up with monotonous frequency to investigation or trial on such charges as sale of import-export licenses, a business transaction so routine and necessary as to seem almost commendable. As anyone in Djakarta knew, a cabinet official who earned a salary of 2,500 *rupiahs* per month but owned a Rp. 250,-000 car and Rp. 2,500,000 house and scaled his standard of living not to his salary but to his extras, would have difficulty if he ever tried, as the military occasionally said that he should, to explain the sources of his wealth.

The top military command, which regarded itself as the custodian not only of the nation's security but also of its morals, was at least as ostentatiously corrupt as the politicians. Djakarta headquarters usually condoned its own peccadilloes, but it grew incensed over regional commanders who smuggled millions of dollars worth of rubber and copra to Singapore and banked the proceeds abroad.

The government had adopted and refused to abandon the diametrically conflicting policies of attempting to maintain the low wages, low prices, and low social pressures of the colonial past while at the same time raising consumption, expenditures, and expectations to the level of a wealthy independent nation. It was not only the civil officials, consequently, who were trapped in an impasse. It was virtually everyone, up and down the social and economic scale. Salaries and wages, fixed by the government in wildly inflated *rupiahs,* bore no logical relationship to price indices for rice and textiles. Soon, on a full month's legal income, no one with any pretension to status could sustain himself and a family for as much as a week. The day laborer had to hold two jobs, shirk both, and put his wife out to work even to get by, and to pilfer almost anything portable in order to support his children. Even the peasant was up against it. The government tried to buy up his rice at confiscatory prices, promising in return to supply him with textiles and other commodities at one tenth their worth or cost. It was a rare peasant, just as it was a rare laborer or civil servant, who did not decide that rather than starve within the law he preferred to live by his wits outside the government's futile regulatory system.

The students too were trapped, a new generation of almost frighteningly quick and eager *pemuda-pemudi* (male and female youth), as Sukarno insisted upon calling them, to whom educational opportunity of a superior order was now indeed opening up. They lived, however, in a world of incoherence while they studied in a world of logic. The adjustment between the two was made no easier by the fact that soon they were constantly being recruited for political rallies in ecstatic support of Sukarno's demands, "spontaneous" demonstrations of "channeled anger" which not infrequently turned into riots.

Of all the provocations to demonstrations, riots, and public ovations for Sukarno, no cause was more potent during the whole of the postindependence period than that of Irian Barat, that is, Western or Dutch New Guinea, which for Bung Karno constituted an Indonesia irredenta. The Irian Barat cause stirred Bung Karno to oratorical frenzy, the Indonesian public to hysteria, the Communist and much of the Afro-Asian world to chanting anticolonial, anti-Western slogans. It stirred the Western world to uneasy re-examination of its own principles and policies and their relevancy to the demand for swift Indonesian-style "emancipation" of Stone Age primitives inhabiting a remote and unattractive land of mountains, jungles, and swamps, to which only the Dutch colonials and missionaries seemed able or willing to bring progress. Irian Barat, to which Sukarno's best claim was his demand for appeasement, became an international albatross destined eventually, of course, to come to roost on his own backdoor stoop, just as he demanded that it must, although its dark and sinister shadow obviously served his purposes far better than its carcass.

During the early and mid-fifties, Bung Karno was acquiring an increased sense of his own power in a situation in which he made his own rules, alleging national liberation and the search for "national identity" and self-realization as justification for all of his excesses. He was acquiring also an increased contempt for all "conventional," "liberal," "Western democratic" theory and practice and for all who were guilty of what he later termed "textbook thinking," "anticommunistphobia," and commitment to "the old established order" in resistance to the "just aspirations" of the "new emerging forces." The record of failures on the part of three cabinets of the mid-fifties—failures for which Sukarno's interference was in large measure responsible—proved conclusively to others as well as to Sukarno that the Djakarta politicians, whatever might be the reasons, were not up to their jobs and that the Djakarta version of liberal democracy did not and could not work.

The first Ali Sastroamidjojo cabinet (July 30, 1953–August 11, 1955), for instance, was spectacularly indecisive, incompetent, and corrupt. It did score one major triumph, namely the staging of the Afro-Asian Conference at Bandung in which Sukarno, not Ali, was the featured Indonesian performer, and international prestige, not domestic progress, was the objective. Toward Ali personally, his long-time nationalist revolutionary confrere, Sukarno did not even bother to conceal his personal contempt. The successor Harahap cabinet (mid-1955 to early 1956) was a failure for quite a different reason. Some of its members were highly competent personally; most of them were honestly reformist in policy; none of them was a Sukarnophile. They presided over Indonesia's first national elections, which merely demonstrated the fragmentation of political power. They also provided a brief interlude of tolerably good government. They failed, however, either to achieve any lasting results or even to survive very long in office. Precisely because they undertook basic reforms they made themselves vulnerable to lethal attack which Sukarno himself often inspired. The second Ali cabinet (March 20, 1956–November 27, 1957) was even more impotent than the first but managed to hang on for over a year, mainly because nobody, Sukarno included, would take responsibility for deciding what to do next.

For both Sukarno and for Indonesia, the year 1956 was by far the most critical since 1945. It was a year of chaos, when every individual national leader was privately and publicly seeking for the "way out," but everybody blocked everybody else's exit. In the past Bung Karno had always provided the nation with the formulas which inspired action, but in 1956 Bung Karno, like everyone else, seemed to be baffled. Bung Karno, in fact, seemed to be seeking not the nation's "way out" but his own private escape from the apparently irresolvable dilemma. While the nation floundered, Bung Karno spent a great part of the year abroad, preparing, however, as it presently developed, to resume his role as seer and prophet of the revolution.

Bung Karno's transformation through tourism traces back to one fateful day, March 12, 1956, when Secretary of State John Foster Dulles dropped in at Djakarta, where his welcome was not expected to be cordial. Secretary Dulles sweetened his reception by delivering to President Sukarno an invitation to pay a state visit to the United States, an invitation for which Bung Karno had long been angling. The Russian ambassador to Djakarta next day delivered an invitation to Moscow. The Chinese Communist ambassador delayed only a few days before delivering an invitation to Peking. Other ambassadors, from East and West, headed for the palace, gilt-edged cards in hand, to advise Bung Karno that he would be welcome wherever and whenever he cared to call. Bung Karno, who had made a state visit to India, Pakistan, and Burma in 1950, one to the Philippines in 1951, and a pilgrimage via Cairo to Mecca in 1955, was not difficult to persuade. Ever since 1956 he has made himself readily available.

Bung Karno's 1956 state visits developed into a series of triumphal processions through the United States, the Soviet Union, Communist China, and various intercontinental way points of somewhat less immediate political significance. He was accompanied by an entourage of some fifty prominent Indonesians, some of them hitching a ride at the last moment, all of them copiously provided with official dollars. By way of incidental diversion, they made book with each other as to which country would most enthusiastically and most adroitly receive them. They did not fail to note, for instance, that the United States picked up the checks for only the strictly official members of the party and observed a marked decorum regarding extraofficial entertainment. In Russia and China, particularly in Russia, where Bung Karno was assigned a very charming interpreter who later joined him elsewhere, virtually anything for anybody was on the house.

Wherever he went, Bung Karno turned in a superlative performance, one which bedazzled almost everybody, and nobody more than himself. He radiated personal magnetism. He corked or uncorked the oratory to suit the audience and the occasion. He handled radio, television, and the press as deftly as he kissed the babies, the babes, and the elderly ladies. Everywhere he carried the message of revolution and nationalism as the great, the irresistible, the forward-looking forces of the century. He won a standing ovation from the United States Congress by warning it that if it did not adjust in time to the forces of nationalism it would pour out in vain its "Niagaras of aid." In the Soviet Union he set audiences of 100,000 to shouting "Merdeka" and "Hidup Bung Karno" whenever he pledged the undying friendship of the Indonesian for the Russian people. He was greeted on arrival in Peking by a million wildly enthusiastic welcomers, including stilt dancers, jugglers, and musicians who had entertained the crowds while they waited, pretty girls who pelted him with flowers, and just about everybody else who was ambulatory. Bung Karno progressed from sightseeing and charming and admonishing in the United States, to orating and pledging in the Soviet Union, to starring in a series of people's democratic carnivals in China. Everywhere, of course, he not only talked but looked and listened and stored up impressions, to the analysis of which he brought the canny mind of a highly experienced politician.

Bung Karno's 1956 travels stirred Bung Karno at least as much as they stirred his hosts. The press, the newsreels and Bung Karno himself brought back reports which entranced the Indonesian people. Bung Karno had demonstrated that he could command the admiring attention of a world audience just as readily as he could command that of the Indonesians. The outside world, quite obviously, was even more eager to woo Sukarno and Indonesia than Sukarno and Indonesia were to woo it. Competition among the United States, the Soviet Union, and Communist China could just as obviously be turned to Sukarno's and to Indonesia's great advantage. In Indonesia, during the previous years, many people had begun to ask themselves whether their nation was not, perhaps, the "sick man of Asia" and whether the illness was fatal. Suddenly Bung Karno had made both himself and Indonesia seem to be Asia's most dazzling prospects as partners in pioneering a new world order. It is still far from clear whether the ultimate effect upon Bung Karno and upon the nation as then constituted was tonic or toxic, but quite certainly the immediate contact was electric.

On his return to Indonesia Bung Karno began formulating both in private and in public his various travel impressions. Although public formulations differed and reports of private formulations conflict, it is still possible, on the basis of his speeches and his actions, to report with some confidence what he actually concluded. In the United States he saw a nation which had achieved a high degree of personal freedom, technical progress, and material abundance. From his point of view, however, the American revolution had long since run its course; America's institutions, he thought, had become static and offered little inspiration to an aspirant new people; its confidence in its own future, furthermore, seemed badly shaken by the spectacle of Communist expansion. In the Soviet Union and in Communist China, by contrast, he observed revolutions which were still in process, populations animated both by revolutionary zeal and political certainty, people so successfully disciplined, he believed, that they escaped both the fear and the frivolity he sensed in the United States and the futility he deplored in Indonesia. The Communist countries, he conceded, lacked personal freedom. They had deliberately set their own priorities, however, and they had chosen first to attain freedom from want and later would find freedom of expression. Indonesia, he insisted, would find its own way in accordance with its own values, setting no priorities, acknowledging no necessity either to choose between or to combine freedom from want and freedom of expression, the latter a concept originating in the West, peculiar to the West, and not necessarily, he intimated, to be equated with Indonesian Merdeka.

Bung Karno's travels apparently persuaded him also of something that had been quite apparent for years. Indonesia was lagging desperately in comparison with the rest of the world. If anybody was ever going to be able to do anything about it, it would have to be Bung Karno and soon. Otherwise not only the existing Republic of Indonesia but Bung Karno too was finished.

Bung Karno's observations abroad had not decided for him the course he would take, only that he must act. Obviously, then, he would do something characteristic both of Indonesia and of Bung Karno, something flamboyantly revolutionary. Bung Karno's problem was one with which the Emperor Meiji, among others, would have sympathized. It was to create a whole new ideological base on which to reconstruct a desperately troubled nation. Almost singlehandedly, but supremely self-confident, Bung Karno undertook this self-imposed assignment. He set himself, in the phraseology of the 1945 Declaration, to arrange "circumstances" "within the shortest possible time." In a few days or at most a few weeks of relatively consecutive thinking time, he arrived at a *konsepsi* (concept) calculated to reshape Indonesia's political, economic, and social destiny. It did, but not in a manner which even Bung Karno would then have predicted.

"I AM CRAZED . . . I AM OBSESSED . . ."

During the climacteric seven years from 1956 to 1963, Bung Karno's intellectual progression—or, more accurately speaking, his retrogression—manifested itself in three stages, each corresponding to a time of reintensified national desperation induced by his ideological and presently his military adventurism. Shortly after his return from the Soviet Union and from Communist China, Bung Karno first devised in late 1956, then disclosed to the nation in early 1957, his now historic *konsepsi* of a revolutionary new formula for resolving all of Indonesia's problems. Later, as problems swiftly worsened while he implemented his *konsepsi,* he announced in 1959 that *Repolusi* was in itself the magic formula. Finally, in 1963, as problems became overwhelming, he revealed that he himself constituted the incarnation both of Indonesia and of revolution and that all would be sustained by destiny in defiance of any mundane obstacles. The personal, national, and international tragedy of Bung Karno and of Indonesia thus came to assume truly fantastic dimensions. The great acceleration in deterioration, however, dates from February 27, 1957, the day that Bung Karno, after tantalizing the nation for weeks with hints and peeks, formally unveiled his private—and ultimately the nation's official—*konsepsi* of the "way out" of Indonesia's monumental dilemma.

By February 27, 1957, the Indonesian nation was ready for any panacea. The second Ali cabinet had been teetering for a year in political contortions even more frenzied than the national norm—

attempting, for instance, to outguess three regional military commands which were conspiring to overthrow it. Bung Karno had deliberately exacerbated the difficulties of the politicians while he himself was assuming an oracular stance. Leaving nothing to chance, he had called upon Chaerul Saleh to mobilize the nation's *pemuda* to implore him not to prolong the awful suspense. Finally, on February 27, after the *pemuda* had made sure of a nationwide radio audience for the occasion and had triggered the demonstrations to follow, Bung Karno pronounced the incantation. The *konsepsi,* in two compound words which Bung Karno then or later expanded upon by multiples of millions over tens of thousands of miles of itinerant oratory, was *musjawarah-mufakat* and *gotong-rojong.*

Musjawarah-mufakat, according to Indonesian tradition, which by now had to be explained to many leading Indonesians themselves, was the process whereby in the villages each individual had the opportunity to express his views in council, and the village elders afterwards, without resorting to any such formality as a vote or a decision, relied upon a Quaker-like sense of the community to guide them in their actions. The consultation was called *musjawarah* and the consensus was called *mufakat.* *Gotong-rojong* was already long established as a charter slogan of the revolution, but it too required elaboration. Originally, *gotong-rojong* had meant cooperation among villagers who helped to harvest each other's rice or to build community roads, irrigation ditches, and mosques, never keeping book about help offered and benefits received but practicing an unself-conscious system of communalism. In the new Sukarno apocalypse, *gotong-rojong* was to signify more especially "spontaneous" mass enthusiasm for whatever crusade Bung Karno might embark upon.

By reverting to *musjawarah-mufakat* and *gotong-rojong,* Bung Karno kept reiterating, Indonesia could practice a system of "Guided Democracy" that would be true to its own ideals and traditions. It must reject "Western," "liberal," "head-counting" democracy along with the political parties, which forced a divisive vote and created unbridgeable chasms. Everyone must now voluntarily suspend debate and cooperate in achieving universally agreed upon objectives. He, Bung Karno, would create a new Consultative Assembly in which all political factions and all regional or "functional groups," the latter including intellectuals, peasants, youth, women, artists, and the like, would be represented. The Assembly would compound unformulated guidance in accordance with which he himself would steer the other agencies of state. The special Sukarno spin to the *konsepsi,* however, was not only that Indonesia would renounce disputatious Western-style democracy in favor of the intuitive practices of its own past. It was that "guidance" was to be channeled through a body in which there would be happily commingled all formerly inimical factions, including the Communists. The PKI comrades, Sukarno stated quite explicitly, were hereafter to have their "fair share" of responsibility and of positions, including cabinet posts.

Bung Karno's *konsepsi* shook the nation and all but shook it apart. To a great many of the nation's leading citizens, it seemed an invitation to anarchy, military dictatorship, or communism. The PKI, to be sure, acclaimed it. The Djakarta military command, characteristically, hesitated. The Sumatran commands denounced it, reintensified their defiance of Djakarta, gained allies in Sulawesi, and threatened outright insurrection. The Masjumi (liberal Muslim) and the Socialist Party leaders analyzed and rejected the whole scheme. Most of the other parties equivocated. The Chaerul Saleh *pemuda* staged pro-*konsepsi* demonstrations and maintained surveillance over Masjumi and Socialist leaders. They painted up acres of whitewashed wall surfaces with big red and black letters spelling out many variants of "Hidup Konsepsi," and "Awas [Beware] Anti-Konsepsi," and the wall owners, after a couple of violent object lessons as to the consequences of erasure, let the messages stand.

Bung Karno attuned his ear to the loud, clear cry of the guided *pemuda,* but he hearkened also to the muffled voice of the politicians and tempered his *konsepsi* to the expediency of the moment. He appointed his Consultative Assembly but retained Parliament. He constituted his new cabinet with himself as Prime Minister, but he did not appoint any outright Communists to it. Although he extended repeated invitations to the political parties to practice self-immolation, he himself did not yet pile or ignite the funeral pyre. He referred with great oratorical fervor to previous cabinets which had included three major parties but excluded the fourth—the PKI—and were therefore, he said, maimed and crippled. "I can't and I won't ride a three-legged horse," he told the cheering mobs. Nevertheless, Bung Karno soon rode off on a slightly domesticated *konsepsi* which looked to many observers like a cross between a centipede and a chimera with the head of a Hydra and the complexion of a chameleon. The nation shied and it took Bung Karno a good two years to bring either his mount or his people under control. By that time both had undergone a drastic process which Bung Karno described as "retooling."

According to Bung Karno's private system of reckoning, the years 1957, 1958, and 1959 were, respectively, "the Year of Decision" and "the Year of Challenge," climaxing in "the Year of the Rediscovery of the Revolution." By anyone's reckoning, these were years of frenzy, packed with decision, challenge, and revolution enough to satisfy the most insatiable craving for action. They were years, therefore, of *peristiwa* too numerous and momentous to be designated merely by date.

The first great *peristiwa* of 1957, the Year of Decision, was the February 27 announcement of the *konsepsi,* about which many Indonesians, uncharacteristically, reached a firm decision, and the decision was not in favor of Bung Karno. Major areas of Sumatra and Sulawesi not only rejected the *konsepsi* but set up autonomous regimes under the regional military commanders. They welcomed distinguished defectors from Djakarta—ex-Ministers of State (two ex-Prime Ministers among them), the president of the Bank of Indonesia, and others of almost equal prominence, all of them branding the *konsepsi* and the Sukarno policies as ruinous madness. Bung Karno, meanwhile, devoted himself to a great extent to interinsular and intercontinental travels, in the course of which he delivered to millions of auditors in millions of words his *pro-konsepsi,* anti-insurrection message. Into his orations he laced generous infusions of anticolonial, pro-Irian Barat, "anticommunistphobia" propaganda. Then, on November 30, there occurred the year's second great *peristiwa,* one which shook Bung Karno himself as deeply as the *konsepsi* had shaken the nation.

As Bung Karno stepped from his car that November day to enter a building in the Tjikini district of Djakarta, where his own children were participating in a school ceremony, two *pemuda* threw hand grenades which killed several adult bystanders, injured other adults and also some children, and just barely missed Bung Karno himself. The *pemuda* were later identified and executed as fanatical Muslim disciples of an army-coup conspirator, Colonel Zulkifli Lubis. But Bung Karno's own person, like his ideology, it was now apparent, was no longer inviolate. Bung Karno was unnerved and his nation was appalled, but his *karma,* it seemed, was working overtime. During subsequent years it remained on a twenty-four-hour shift.

The Tjikini Affair was merely the first of four publicized assassination attempts, and Djakarta rumor mentions numerous others. On March 9, 1960, a "mad" air force lieutenant strafed the presidential palace. On January 7, 1962, "Dutch agents" from New Guinea threw hand grenades at the presidential car in Makassar. On May 14, 1962, a "fanatical Darul Islam traitor" fired at almost point-blank range during a special prayer ceremony in the palace mosque. Sukarno each time miraculously escaped.

"The heavens preserved me for the nation," explains Bung Karno. His trust in his destiny does not deter him, however, from taking precautions. He is surrounded by personal bodyguards. His special palace guard has again and again overflowed the quarters planned and built for it. In Indonesia he travels by land only in a heavily guarded, fast-moving convoy. He prefers even for short trips—to his Bogor Palace, for instance—to travel by helicopter. The plane, a gift from President Kennedy, picks him up and puts him down within the Bogor Palace grounds, but unfortunately, he complains, it blows the petals from the pond lilies. A Belgian-manufactured bulletproof vest, say the "well-informed" insiders, is an indispensable item in his wardrobe. He regularly consults soothsayers, some of whom, say the "well-informed," are dealers in black as well as in white magic. And he is never without his kris, a splendidly wrought and jeweled dagger which from ancient times, it is said, has conferred invulnerability upon its possessor.

To refresh himself after his brush with destiny on November 30, 1957, Bung Karno traveled abroad, stumping everywhere for the Irian Barat cause. Duly refreshed and newly outraged by the failure of the United Nations to endorse his case, Bung Karno returned to Indonesia to fulfill his promise to "take another way" in pursuing his Irian Barat campaign, one which would "startle the world." In late December, accordingly, he allowed Chaerul Saleh's *pemuda* and the PKI labor unions to begin and the army to complete the seizure of Dutch-owned business companies, banks, shipping lines, tin mines, rubber plantations, even such private properties as homes, cars, refrigerators, radios—everything which the Dutch could not take with them in their precipitate enforced departure. Meanwhile, as the Indonesian economy and the anti-*konsepsi* elements shuddered under the impact of nationalization and almost equally swift deterioration, Bung Karno was completely revising the strategy of his *konsepsi*. He denounced the anti-*konsepsi* "traitors" and acclaimed three mutually inimical sets of allies, each of whom he pitted against the other in order to maintain himself in control: Comrade Aidit and the PKI, Saudara Chaerul Saleh and the "Generation of '45" (i.e., both the old and the new *pemuda*), and General Nasution and the armed services.

Early in 1958 ("the Year of Challenge"), stirred to drastic action by the memory of the Tjikini Affair and the consequences of nationalization, Bung Karno gave the command to Nasution to put down the regional insurrectionists by force of arms. He thus precipitated into its violent phase the *Peristiwa* PRRI, the "war of brothers" which the Sumatran and Sulawesi insurrectionists, among many others, had believed could not occur and had neglected to prepare for. The central command succeeded swiftly and ably in its campaigns. By midyear Bung Karno could tour the nation in triumph, announcing the collapse of the rebel cause, to which, parenthetically, the United States had lent timid, tardy, and ineffectual support. With a covey of twelve ambassadors, including the American, Bung Karno ventured even into the easternmost islands. There, at Dobo, he shouted "Merdeka" across the Alfura Sea toward Irian Barat for the Papuans, the Dutch— and somewhat more remotely, the United Nations and the United States—to take notice.

In 1959 ("the Year of the Rediscovery of the Revolution"), Sukarno threw the nation for the first time since 1945 back into revolutionary high gear. He reverted by decree to the brief, vague, but authoritarian "Constitution of '45" ("magically endowed," he said). He "suspended" the Constituent Assembly—but not as yet the Parliament; altered his cabinet to add still more "Generation of '45" and more military representatives, and governed thereafter by emergency decree. The most dramatic of his decrees was that of August 24, 1959, "reforming" the economy. Runaway inflation was the most obvious symptom of a deep-seated economic disease brought on by reckless attempts at impossible controls, and Bung Karno treated the symptom. He did so by declaring a 90 per cent currency devaluation which so nearly bankrupted not only private individuals and business concerns but government offices as well, that the National Bank promptly printed up vast amounts of new currency just to stay in business.

While the inflation gathered new speed, Bung Karno directed his next economic and political "reforms" against the resident Chinese, identified as "economic exploiters" and "political provocateurs" by the government propagandists. The army, acting on Bung Karno's orders, in 1960 closed out the great majority of the rural Chinese traders, near-monopolists as village dealers in local produce and daily necessities, small capitalists who looked to Communist China for protection. As economic conditions worsened, naturally, little *peristiwa* multiplied. Some of the Chinese, for instance, chose to resist military foreclosure and forced evacuation. Djakarta thereupon found itself involved in a rancorous dispute with Peking, one in which Peking was the first to subside. Communist China repatriated tens of thousands of its nationals, relinquished claims to compensation for their properties, and soon began talking again of everlasting friendship and understanding. Sukarno, it appeared, had achieved yet another major victory. When rice and textiles went off the market, the stocks of the Chinese shopkeepers having been sold off and not replenished by the new owners, Bung Karno coined a new slogan—*sandangpangan,* signifying bountiful, government-subsidized food and clothing—which added a hopeful if empty obbligato to the national uproar.

Bung Karno's decrees, clearly, had long since outdistanced his *konsepsi*. In mid-1959, in his Independence Day (August 17) oration on "The Rediscovery of the Revolution," he retailored his ideology to his tactics. The address was promptly hailed as the Indonesian Political Manifesto, or "Manipol" in abbreviated slogan form. From it a working party headed by Comrade Aidit extracted a code called USDEK, an acronym formed from the initial letters of five key slogans which Manipol enshrined. The slogans included "Guided Democracy" and other variants—"Guided Economy," for instance—of Bung Karno's revivalist revolutionary formula for achieving the "pure and sacred" "Indonesian identity" in a "just and prosperous society" "free from 'l'exploitation de l'homme par l'homme.'"

Manipol-USDEK is a political acrostic shrewdly calculated to appeal to the Indonesian love for the slogan, the symbol, and the shibboleth, all of which acquire magical powers which transfix those who invoke them or those upon whom they are endlessly invoked. Manipol-USDEK soon yielded in oratorical priority to NASAKOM, and NASAKOM in turn to NASAKOMIL—the coalition in government of all factions based upon nationalism (*nasionalisme*), religion (*agama*), communism (*komunisme*), and the military (*militer*). Manipol-USDEK and NASAKOMIL have had to share the antiphonal chorus with a dozen other cryptograms which are represented as ideology, all of them together constituting total, but very inefficiently totalitarian *Repolusi*.

Sukarno's key ideas ever since 1927 have been Merdeka and *Repolusi,* and by 1959 he had come full circle in forcing each concept to its ultimate and irreconcilable contradiction. To Sukarno in 1959, *Repolusi* had come to signify revolution for the sake of revolution itself. Commitment to total, self-perpetuating revolution involved acknowledgment that orderly devices had failed, and the decision, rather than trying yet once again on the basis of learning from experience, to reject the validity of experience as a guide. It implied deliberate recourse to fervor and ferment in defiance of all predictable consequences, in expectation of results so startling that they themselves would maintain the momentum of Merdeka. For Bung Karno, then, *Repolusi* has become a rite, Merdeka has become a cult, and all wisdom is comprehended in the new slogan "The Freedom to be Free." At this point, if not long before, Bung Karno took leave not only of law but of meaning.

Bung Karno's state of mind since 1959 is most clearly revealed in a passage from the Political Manifesto that is at once incendiary and chilling, a personal testament to the ultimate effect of revolution upon the revolutionary:

I tell you frankly: I belong to the group of people who are bound in spiritual longing by the romanticism of revolution.

I am inspired by it, I am fascinated by it, I am completely absorbed by it, I am crazed, I am obsessed by the romanticism of revolution. And for this I utter thanks to God Who Commands All Nature!

There are people who do not understand revolutionary logic. . . . This is revolutionary logic: once we start off a revolution we must continue that revolution until all its ideals have been implemented.

This constitutes an absolute law of revolution, which can be denied no longer, that can be debated no further!

Therefore do not say, "The revolution is already over," whilst revolution is on the march; and do not attempt to dam up or to oppose or slow down a particular phase of revolution which is but a consequence of prior phases of the revolution!

There are also people who, oh yes, understand and agree about all the phases, but they ask: "Do we need to be always inflaming the spirit of revolution?"

"Is it necessary for everything to be done in a revolutionary way? Could it not be done by means of 'Alon-alon asal kelakon'—'slow but sure'!"

Good heavens! "Slow but sure!" That is not possible. That is not possible, unless we want to be crushed by the people! . . .

This world today is a revolutionary ammunition dump. This world today holds revolutionary electric power. This world today is "loaded with revolution."

Three-quarters of the whole of mankind on the face of this earth . . . are in a revolutionary spirit.

It has never before happened that the history of man has gone through such a revolution as this at present—so strong and so tremendous, so wide-sweeping and universal—a Revolution of Humanity which at the same time surges, flashes, thunders, in almost every corner of the earth. . . .

We see the red glow of fires reflected in the Eastern skies, the red glow of fires reflected in the Northern skies. . . . We see that all the skies around us are glowing with the fire of revolution. . . . [So] it is forbidden to us to go "slow but sure," forbidden to us to creep like snails, to crawl like tortoises . . . forbidden to us to nurture revolution-phobia!

Look and take heed! A state which does not grow in a revolutionary way will not only be crushed by its own people, but also will soon be swept aside by the typhoon of universal revolution which is the most important phenomenon in the world at the present time. . . .

The states and nations which are already old, and the states and nations which feel that they are already "settled," will also eventually be shaken up by that typhoon of universal revolution, if they do not adjust themselves to the changes and upheavals leading toward the formation of a new world, free from colonialism, free from *exploitation de l'homme par l'homme,* free from oppression, free from exploitation, free from color discrimination, free from spying upon one another with atomic bombs and thermonuclear weapons in their hands.

This is why I, who have been given the topmost leadership of the struggle of the Indonesian nation, never tire of appealing and exhorting: solve our national problems in a revolutionary way, make the revolutionary spirit surge on, see to it that the fire in our revolution does not die or grow dim, not even for a single moment.

Now, come on, keep fanning the flames of the leaping fire of the revolution. *Let us become logs to feed the flames of revolution.* [Italics added.]

In this text Bung Karno expounded his new gospel of the sacred obligation of the Indonesian people to "complete" the "unfinished revolution," to renounce, therefore, all devices of gradualism and conservatism and to seek the "true Indonesian identity" through genuinely and exclusively revolutionary action. The true revolution, he said, was sabotaged after December 27, 1949, by the "counterrevolutionaries" and the "neocolonialists," who led the nation through "deviation" and "error" to the very brink of an "abyss of annihilation." At any risk, indeed at any cost, the nation must now revitalize its revolution and drive it to its predestined fulfillment.

Reinspired by his own revolutionary dogma, Bung Karno devoted himself in 1961 to preparing for what he already envisaged and later christened "the Year of Triumph" (1962). He undertook to deal with all of Indonesia's domestic and international problems by concentrating on one bold program: not national development, but an all-out campaign of "mobilization of the people's potential" and of "confrontation in all spheres" for the "fulfillment of the revolution" by acquisition from the Dutch of Irian Barat. As a kind of divertissement, he ordered all-out effort also with regard to the 1962 Asian Games, to which Djakarta was to play host. Under Bung Karno's flaming leadership, the Indonesian public devoted itself to this double-feature extravaganza with a wild enthusiasm which led foreigners to a conclusion that became a favorite quip of the cocktail circuit: "Nero did it with bread and circuses. Sukarno does it with circuses." "Last things first," was the stock reply.

For the Asian Games the Japanese were induced to spend $14 million in war-reparations money to build and equip a 409-room luxury hotel. The Russians supplied $17 million in aid and a corps of engineers to build a spectacular sports complex inclusive of various stadia and an Olympic Village. The Americans stretched their aid program to provide for a divided highway complete with a handsome clover-leaf. American highway-building equipment and material, it might be noted, was sometimes diverted to the Russian stadium site, and the whole American project, as Bung Karno pointed out, fell badly behind schedule. Still, the clover-leaf provided a panoramic view of the sports area. The main Russian stadium, it might also be noted, sustained a nearly disastrous bit of arson in the course of construction; once rebuilt it did not even carry a brass gift plaque, such was Bung Karno's sensitivity and possessiveness toward the "Bung Karno Stadium." The Japanese were not very happy either about their hotel, which was turned over to the management of an American airline. The Asian Games area was brilliantly lighted even though blackouts are chronic elsewhere in Djakarta, and two splendid new fountains were installed on a main avenue of approach even though domestic water taps are often dry. In addition, by way of urban renewal in the games area, there were also built half a dozen new office, bank, and other buildings, one of them an American AID headquarters which did not venture to display a sign. Another was a new British Embassy, two years later to be stoned, ransacked, and burned by Bung Karno's guided mobs.

The Asian Games induced a nationwide state of euphoria. Food and clothing moved into phases of shorter and shorter supply and higher and higher prices, but national prestige seemed to shine with brighter and brighter luster. The Games turned out in fact to be a triumph of Indonesian planning, organization, hospitality, and athletic prowess. They were also, however, a triumph of Indonesian political manipulation at the high level and of rabble-rousing at the low. The Indonesian games officials, with Bung Karno personally calling the plays, craftily excluded Taiwan and Israel from participating. They then manipulated the other delegations into accepting the *fait accompli* rather than risk last-moment cancellation of the contests and world-wide derision. In the end, the Indonesian hosts came close to adding injury to insult. Besides staging angry demonstrations against those visiting teams and officials who objected to Indonesian substitution of politics for sportsmanship, they instigated a riot at the Indian Embassy and a near riot at their own new Hotel Indonesia.

While preparing for the Asian Games, Bung Karno had turned to Moscow for massive assistance for his Irian Barat campaign. From Moscow in early 1961 he gained a billion-dollar line of credit for ships, planes, jeeps, guns, and almost anything else he cared to order, as well as a resounding reindorsement of his Irian Barrat claim and a declaration of intent to help him assert it. Beginning in late 1961, Bung Karno took delivery on an imposing armory of Russian submarines, destroyers, MIG's, Turbonovs, rockets, and missiles, along with Russian technicians to make sure they were operable. In late 1961 also he began landing a few dozen paratroop infiltrators in Irian Barat; in early 1962 he dispatched a few hundred more. He had already stirred the whole Indonesian nation to a frenzy of volunteering, marching, singing, shouting, drilling, and demanding the joy of shedding blood in the liberation of their "Papuan brothers." Regional, possibly world war threatened.

"We don't care! We don't care! We don't care!" Sukarno shouted to his audiences after reporting to them the fears of the outside world that nuclear war was imminent. The Secretary-General of the United Nations thereupon designated an American mediator who negotiated a settlement which amounted to all but unconditional capitulation on the part of the Dutch to Bung Karno's demands. The minimum concessions to be exacted from Indonesia, on the basis of which the Dutch were pressured into handing the Stone Age Papuans over to Bung Karno's guardianship, were that there would be a two-year transition period and a later referendum. Bung Karno, however, demanded and got the right to fly the Indonesian flag in Irian Barat "by cock-crow" on

January 1, 1963, just as he had promised the Indonesian nation that he would. He gained commitment regarding outright physical possession on May 1, 1963. Long before that he announced that "a referendum will not be necessary" and made it clear that Indonesia's Year of Triumph was a beginning, not an end, to Indonesian expansionism.

Naturally, Bung Karno did not achieve his 1962 triumph without incurring heavy costs. He virtually bankrupted the nation and what was more, he mortgaged it to the Soviet Union for something well over $1 billion and far more than canceled out any possible benefit from some hundreds of millions of dollars in American aid. He created an Indonesian military colossus which he now attempts to hold in check by encouraging PKI challenge to its authority, while at the same time promising it new military adventure. To the general Indonesian population he denied all but the barest minimum of food and clothing, much of that coming by courtesy of discreetly anonymous American aid. He bought the dubious loyalty of a palace clique of official rogues and sycophants by letting them enjoy illegal wealth and luxury. His various policies set the national economy moving so fast and far in reverse that Indonesia constitutes a staggeringly greater problem of national rehabilitation and development in 1963 than it did in 1949. The situation became so explosive that even Khrushchev, on his 1962 good will visit, counseled caution while he dunned for payment. Bung Karno had already defied the Dutch and the Chinese, not to mention his domestic enemies and all accepted conventions of personal or national behavior; in 1962 he defied the Russians also by evading both their requests for payment and their proffers of advice.

Since defiance was obviously the dynamic force which kept Indonesia from smashing up, Bung Karno had to cast about thereafter for some new ogre to exorcize. He found it in the British presence in the neighboring, newly emerging Federation of Malaysia. The former Malaya and the new Malaysia, being the very antithesis of Indonesia, were natural targets for Bung Karno's animosity. Malaya and Malaysia symbolized such antiquated phenomena as political stability, economic solvency, racial harmony, military restraint, and national development. The Malaysian states, in other words, had achieved domestic progress by foregoing national and international agitation. They cooperated with the Western world in resisting Communist advances, financed their own national-development programs out of the profits of free enterprise and Western investment, and regarded good government as more important than mass movements. While the whole Malaysia area was achieving truly remarkable progress, Indonesia was deteriorating steadily, and the contrast was one which many Indonesians, including Bung Karno, found hard to explain and even more difficult to tolerate.

Bung Karno had been so preoccupied with his campaign to acquire Irian Barat that he had given relatively little attention to the newest developments next door, even in adjacent British Borneo. There the Crown Colonies of Sarawak and North Borneo and the Sultanate of Brunei were preparing to join with Singapore and Malaya to form the new Federation of Malaysia. On December 8, 1962, however, a Brunei politician, Azahari by name, a veteran of the Indonesian revolution and an associate of the PKI, staged an armed insurrection designed, he said, to "restore" the Sultan of Brunei to sovereign authority over all of British Borneo. Azahari, who directed his insurrection from the safe vantage point of Manila, called upon both the Philippines and Indonesia for military support. The Sultan of Brunei in turn called upon the British for military protection. The British put down the insurrection within a week, but Sukarno, who sent no immediate aid, hailed the Brunei insurrectionists as "heroic freedom fighters" whose cause Indonesia would vigorously espouse.

Sukarno branded Malaysia a British "neocolonial" conspiracy to "encircle" Indonesia. His military command soon began staging small guerrilla nuisance raids across the Sarawak border and little piratical attacks upon traders and fishermen in the Straits of Malacca. From then on, save for brief lulls while seeking to dictate through negotiation, Bung Karno preached and practiced a policy which he called *konfrontasi* (confrontation), defined first as a policy to "frustrate," then as one to "smash" Malaysia. General Nasution, Comrade Aidit, Saudara Chaerul Saleh and their respective cliques began at once noisily to support *konfrontasi,* sustaining the uproar even during the intervals of Sukarno's own relative self-restraint.

The year 1963 is not one upon which Bung Karno has yet

chosen to confer a name. Had he done so, he would probably have christened it "the Year of Confrontation," as indeed it was, but not always in the sense that he intended. In actual fact, of course, Bung Karno has long been practicing confrontation vis-à-vis the outside world. He has faced it with a long series of very difficult decisions in determining just how far it can go in endorsing or at least in condoning his own recklessly irresponsible policies. The decision became especially difficult for the Western world when Bung Karno made himself militantly intransigent about Irian Barat. The choice then lay between a Dutch colonialism which was in fact benevolent and an Indonesian nationalism which was in fact militant and colonialistic. In 1963, however, with regard to Malaysia, he made the choice rather easier. Bung Karno then vilified and threatened not a European colonial power but an independent Asian nation, although, to be sure, he tried to divert attention to the "neocolonial" British and their "puppets." In 1963, not only Westerners but also a respectable number of respectable Asians concluded that Bung Karno's case was a bad one.

Indonesian-Malaysian *konfrontasi* became in fact confrontation between the irresponsible and the responsible forces of Southeast Asia. Huge, heavily armed Indonesia, with a record of belligerence and deterioration, was menacing small Malaysia, a conspicuously peaceful, prosperous, and progressive nation. Bung Karno, a demagogue and a dictator, was alleging provocation while he himself provoked Tengku Abdul Rahman, a notably relaxed and reasonable man, into objecting to being burnt in effigy as a "British stooge." It had been possible for well-intentioned observers to argue that the Dutch, by making bigger concessions earlier, could have placated Bung Karno and eased Indonesia's tremendous problems of national development. It was scarcely possible to argue very convincingly that Tengku Abdul Rahman, by abandoning his Malaysia project, or by progressively and always more drastically modifying it in response to Bung Karno's demands, could have enhanced either Malaysia's or Indonesia's prospects for healthful development or could have shored up the defenses of a free Southeast Asia. With regard to *konfrontasi* of Malaysia, Bung Karno's own performance was transparently an attempt to achieve by ultimatum and duplicity what he could not achieve by right, and his image was difficult to portray as other than malevolent.

Bung Karno, to begin with, acclaimed the "patriotism" of the Brunei "freedom fighters" who had quite certainly received official Indonesian incitement to insurrection, some of them Indonesian military training as well. His real intent was to annex Brunei (and its oil revenues), and Sarawak and North Borneo as well. Bung Karno failed, however, to gain much international or even much spontaneous domestic support, or even panicky international effort toward appeasement. He discovered, furthermore, that American officialdom, alarmed by public and congressional objection to his ruinous policies, was becoming increasingly reluctant to provide the new American-aid money, of which he was desperately in need, if only to re-establish credit for his 1963 round of state travels. Bung Karno got himself as far as Tokyo on his annual "good will" tour before he seemed to realize that unless he went soft on *konfrontasi*—soft, also, on nationalization of American oil interests in Sumatra, which at the moment he was proposing to seize—he would have to rely altogether upon the Russians or the Chinese for his future financing. Neither was in a position or in a mood to be very generous.

To almost everybody's almost incredulous amazement, in late May, 1963, Bung Karno performed his most dramatic *volte face* since the August, 1945, kidnaping episode. He entered into new agreements with the American oil companies, and he staged a reconciliation with the Tengku. American-aid funds thereupon began to thaw, and Sukarno proceeded on his international rounds. Soon after his return to Indonesia, however, he began to zigzag. He did not renounce the oil agreements, at least for the time being, but he once again unleashed *konfrontasi*. His pretext was that Tengku Abdul Rahman, who had just negotiated with the British the final agreements regarding Malaysia, had "treacherously" "broken his promises."

Bung Karno's renewal of *konfrontasi* signaled an increase of nuisance raids into Sarawak and privateering in the Straits of Malacca. It triggered monster anti-Malaysia, anti-Tengku, anti-British demonstrations, plus the accustomed show of military, PKI, and high official outrage. Malaysia, Bung Karno orated, "is against our wishes and against our revolution" and therefore it should be "smashed." Once again, however, Bung Karno failed to stir up quite the national or international pandemonium he expected, and once again the American-aid pipe line began to dry up. The Soviet Union, meanwhile, was so cautious in its endorsement of *konfrontasi* as to be almost noncommittal. Communist China, on the other hand, was almost embarrassingly committal: it frightened the Philippines, which, itself seeking to gain North Borneo, was siding with Indonesia against Malaysia and found itself suddenly in the Peking camp.

After repeatedly shouting "Smash Malaysia" and hearing few sympathetic echoes except the controlled Indonesian amplification of his own voice, Bung Karno felt constrained to attend a "Little Summit" in Manila (July 31, 1963), there to negotiate with Malaya's Tengku Abdul Rahman and the Philippines' President Macapagal. On his arrival in Manila he threatened to depart forthwith unless the Tengku agreed to delay the formation of Malaysia, to accept a referendum in the states of Borneo, to close down British military bases, and to make various other concessions, both big and small, any one of which would have meant, sooner or later, no Malaysia. But the Tengku stood reasonably firm, and Bung Karno ensnared himself in his own strategy. He argued that Indonesia's case against Malaysia was based primarily on the principle of self-determination of nations, a principle which he himself had specifically rejected with regard to Irian Barat, but the Irian Barat case, he said, was "different." For failure to gain any other significant concession, he was obliged to settle for a resolution to call upon the United Nations' Secretary General to "assess" the situation in British Borneo. Bung Karno was so certain that U Thant himself would insist upon a referendum, which would allow time for a very great deal to happen in the interval, that he even agreed in advance to accept U Thant's findings. U Thant, however, after consulting with the British, decided upon a quick "assessment" of the validity of the 1962–63 Sabah (North Borneo) and Sarawak elections as an expression of self-determination. Bung Karno thereupon devoted himself to vigorous but unsuccessful efforts to sabotage the assessment, which he represented as fraudulent and British-manipulated. When U Thant pronounced on September 15 in favor of Malaysia, Bung Karno rejected his findings, refused to recognize Malaysia, and yet once again reactivated *konfrontasi*. Malaysia promptly broke off diplomatic relations and Bung Karno retaliated by ordering the ransacking and burning on September 18 of some fifty British buildings in Djakarta, including the embassy, the seizure of various British business interests, and then an embargo on all Indonesian communication and trade with Malaysia—trade which is important to Malaysia but absolutely vital to Indonesia.

By late 1963, save for his astounding record of survival and triumph to date, it would have seemed safe to conclude that Bung Karno had at last overreached himself. Indonesia was unreconstructable, indeed it was virtually ungovernable in consequence of his chaotic, anarchic policies. American aid administrators, despairing at last of results beneficial to Indonesia or to the United States, had suspended new programs and were continuing the old only because cancellation would have meant starvation and rioting.

The Sukarno regime could no longer maintain the fiction of any form of solvency, only the dangerously accelerating exhibition of hysterical defiance. It would require billions of wisely spent American dollars and thousands of competent, dedicated Indonesian leaders to restore anybody's confidence in the nation. Neither the unlimited supply of safeguarded dollars nor the uncorrupted Indonesians were even distantly in view. Bung Karno himself no longer inspired respect, let alone credence or even despairing hope—not among Indonesians, Americans, Russians, Chinese, Malaysians, or for that matter, his newest allies, the Filipinos. He inspired only the fear that from the inevitable debacle there would emerge someone and something which from almost anybody's point of view would be even less tolerable.

Bung Karno was once Southeast Asia's most dazzling new leader, and Indonesians were Southeast Asia's most attractive people. The Indonesians themselves, however, have been so dazed by their own dazzle as to require prolonged national therapy in order to recover. Bung Karno, a quarter of a century after he emerged as Indonesia's radiant national hero, has now been exposed as a national and an international menace. Ten years ago, as the reckless but nevertheless dashing Father of His Country, Bung Karno had seemed on the point of committing involuntary infanticide upon a singularly attractive progeny; in 1963 he seemed in fact to have fathered in his own regime a Mongoloid monster. The ultimate and the tragic irony of the Sukarno charisma is that it should have created what even the charismatic disciples no longer care to contemplate.

"Saja Indonesia, saja Repolusi" (I am Indonesia, I am the Revolution), Bung Karno has said on occasion to his close associates, and he has recently begun to make the statement even in public. The identity at times seems all too frighteningly exact. But history is rarely kind in its judgments of those who believe "L'état, c'est moi," and "Après moi le déluge." Indonesian history and Indonesian historians may prove even more unkind than most.

Mohammad Yamin, Indonesia's first contemporary historian —"historian," that is, in the Indonesian ultranationalist sense— did not altogether accept one of Sukarno's earlier concepts of his own role. Sukarno, if one can believe a story which is rather too well supported to be mere fabrication, used to fancy that he was the reincarnation of Gadjah Mada, the great warrior Prime Minister of the fourteenth century who created the Modjopahit Empire. Mohammad Yamin, who compiled—or rather invented —the modern biography of Gadjah Mada and illustrated it with his own portrait, believed that he himself and not Sukarno was the reincarnated Modjopahit hero. Sukarno, he said—on one occasion, at least, to Sukarno himself—was more probably Ayam Wuruk, the amiable, accomplished, but basically weak king who undermined the empire Gadjah Mada conquered for him. Since Gadjah Mada, both in legend and in fact, although not in Mohammad Yamin's hagiography, was a man not only of genius but of singularly repellent character, conduct, and countenance, it is difficult for an outsider to understand why Sukarno and Yamin should either claim or dispute the reincarnation. Nevertheless, there are those today who see in President Sukarno either another Gadjah Mada or another Ayam Wuruk or a composite of the two. Practically everybody, however, sees in Bung Karno today the Big, Big Bung, and indeed, whether more or less indulgently, the Bad, Bad Bung. The dramatically delinquent father of an overgrown, underdeveloped adolescent nation, the Bung Besar-Besar is Southeast Asia's most recklessly potent Papak and Pemuda Repolusi.

Tengku Abdul Rahman:
Bapa Malaysia

Fifteen years ago Tengku Abdul Rahman would not have been
picked by many of the political pollsters as a man at all likely to
become Prime Minister of the Federation of Malaya, then only
dimly foreseen, let alone of the then not even contemplated
Federation of Malaysia. Twelve years ago his own Malay associates were rather dubious about selecting him to head a forlorn political party, the United Malay National Organization (UMNO),
which Dato Sir Onn bin Ja'afar, its brilliant and showmanlike
founder, had almost wrecked. Tengku Abdul Rahman himself
was not and is not brilliant or even, by choice, very industrious.
His best friends smile deprecatingly, as does the Tengku, about
his capacity for retaining facts and figures or his grasp of intellectual profundities. Nor is he a showman. His sense of the
theater is that of a keenly appreciative spectator, and he is quite
likely to be pointing his own camera from the dais when he
should be posing. As a state figure, he is a bit too plump and
casual to create an impression of imposing presence. He seems
more stuffy than stately when he is decked out in gold and silver
brocades for some official occasion. As for speechmaking, his
delivery is good enough if he keeps his eyes on the script; but
his eyes, behind big horn-rimmed bifocals, have a tendency to
wander. His voice is likely to break into chuckles at some of his
own witty interpolations. Self-enjoyment then prompts him to
interpolate still more, and as every politician knows, wit is not
always catnip to the voter.

The Tengku all the same is probably Southeast Asia's most

successful Prime Minister. He is successful, that is, in the sense that he is running a good government, which is not, of course, everyone's criterion of good political performance. Tengku Abdul Rahman may be successful precisely because he is not constantly on guard either to avoid giving offense or even to maintain himself in position. He obviously likes his job and the pay is good— M$4,000 per month (U.S. $1,333.33), plus quite a lot of extras. But the Tengku prefers to be himself rather than a public property, and he can always retire to being pensioned petty royalty. His present M$228 per month stipend as a prince of the State of Kedah can be modestly supplemented by rents from those few inherited properties he has not sold off to pay his own debts or to help his friends. Being royalty, he is not overwhelmingly impressed by his position as Prime Minister, nor, being genuinely democratic royalty, is he overwhelmingly impressed by the pretensions of the politicians, especially his rivals.

The Tengku did not exactly bid for the job as UMNO leader back in 1951, but he did make himself available. As UMNO president, he was gradually—and on the whole willingly—maneuvered into the job of head of government. He is motivated now, it is quite apparent, by a deeply felt desire to serve the state to the best of his ability. But he is guided also by two other considerations which are rare among the world's politicians. One of them is a shrewdly realistic estimate of his own capacities and of what assistance he requires. The other is a conviction that the good life includes not mere fame and power but leisure, sports, friends, and family, and that he is going to enjoy these latter amenities right here and now.

The Tengku, in being completely himself, frequently departs from the paths of political and diplomatic rectitude by speaking his mind. He then leaves to his associates the task of tidying up the debris. He refuses to get ulcers by following the urgings of some of his friends that he try to become prompt, precise, and perspicacious. Not long ago he seemed to be yielding to pressure to the extent that he suffered for a time from insomnia. His malaise was cured less, perhaps, by the medication prescribed by his physician than by his own reaction to such solicitous display of public sympathy as an offer on the part of some elderly UMNO ladies that they sing him to sleep.

To those who are satiated with publicly and self-glorified makers of new nations, the Tengku often seems too good to be true, or at least too good to last as head of a Southeast Asian government. Both his friends and his enemies think at times that they had better focus attention upon his faults. The fact is that he has so many and admits to them so disarmingly that he becomes a paragon of self-deflation. He is by nature indolent, imprudent, self-indulgent, frivolous, and extravagant. He has little truck with good books, good music, or publicized good works. He drinks brandy, smokes cigars, plays poker, and in his youth he sowed wild oats. It should also be pointed out, however, that he observes the rigorous self-discipline of the Muslim fasting month. His apprehension at the onset of *Puasa* and his relief at its termination fuel Kuala Lumpur society's small talk and his own.

The Tengku does not and cannot cast himself as the projection of a studiously contrived image, either as the quite extraordinary ordinary man which he is, or as the sacrosanct father of his people. A recent careless lapse in allowing himself to be formally designated by earnest youths as "Bapa Malaysia" seems unlikely at the moment to lead to anything worse, for the personality cult is not to his liking. The Tengku's unadorned personality, in fact, is no model for earnest youth, although for many adults it seems a vindication of their own errors.

In other words, Tengku Abdul Rahman is easy to like and hard to dislike because he does not insist upon excelling in any other virtue than getting people to reconcile their differences and to get on with whatever job most needs to be done. In a nation where the center of the stage is disputed by mutually suspicious and jealous Malays and Chinese, with Indians lurking loudly in the wings and the British in the prompter's pit, the Tengku's genius for liking others and making himself liked, rather than for upstaging his associates, is something which the Japanese would probably designate as a national treasure.

The Tengku's fairly widespread reputation for personifying in his career not the rewards of excellence but the compensations of mediocrity in itself invites a bit of reverse debunking. His "mediocrity" is that of a genuine, honest, intelligent human being, the man who regards it as more important to be a good citizen than to be a prominent one. He manages to be both without being either pious or overbearing. His is almost the "mediocrity" of the golden mean. While it is refreshing to find in him a national leader who is not bedazzled by his own fluorescently lighted image, it is well to remind oneself that quiet self-deprecation is an art which only a truly superior public man can practice for long. The Tengku has been practicing it for over a decade with few symptoms as yet of becoming pompous. He does occasionally get huffy these days about real or imagined breaches of protocol. He is subject to quite a lot of criticism for "despotic" management of his own party and the Alliance to which it belongs. He tolerates quite a good deal more wheeling and dealing on the part of his cronies than would, say, De Gaulle, if he had any. The Tengku may yet become more the stereotype than the maverick among the leading figures of the emerging nations, but his record to date does not give much grounds for either the fear or the hope.

Tengku (Prince) Abdul Rahman Putra al-Haj was born on February 8, 1903, in Alor Star, the capital of the northwestern Malay State of Kedah, then a dependency of Siam. He is the fifth surviving son of the Sultan Abdul Hamid Halim Shah (d. 1943), one of the forty-five legitimate children whom the Sultan sired by his eight legal wives before he died, quite mad, at the age of seventy-nine after a reign of sixty-one years. The Tengku, to continue the enumeration, was the seventh child of the Sultan's sixth wife, a circumstance which made his prospects for succession to the throne fairly remote. Even though the sixth wife was the Sultan's favorite, the Tengku was her own fourth son.

Tengku Abdul Rahman was born at a period when the Sultan, who was subject during most of his life to recurrent spells of insanity, was climaxing a career of reckless extravagance which bankrupted the state. In 1906, in celebration of the marriage of his eldest son, the heir apparent, and of four other sons who also happened to be of marriageable age, the Sultan staged a three-month wedding party. State offices were closed for the duration; practically everyone in the state was invited and all the neighboring royalty as well; and save for activities connected with the wedding party, almost all constructive labor was suspended.

The Sultan financed the blow-out with loans from the Penang moneylenders. He was so lavish with his hospitality—providing for his more distinguished guests, it is said, some thirty cases of champagne per day and unlimited quantities of fine Egyptian cheroots, in addition to full board and lodging—that the final reckoning came to M$3-4,000,000. By that time the Kedah State treasury was bare, and the Siamese government, to whom the Sultan appealed for rescue, agreed to bail him out only on condition that he accept a financial adviser. This adviser, who turned out to be an Englishman, was an advance party of one who preceded the British government's extension of "protection" to Kedah in 1909.

The Tengku—fortunately, perhaps—saw little of his father except on Fridays, when the Sultan's usual schedule took him first to the mosque for prayers, then to the palace of Makche Menjelara, the Tengku's mother. From all accounts Makche Menjelara (d. 1941), or Mak Chek as she was usually called, must have been a most extraordinary member of the harem. She was not a Malay but a Siamese-Burmese, the daughter of a Thai provincial Governor of Burmese descent, who, having plenty of female children, had sent her as a young girl to Kedah where she lived as a foster child to one of the sisters of the previous Sultan. She grew up to be both beautiful and intelligent. By her beauty, she attracted the Sultan, and by her shrewdness—the business acumen more characteristic of the Burmese and Thai women than of their men—she made herself rich. She acquired properties not only in Alor Star but in Bangkok as well, and she very wisely kept her own finances quite separate from those of her husband.

As a mother, Mak Chek seems to have combined discipline with affection and to have maintained at the same time an agreeable tolerance toward the leisure-time occupations of her children. The Tengku lived in her "palace"—a curious three-story Chinese pagodalike structure, long since vanished—but he wandered about Alor Star almost like any other barefoot, bare-bottomed *kampong* child. He was in and out of the trees, the river, the stalls of the wayside food venders, and the homes of the neighbors, like one more member of the pack of boys who constituted one of the liveliest elements of a sleepy town.

The Tengku's education was spotty from the first, and what his teachers remember best about him is his capacity for inattention and for enjoyment. He started out at the age of four in a sort of kindergarten where Malay was the language of the morning, English that of the afternoon. He progressed to the government-sponsored English school in Alor Star, but when he was ten he was sent to study in a Siamese school in Bangkok. There he lived with his brother, Tengku Yusoff, who had been brought up as a ward of King Chulalongkorn and had studied at Rugby and at the Royal Military Academy at Woolwich. Tengku Yusoff had returned to Kedah with an English wife, but upon encountering both British and Malay resentment toward his marriage had settled into Thailand as a captain in the Siamese Army. Abdul Rahman remained with him in Bangkok for about a year. When Tengku Yusoff died suddenly of pneumonia in 1915, the younger brother returned to Malaya. There he entered first a Malay-language school in Alor Star, then in 1916 transferred to the English-language Penang Free School.

The Penang Free School, the oldest and by common repute the best secondary school in Malaya, was then attended mainly by sons of well-to-do or rich Chinese or Indian families and by sons of British families who had not yet been sent back to school in England. As a Malay, the Tengku was in a small minority, and as a royal prince, whose mother rather ill-advisedly outfitted him with gold-embroidered bed pillows and similar tokens of affection and rank, he was soon obliged to establish the fact that he was good with his fists. So far as his no-nonsense British masters were concerned, he had also to establish the fact that he could pass examinations, which he did, although without much margin.

In early 1920, as soon as passage could be engaged after the end of World War I, Tengku Abdul Rahman sailed for England to continue his studies as the recipient of a newly established Kedah State scholarship. It was his intention to enter Cambridge, but the Kedah state government had prudently arranged for some preliminary tutoring. On arrival in England, therefore, Tengku Abdul Rahman proceeded to the village of Little Stukeley, near Huntington, where the rector took in foreign students for special coaching. The Tengku, who found country life and sports more agreeable than study, quickly acquired a favorable local reputation as the athletic "Prince Bobby." He made little academic progress until he was moved to Cambridge. There he enrolled with a private tutor, who managed, in the course of about six months, to cram in enough learning that he qualified for matriculation.

Once enrolled in St. Catherine's, one of the smallest of the Cambridge colleges, the Tengku's first really memorable encounters were not with intellectual stimulus but with race prejudice. When he applied for residential quarters in the college, he was informed that none were available. He was subsequently advised that the college was "built for English students." He was eager to play football for the university, but although he was clearly an outstanding player and his name was proposed, he was never called for the freshman trials. The Tengku's reaction in each case was characteristic. First he got angry, then he shrugged his shoulders and made the best of it. He found his own "digs," where he enjoyed more independence than he would have had inside the college. He played football for St. Catherine's, if not for the university, and found plenty of time to travel about attending country matches.

The Tengku managed to travel about quite a lot, for his £800 (U.S. $4,000) per year allowance enabled him to live in style and to drive a £525 Riley, a red and aluminum sports model. Addiction to football, horse racing, dog racing, dancing, and miscellaneous other diversions left him little time for study and almost none for lectures. He propelled his Riley with such speed and verve from one extracurricular engagement to another that he began collecting convictions for traffic offenses in Cambridge, London, and elsewhere. He scored a grand total of twenty-three, not all of them in this early period but over the sixteen years which he spent at various times in England, more vigorously in pursuit of pleasure than of a degree. Just as he forgot to watch his speedometer, he also forgot to watch his calendar, and his leisurely academic progress was the result not only of failing his examinations but of failing on at least one occasion even to appear on the right day to take them. In December, 1925, he managed to become the first Kedah prince to receive a B.A. degree from an English university, but the academic basis of the distinction does not invite close scrutiny. He then started what was to be a marathon pursuit of a law degree, ending at last in 1949 after repeated failures and prolonged interruptions. Then, at the age of forty-five, almost as much to his own surprise as that of his friends who had managed to fix his attention on law by reading it aloud to him, he just barely made the pass list. The Tengku happily celebrated what he called the "silver jubilee" of his matriculation.

The Tengku's true distinction, perhaps, consists in not taking himself altogether seriously, and one of the results has been that until recent years almost no one else took him very seriously either, least of all in politics. His first real experience in politics occurred when he was still an undergraduate. On that occasion he played chauffeur to a young British Liberal friend of his who ill-advisedly chose to campaign for Lloyd George in a working-men's district, provoking such outrage that both young men had to decamp as swiftly as the Riley could gather speed. This episode, his friends thought, taught him little except the social value of a political anecdote. One of his later experiences, after he had already passed a prolonged apprenticeship, came when he decided in 1946 that it was time for the Malay students in London really to organize for political action as did the other students from the colonies. He therefore revived the Malay Society of Great Britain, which he had helped to found back in 1927, but in doing so ran into near insubordination on the part of his associates. Some of them claimed, with considerable justification, that he wanted them to do all the hard work. As a politician, his friends in London thought, the Tengku was a wonderful cook. The evenings when the Malay students huddled in out of the London cold to eat highly seasoned Malay food and to talk of home in the flat of one or another of the set generally turned out, when the Tengku was in charge, to be at least as culinary and social as political in tone, the Tengku having a deft hand with both the skillet and the bottle.

Reports of the Tengku as a playboy prince, however, do not take into account quite a good deal of evidence that, unlike all too many of the other Malay princelings, he was quite earnestly if unmethodically attempting to become a useful citizen. In the long intervals between periods of study in England, he entered the Kedah Civil Service, and in it he worked hard. Beginning in 1931, he was assigned to a series of minor posts, but soon achieved the rank of that all-purpose administrator, the District Officer, i.e., the legal, police, sanitation, agriculture, education, and tax officer all in one, with extra responsibility for community morale.

As District Officer, the Tengku earned about M$300 per month, a figure which contrasted rather sharply with the £800 annual allowance (M$1,000 per month) he had enjoyed in England. He achieved a considerable reputation as champion of the rights of the poor and became immensely popular with the people of his district but not with the senior British and Malay officials back in Alor Star, to whom his reports were infrequent and disquieting. On one memorable occasion, when the taxi drivers of Sungei Patani were being forced arbitrarily to form a company, the Tengku sided with the drivers against the government. For this offense he was given twenty-four hour notice of transfer. Next morning a convoy of Sungei Patani taxi drivers showed up to escort him in style to his new post in Kulim. He was District Officer at Kulim when the Pacific War broke out.

One of the Tengku's exploits at the very beginning of the Japanese invasion of Malaya has now become a part of Kedah State folklore. The British and the Kedah court decided, when the Japanese advance began, to transfer the Sultan from Alor Star to the presumed safety of Penang Island. They packed him into the royal Rolls Royce and pointed it southward, trailing the car at some little distance to make sure he was not surprised from the rear. Tengku Abdul Rahman, alerted to the maneuver and determined that the Sultan should remain in Kedah with his people, waited at a road fork not far from Butterworth and the Penang Straits ferry. He ambushed the royal yellow Rolls, and kidnaped his father, Rolls, driver, and all. He spirited them off to Kulim and from there to a quiet *kampong,* one which has just recently been rechristened Kampong Raya (Hamlet Royal) to memorialize the event. When the British and Malay officials caught up with the Tengku by telephone he admitted to the crime. Although he was threatened with arrest, he defied orders to deliver the Sultan to Penang. When the Japanese staged heavy air raids soon afterwards on Butterworth airfield and Penang Island, he was moved to point out that the Sultan was safer right there near Kulim.

The Tengku remained in Kedah State government service throughout the Japanese occupation, when Kedah was placed under the administrative control of Thailand. On more than one occasion, according to the report of those who should know, he boldly confronted the Japanese authorities on behalf of his people.

At the time of the Japanese collapse, when Kedah, to an even greater extent than the rest of Malaya, was seething with the intrigues of Communists, nationalists, feudalists, and others, many of whom were armed, the Tengku was largely responsible for the fact that British troops reoccupied the state without any incidents of violence. Nevertheless, the taint of collaboration with the Japanese attached to many royal names in 1945 and accusations were made also against the Tengku. It was not for some time that his name was completely cleared. Meanwhile, both Kedah and Malayan politics had become vastly complicated as small nationalist organizations mushroomed all over the country, most of them with but vaguely defined programs and bitterly jealous of each other. The Tengku, despite the geniality which characterized him in most of his dealings with individuals and groups, tangled both with left-wing extremists—especially the Communists—and with right-wing feudalists—especially his brother, the new Sultan. In 1947 he left for England again, motivated more by the desire to absent himself from Kedah State than to present himself before the British bar examiners, whom he decided to face yet again—as he did, successfully, two years later.

In early 1949 Tengku Abdul Rahman returned once again to Malaya and joined the Legal Department of the Kedah State government. It soon became obvious to everyone, including himself, that he had no future in Kedah. His personal and political relations with his brother, Sultan Badlishah (d. 1958), an arrogant feudalist who had come to the throne in 1943, were bordering on the explosive. Tengku Abdul Rahman welcomed the opportunity, therefore, to go to Kuala Lumpur as Deputy Public Prosecutor. He did not resist very vigorously, if he did not actively encourage the pressures which a few of his friends began putting upon him to devote himself more and more to politics. Finally, in 1951, circumstances conspired at last to unleash the Tengku's special talents, which clearly were not for jurisprudence but for public life, and a career which hitherto had been unillustrious began to brighten.

The United Malay National Organization at that time was experiencing a major crisis. Under Dato (later Sir) Onn bin Ja'afar, the UMNO had been largely responsible for persuading the British to modify their immediate postwar proposal regarding the future status of Malaya. The British had worked to create a Malayan Union, in which the sultans would have been relegated to the background, a new central government would have gained sweeping authority, and the British themselves would have remained in the ascendant. Rallied by Dato Onn, the Malays balked. The British then consented to form a less highly centralized federation in which they would allow an increasing degree of democratic self-government. But the UMNO, having achieved its first major objective, soon split wide open. It repudiated a proposal by Dato Onn that it achieve interracial cooperation in building the new nation by accepting Chinese and other non-Malay members into the organization. It also repudiated Dato Onn himself. This was the time for a new leader, and the Tengku, it happened, was chosen. He himself has always acknowledged a major debt, however, to Dato Onn, to whom he was never personally or politically very close but from whom he inherited a very great deal.

Dato Onn (b. 1895), Malaya's first great nationalist, might pass as the prototype of the Southeast Asian leader of an early revolutionary period. Thoroughly indoctrinated in the intellectual tradition of the colonial motherland against which he was rebelling, Dato Onn proved at critical moments so obtuse to the aspirations of his followers that he seemed to be leading away from the goal which he himself had announced. He had been educated in England and on his return to Malaya he had set himself to practice his British-style eloquence, wit, and sportsmanship as professional gadfly of the British administrators, with whom, socially, he consorted on terms of the greatest mutual esteem while other Malays looked on in incomprehension. More Arab than Malay by racial background, more European than Asian in personal outlook, Dato Onn was also by temperament more pirate than politician, piracy having been, in fact, the avocation of some of his ancestors. By instinct, he was more feudalist than democrat, for he belonged to a family of virtually hereditary court officials of the Johore sultanate.

Eventually Dato Onn earned a knighthood but forfeited the Prime Ministership. He knew how to handle the British, but he never learned how to handle the Malays other than those of his own small class, the older scions of the court families; and he bungled badly when it came to dealings with the Malayan Chinese. He gloried in his gift for the winged word, but his political principles became so subtle that few could follow and fewer still could trust them. In 1951 he attempted to bring the Chinese into the UMNO, but before the Malays were ready; later, after the Tengku had succeeded in bringing them in (early 1953), Dato Onn protested that Malaya was being converted into a "twentieth province of China." He himself wanted independence, but he made the incredible blunder, and led his followers into the same dead end, of denouncing the Tengku for demanding it "too soon." When he formed his own anti-UMNO party, the Independence of Malaya Party, he took puckish pleasure in the abbreviation IMP. Even a Britisher could have told him that IMP translated into Malay would come out as *hantu,* meaning not merely a mischievous but a malign spirit, and *hantus* draw few votes. Later he transformed his IMP into the Party Negara but so neglected organizational details that in the course of a year or so branch after branch vanished without leaving a trace. Given a good campaign manager, Dato Onn might have put on a really good political show. But Dato Onn was himself unmanageable, and he preferred to startle rather than to manage others. So at the end of his career, which set in shortly after the peak, he was a picturesque and popular old fossil, frail and toothless and cheerful, but not a serious political influence.

For all his aberrations, Dato Onn performed at least three major political services, of which the Tengku inherited the benefits. He personally initiated the nationalist and independence movement and gave it irresistible momentum; he chose the course of peaceful rather than violent revolutionary devices; and he passed into political decline before doing any great damage to the movement, either by reason of any frenzied efforts of his own to remain in control or by reason of any frenzied efforts of others to oust him. As the first great Malay nationalist leader, Dato Onn is still honored today, and Tengku Abdul Rahman inherited from him a foundation, not a ruin, on which to build.

Tengku Abdul Rahman emerged on the national scene, then, just as Dato Onn started into eclipse. At this point the UMNO had found itself without a clear-cut program or acknowledged leader, without anything but the shakiest sort of organization.

The Tengku's friends, who knew his gift for sustaining amity and suspected that he might have popular appeal if not administrative skill, maneuvered him into the party presidency (August 26, 1951). The most influential of these friends was a man who might have had the presidency for himself, Tun Abdul Razak, then and now the Tengku's closest associate, and his probable successor.

Tun Abdul Razak (b. 1912; the court title "Tun" was conferred upon him by the Sultan of Pahang), who considered himself "too young" for the UMNO presidency and urged it upon the Tengku instead, is a rigorously self-disciplined intellectual, as the Tengku is not, a man of outstanding drive and ability who lacks but values the Tengku's warmth. Tun Razak can be relaxed and genial among his intimates, but in the office he is something of a martinet and in public rather a monochrome. The son of a high hereditary chieftain of the State of Pahang, he received his early education in Malaya, chiefly in the Malay College of Kuala Kangsar, a school established by the British for the express purpose of educating promising young Malays for the civil service. After acquitting himself with distinction in several government jobs, Abdul Razak was awarded a scholarship to go to England to study law, where once again he achieved an outstanding record. He managed in his spare time to organize and operate a sort of private tutorial service whereby he and his friends read both law and the law to the Tengku, who has them to thank that he finally managed to pass his examinations. Razak was a leading figure, naturally, in the Malay Student Association and succeeded the Tengku as its head.

Upon his return to Malaya in May, 1950, Razak almost immediately became prominent in the UMNO, to which he was elected vice-president when the Tengku became president. He had meanwhile re-entered government service and in it he rose to the post of Chief Minister of the State of Pahang. In 1955, after winning a seat in the new national Legislative Assembly, he became a member of the Council of Ministers under the Tengku as Chief Minister. His particular achievement during the preindependence period was the drafting of a new national educational program. Following independence he served in various ministerial posts. Today he is the chief assistant to the Tengku, holding posts concurrently as Deputy Prime Minister and Minister for Rural Development.

Since 1959 Tun Razak has devoted himself primarily to the program which may prove to be the most critical to the continued peace and prosperity of the new nation, the implementation of the rural development aspects of the Five Year Plan. For this program he has established a command-post type of headquarters, the central feature of which is a "Control Room" in which key officials are assembled almost daily to report progress, analyze faults, and devise remedies. The Control Room is equipped with enough motion picture projectors, tape recorders, microphones, exhibits, models, graphs, charts, maps, and sliding panels to impress even visitors from the Pentagon. Command post sessions sometimes develop into lengthy inquisitions to determine exactly who is to blame when danger signals flash on the control grid.

Not content to sit in his operational headquarters pushing buttons and papers, Tun Razak spends a good deal of time on the road, often dropping in unannounced at project sites. He manages in this way to keep his staff on the alert, but he gives rise to a good deal of criticism that his methods are mechanical, his standards arbitrary, and his disposition despotic. The criticism, it seems, comes less from the traditionally relaxed Malays, whom one might expect to be upset by his demand for efficiency, than from the energetic Chinese, who appreciate his drive but mistrust his motives. Many of the key Malayan Chinese feel that Tun Razak suspects them of nefarious economic manipulation. While many of them admit to infringing regulations a trifle, they say that infringement would not be so necessary if only Tun Razak would relax, for instance, about letting important contracts go to the Chinese, especially when they are the only ones capable of handling the jobs. Widespread misgivings about Tun Razak among the Malayan Chinese, misgivings which he fully reciprocates, lead to a good deal of speculation whether the Alliance and the Alliance government can hold together when and if Tun Razak actually does succeed the Tengku.

With Tun Razak as his chief prop, often his chief goad, Tengku Abdul Rahman worked hard to convert the UMNO and the Alliance into the paramount political grouping in Malaya, Malaya into an independent nation, and the independent Federation of

Malaya into the most successful of Southeast Asia's new national experiments. The Tengku demonstrated that despite his reputation as a playboy prince, as national leader he could repeat the same serious and sustained attention to business he had shown as a District Officer. He may actually have succeeded the better because his interest was never excessively serious and his effort was never indefatigably sustained. In extremely troubled times, when dealing with extremely delicate problems, the Tengku could still thoroughly enjoy a brandy or two or three in company with British colonial officials who, as everyone including the Tengku knew, were trying to put something over on him and sometimes did.

The Tengku, in his new role as national leader, had to cope not only with the British but with the Malays, the Malayan Chinese, the Malayan Indians, and the local Communists (mainly Chinese). The Communists were engaged in a bloody jungle war to coerce the Chinese, terrorize the Malays, murder the British, and convert Malaya into a Communist state. The "Emergency," which had begun in 1948, entailed all-out effort on the part of jungle guerrillas, equipped with arms parachuted to them during World War II when they belonged to the anti-Japanese underground, to sabotage the administration and to paralyze the vital tin and rubber industries. The British poured in troops and money. Gradually they developed the strategy of sealing off much of the rural population into strictly policed "New Villages." By drastically reducing contacts between the villagers and the guerrillas, and by rigorously patrolling all roadways, the British denied the guerrillas access to food, medical supplies, and ammunition and gradually isolated them in the deep jungle.

For success in their program of simultaneously fighting the guerrillas and rebuilding the nation, the British needed the loyal cooperation of the Malayan people. It was one of the miracles of postwar Southeast Asian national and nationalist history that they got it. They got it by making major concessions to the nationalists, and the nationalists drove a hard bargain. With the Tengku as their leader, however, they chose to negotiate with the British rather than fight them; they chose to fight the Communists rather than appease them or collaborate with them; they gained their objective of independence without destroying the basis for quick national growth. The Malayans thus achieved independence with both nationalists and ex-colonialists still willing and able to work together for the development of the new nation.

The early phase of the Tengku's leadership of the UMNO (1951–1955) corresponded with the height of the Communist Emergency and of the Malayan campaign to convert vague British assurances of independence into a definite agenda and timetable. Tengku Abdul Rahman devoted himself first to building up the strength of the UMNO, then a haphazard conglomerate which lacked discipline or organization. After 1952 he grafted together the UMNO and the MCA (Malayan Chinese Association) to form the Alliance, to which presently was added the MIC (Malayan Indian Congress). This tripartite, triracial coalition operated in theory on the basis of reconciling its differences in party councils and presenting a united front in public. In practice it operated pretty much on the basis of *ad hoc* arrangements and kept threatening to fall apart.

The Tengku himself did not devise the strategy of the Alliance; he just accepted it. Some of the Malay and Chinese politicians in Kuala Lumpur had decided to contest the 1952 municipal elections as colleagues rather than as rivals and had won a dramatic series of victories. The Tengku saw the advantages of the arrangement and decided to extend its scope. So did another gentleman of political influence and vision. He was Dato Sir Cheng-lock Tan (1883–1960), "the grand old man of Malacca," founder (1949) and President of the MCA, a gentleman whose history is worth recounting.

Dato Sir Cheng-lock Tan was the leading member of a prominent Chinese family of Malacca which, having lived in Malaya for many generations, had acquired both British nationality and the British outlook. As the acknowledged doyen of the wealthy, conservative, English-educated Chinese community, Sir Cheng-lock had associated himself inevitably with others of the Westernized "towkay" class. Both Sir Cheng-lock himself and the MCA were fairly remote not only from the great mass of the local Chinese, who were Chinese educated and Chinese oriented, but also from the more "progressive" young elite, some of these latter being Communist sympathizers. Thus the MCA was associated in the public mind with capitalism, just as the UMNO was associated with feudalism, and the Alliance, even though ardently nationalistic and independence-minded, was vulnerable to attack for being in fact reactionary. Sir Cheng-lock Tan and Tengku Abdul Rahman managed to circumvent the opposition of various minor parties which ranged from far left to far right and never managed to get together. They made the Alliance the one party to which Malays, Chinese, Indians, and others ranging from mid-left to mid-right could reconcile their differences and cooperate in political action.

The Tengku, Sir Cheng-lock, and the Alliance in 1954 forced a showdown with the British. As was characteristic for Malaya, the showdown was nonviolent, nonacrimonious, and of short duration, and it ended in mutually acceptable compromise. The British were proposing to proceed at rather a leisurely pace about conferring independence. They made new constitutional proposals, for instance, which entailed elections for a majority (fifty-two) of the members of a new Legislative Assembly, the remainder (forty-four) to be appointed by the High Commissioner. They envisioned the achievement of independence as a gradual evolutionary process to be speeded up or slowed down as events indicated. The Alliance demanded immediate elections, sixty elective members of a hundred-member Assembly, and independence within four years. The Tengku headed a delegation to London to enlist public support and to apply pressure. The British were unmoved. The Alliance therefore called upon all of its members to register their protest by resigning from appointive (noncivil-service) office, such as membership in local and district councils or the Federal Council. The majority of the members complied, and the British were confronted with a nationwide boycott which threatened to stall British-Malayan cooperation.

In Indonesia or in Indochina the consequence of the boycott probably would have been an all-out, uncompromising test of strength. In Malaya, the High Commissioner, the Tengku, and various other representatives of both sides got together over brandy-and-sodas on a British warship in the Straits of Johore. From the meeting came some rather vague agreements not to disagree, and presently a semitacit acceptance of compromise. The British scheduled elections for 1955 but the ratio of elective versus appointive members remained as they had earlier proposed. The

High Commissioner undertook, however, to appoint people who could cooperate with the elected politicians, seven of the forty-four appointive seats to be filled only after prior consultation with the party forming the new government. The elections went off on schedule and the Alliance startled both the British and the Tengku by winning fifty-one of the fifty-two elective seats. As leader of the victorious Alliance, the Tengku became Chief Minister, heading a Council of Ministers which ran the administration. The new government proved stable, competent, and cooperative, and after two more missions to London, the Tengku gained absolute assurance that independence would be conferred on August 31, 1957.

Once independence was clearly in prospect, the Tengku turned his attention to the Communist Emergency. He persuaded the High Commissioner to declare a general amnesty (September 8, 1955) for all Communist guerrillas who would give themselves up and he indicated a willingness to negotiate with their leaders. Chin Peng, the Communist guerrilla chief, presently sent a messenger to propose a time and place of meeting. On December 27–28, 1955, the Tengku, in company with Sir Cheng-lock Tan, representing the MCA, and Mr. David Marshall, then Chief Minister of Singapore, met Chin Peng and his aides in a schoolhouse at Baling, near the Thai border. Chin Peng promised that when and if the Tengku gained Malaya's complete independence, including control over internal security, the Communists would lay down their arms. He demanded, however, that they then be accepted back into society with no questions asked, and that the Communist Party be officially recognized and registered. The Tengku rejected the conditions, Chin Peng returned to the jungle, and the Emergency dragged on until August 31, 1960, when it was finally declared at an end. Only about 700 jungle guerrillas then remained at large, most of them in hiding beyond the Thai border. The Malayan armed forces have regularly attempted, ever since, with indifferent Thai cooperation, to flush them out.

From the meeting with the Communists at Baling, the Tengku turned his attention once again to preparations for independence. He had to deal with a full quota of crises, most of them now almost forgotten. One of the most serious of them concerned citizenship for the "Queen's Chinese," the Malacca and Penang-born Chinese of Anglophile sentiments who were being converted almost but not quite willy-nilly into Malayans. The Tengku had to convince them that Chinese rights would be respected and Anglo-Chinese culture preserved. He also had to reassure quite a lot of alarmists, both local and foreign, who anticipated collapse of the administration, resurgence of guerrilla warfare, and other calamities which frequently attend the birth of a nation.

Within the context of Southeast Asian revolutionary tradition, Merdeka Day, August 31, 1957, proved to be almost an indecent spectacle of decorum and good will. The Duke of Gloucester, representing the crown, gorgeous in gold braid and white plumes, the Tengku, resplendent in gold and silver brocade with a jeweled kris at his side, presided jointly over a jubilant occasion. At the major public ceremony, a whole gallery of sultans were seated under tasseled gold umbrellas. Rows of diplomats—some of them hustled to Kuala Lumpur by governments which first had to inquire how to spell and pronounce the name—were balanced with rows of Malay and Chinese officials, many of them considerably higher in rank than they had been just a few months earlier. The Merdeka Stadium, rushed to completion for the occasion, was packed by a public which had taken very little notice of whispered predictions that if not today, then tomorrow blood would flow in the streets. The Tengku felicitated the British and the British felicitated the Tengku. Felicity, not acrimony, prevailed in the course of the next few days and months and years. The government operated smoothly, business remained profitable, military and police forces encountered no major new crises, and once sleepy little Kuala Lumpur became a boom-town capital of a booming new nation.

The Tengku soon took to referring to himself as "the happiest Prime Minister" in Asia, and there were few to dispute either that he was or that he had reason to be. His cabinet proved quite competent to handle the business of government. The civil service remained phenomenally efficient, honest, well paid, and under-, not overstaffed. The British hovered paternalistically nearby, maintaining their big military forces to help put down the remaining guerrillas and pouring additional funds into a Federation treasury which was already bulging with profits from a long-sustained good market for rubber and tin. The Tengku soon took time out to start the almost mandatory round of state visits—first to South Vietnam, Ceylon, and Japan (1958), then to the Philippines (1959). He had already visited Indonesia as Chief Minister back in 1955, he had made the pilgrimage to Mecca in 1958, and at times, of course, he had practically commuted between Kuala Lumpur and London. He traveled about Malaya too, and he became aware, despite his growing preoccupation with state outings and tourism, that domestic opposition was building up. Some of the opposition criticized him for "arrogance" and "extravagance," some for neglecting the ordinary people, some for complacency in thinking that the Alliance had a lien on the loyalty of the nation.

In early February, as the time drew near for the 1959 elections, which were to result in the first fully elective Parliament, the Tengku temporarily resigned as Prime Minister. Leaving Tun Razak to run the government, he himself spent the next six months performing immense labors of meeting the public. He visited every state, every city, almost every village of any importance. He spent uncounted hours in conference rooms and on the platform, urging UMNO and Alliance solidarity for the good of the nation. Throughout these months he remained relaxed, cheerful, and confident, and also, said his critics, a bit vague about what it was that the Alliance now offered.

The Alliance easily won the 1959 elections, but by a lower percentage of the vote and with a less favorable total of seats than in 1955 (51.4 per cent of the vote in 1959, versus 55.5 per cent in 1955; 74 of 104 seats in 1959, versus 51 of 52 elective seats in 1955). Tengku Abdul Rahman's opponent in his own electoral district polled 5,542 out of the total of 18,572 votes. "I wouldn't have believed it!" the Tengku kept saying for weeks, when reminded of the strength of the opposition.

The Tengku and the UMNO and the Alliance determined to take drastic steps to strengthen their political machine, even more drastic steps to insure greater public support in the next elections. The most important element of the new Alliance government program was a M$2 billion development plan emphasizing not only big expensive projects, but innumerable small schemes to bring light, water, telephones, clinics, schools, community halls, and land-development programs to the villages and rural areas. The Tengku turned the Rural Development Program over to Tun Razak to run. As soon as it became clear that new projects were well under way, the Tengku announced that the domestic situation was in good order and that he himself would concentrate more and more upon foreign affairs. He did not then and he does not now aspire to make himself a major international figure or his nation an important power. He is thoroughly convinced, in fact, that the nation will prosper most if it concentrates its attention and energy on problems right at home. Nevertheless, the Tengku wants to make his country well and favorably known and to make its influence felt. That aspiration, predictably, has got him into trouble as well as into the limelight.

The Tengku's first really serious venture into international affairs, actually, had already occurred and it should have forewarned him. In January, 1959, in the course of a state visit to the Philippines, he had joined with President Garcia in proposing a Southeast Asia Friendship and Economic Treaty. The proposal aroused immediate and outraged Indonesian repudiation of any arrangement which smacked of anti-Communism or of un-Afro-Asian motivation. A year later there emerged the Association of Southeast Asia (ASA), with the Philippines, Malaya, and Thailand as the co-sponsors and charter members, but Indonesia continued to remain suspiciously aloof.

The Tengku's second major foray into international affairs came in April, 1960, at the London Conference of the Commonwealth Prime Ministers. There he earned considerable applause by spearheading a drive to discipline or expel South Africa unless it ended its practice of *apartheit.* His next move came in 1961 and he soon regretted it. In the course of a round of state visits which took him to Canada and the United States, then to the United Kingdom and Europe, he volunteered to mediate in the rancorous Irian Barat dispute between the Netherlands and Indonesia. The Indonesian government promptly and publicly rejected his proposals, which involved a U.N. trusteeship, and Indonesian government officials impugned his motives. Djakarta's spokesmen were not feeling kindly toward the Tengku. He had been slow, they said, to support Indonesia on the Irian Barat question at the

United Nations; he had given sanctuary to Indonesian rebels during and after the civil wars of 1958; all along he had been conspicuously soft on colonialism and cool toward Afro-Asian solidarity. The Tengku, for his part, made no secret of his dismay at encountering on the part of "brother Malays" categorical rejection of all compromise, and preference for retrogression instead of cooperation.

On May 27, 1961, the Tengku finally emerged, quite by inadvertence, as the key figure in a domestic and international drama, which started out as a minor Southeast Asian sideshow but soon achieved feature billing. Speaking before a luncheon meeting in Singapore of the Foreign Correspondents Association of Southeast Asia, the Tengku started off by announcing that he had nothing sensational to say. Later on, he slipped in a modest proposal of startling implications, the full significance of which, quite possibly, had escaped him. "Sooner or later," said the Tengku, "Malaya should have an understanding with Britain and the peoples of Singapore, North Borneo, Brunei, and Sarawak . . . and think of a plan whereby these territories can be brought closer together in political and economic cooperation."

Singapore's Prime Minister, Lee Kuan Yew, had been pressuring the Tengku for two years to accept Singapore into the Federation, but the Tengku had been adamant: Singapore's extreme left-wing politics, its preponderantly Chinese population and its uncertain economic future were all much too risky. Everyone knew that colonialism could not survive much longer in Borneo, but while the British had been urging a Borneo Federation, the Bornean leaders had been waiting for someone other than the British to lead them. Until the Tengku practically stumbled onto the answer on May 27, 1961, no one had publicly suggested—at least no one of great influence had very loudly suggested—that all five states get together to share and solve their problems. Lee Kuan Yew, who had appeared for the preluncheon drinks but had not waited for the speech, assuming that it would be inconsequential, pounced upon the proposal. So did the press, and so did politicians of all degrees of vision and volume. Suddenly there was talk of a Greater Malaysia, then of a Mighty Malaysia, and then as opposition began to build up against alleged high-pressure tactics, of just plain unassuming Malaysia. Ever since

May 27, 1961, the effort to bring Malaysia into being has thrown the Tengku into close association and sometimes into sharp conflict with some very stagy characters, conspicuous among them Lee Kuan Yew.

Lee Kuan Yew is one of the few people whom the Tengku apparently has to make an effort to get along with, as seems rather a pity; for Lee himself rarely makes the effort to get along with anyone else except the Tengku. Lee Kuan Yew (b. September 16, 1923), formerly known to his intimates as "Harry," is the organizer and head of the People's Action Party, a onetime extreme left-wing organization which has gone through a strange metamorphosis and now looks sober, responsible, and certainly competent. The son of a moderately well-to-do Singapore Chinese whose own father had been legal counsel to the fabulously rich Oei Tiong Ham family of Singapore and Indonesia, Harry Lee was born smart. He achieved one of the most brilliant scholastic ratings ever recorded in Singapore. Not only was he first in his senior Cambridge examinations, but he picked off "double first" honors when he studied law in England. On his return, Harry Lee established himself almost immediately as one of the best and one of the best-paid Singapore lawyers, also as one of the most active and agile of the local labor leaders.

In 1955, in the Tengku's presence and with his blessing, Harry Lee founded the People's Action Party, a party which appeared dangerously radical to the British and to most of the well-to-do or wealthy Singapore Chinese. The PAP found its strongest supporters among labor and student groups that were notoriously responsive to left-wing agitators. The PAP grew quickly, too quickly for even Harry Lee always to keep up with it. Several times he lost control, and rival leaders indulged themselves by instigating disorders which at times turned into riots. Presently the doctrinaire Marxist faction, headed by a young union organizer, Lim Chin Siong, went to jail as subversives, and the lunatic fringe, headed by a rabble-rousing accountant named Ong Eng Guan, was elected to control of the municipal government.

In 1959, Lee Kuan Yew, who no longer liked to be called "Harry," triumphantly reasserted his own control. He managed shrewdly to exploit the martyrdom of the extremists and the dramatics of the exhibitionists to help carry the PAP to a landslide election victory. Lee Kuan Yew then became Prime Minister of the new semiautonomous State of Singapore, first exacting from the British the release from prison of Lim Chin Siong and his colleagues, then attempting to put them into political quarantine by appointing them to made jobs as "parliamentary secretaries."

The new PAP government, much to the surprise of the Singapore conservatives and to the dismay of the radicals, proved efficient and responsible. The Ong Eng Guan clique tried for a while to whip up mass movements, the Lim Chin Siong clique to foment intraparty conspiracy. Before long both sets of dissidents bolted the PAP outright, Ong Eng Guan to form the United People's Party, Lim Chin Siong to form the Barisan Sosialis (Socialist Front), neither very readily distinguishable from a Communist front. Both made common cause against the PAP alongside the Labour Party of former Chief Minister David Marshall, an able, wealthy, flamboyant lawyer, equally at his ease among the working and the investing classes. As a result of a series of political disasters, Lee Kuan Yew found his PAP majority in the fifty-one-member Legislative Assembly whittled down from forty-three in 1959 to twenty-six in early 1962; by late 1962 he commanded only a minority of twenty-five and found himself dependent for mere political survival upon his archenemy, former Chief Minister Tun Lim Yew Hock, the leader of the Singapore right wing and a close friend and confidant of the Tengku.

By 1961, then, Lee Kuan Yew's future, the PAP's future, in fact the future of Singapore itself, was perilous in the extreme. The Barisan was quite certainly conspiring to take over—whether by peaceful or by violent devices was seemingly a matter of its own choice. The Singapore crisis focused the Tengku's attention upon the potential Cuba at his boot tip. Given any real and immediate possibility of merger with Malaya, which was the key point of his party's platform, Lee Kuan Yew and his PAP government could probably survive, for even the Barisan Sosialis, deeming merger impossible, was demanding that the PAP achieve it. Neither Lee Kuan Yew nor the PAP appealed very much to the Tengku. Nevertheless, he liked the Barisan even less, and he prized regional peace and stability above the chancy glory of going it alone. He chose, therefore, to accept Singapore's importunities and at the same time to offset Singapore's wobbliness by the presumed stability of the Borneo states—a stability which proved, on close inspection, of course, to be no such thing. Lee Kuan Yew, the brilliant, arrogant, ruthless politician, found in the Malaysia proposal a cause worthy of his brashest, brainiest efforts. He staged a merger campaign in which he consistently outthought, outtalked, and outmaneuvered the opposition. He was able to gain a 72 per cent victory in a referendum which offered almost every alternative except "No." The opposition campaigned for a blank ballot as a protest vote, only to be threatened at the last moment that a blank would be counted for the alternative it liked least of all—its own, in fact, which it had proposed in the first place only to confuse the issue.

After the referendum, Lee Kuan Yew negotiated so shrewdly with Kuala Lumpur for the best possible conditions of merger, including, of course, the financial and the economic, to which Singapore gave top priority, that he won a final victory almost too great for his own good. Meanwhile, he had set about another formidable task, one which few had expected him ever to undertake, that of popularizing himself. The Singapore government had just installed a television system, and Lee Kuan Yew became the featured performer. With television cameramen as his inseparable companions, he began a series of Sunday tours of the voting districts, rigorously repressing the waspishness in his disposition and cultivating folksiness. Synthetic as his camaraderie seemed to the sophisticates, it was good for carnivals and processions. Even his occasional lapses served an inadvertent purpose that could not have been better calculated. On the spur of the moment, for instance, he ordered the TV cameramen to zoom in on the opposition's goon gangs which had followed to heckle him but fled in panic from publicity. When the formation of Malaysia was delayed from August 31 to September 16, 1963, as a result of Indonesian opposition, Lee Kuan Yew declared *de facto* Singapore independence for the interval. The move was immensely popular in Singapore and served to underscore what was already painfully obvious to Kuala Lumpur: that Lee Kuan Yew was destined to be a star and not merely a featured player in the continuing Malaysia serial.

With Lee Kuan Yew to collaborate and to compete with, the

Tengku has found the last several years full of more excitement by far than any previous period in his life, not excluding that of his negotiations with the British for independence. Then, on top of everything else, suddenly he had Sukarno to cope with, and all, it might seem on superficial analysis, because of a prospective Malaysian citizen, a onetime volunteer in the Indonesian revolution, Azahari by name. As head of the anti-Malaysia, pro-Indonesia Party Rakjat in Brunei, Azahari chose on December 8, 1962, to stage a Mad Hatter little insurrection in the minute British-protected, oil-soiled, Sultanate of Brunei (annual revenue, U.S. $40 million; annual expenditure, U.S. $15 million; accumulated and invested hoardings, U.S. $300 million). Sukarno, who had just won the vast empty jungles of Irian Barat from the Dutch and thus lost a rabble-rousing cause and the last shreds of economic solvency, was interested.

Azahari and his followers had taken up arms, they declared, to restore to the Sultan his traditional domain of North Borneo and Sarawak, and they put out an appeal for Philippine and Indonesian military assistance. The British, responding to the Sultan's call for protection, used Green Jackets and Gurkhas to put down the insurrection. Sukarno failed to send the paratroopers whom Azahari expected, but he set up a clamor denouncing "neocolonialism" and "mercenary atrocities" and pledged undying Indonesian support for the "freedom fighters" of the "new emerging forces" who dared to defy the "old established order." Presently, branding the Tengku a British puppet and a "false freedom-lover," he launched a policy of anti-Tengku, anti-Malaysia, anti-British *konfrontasi,* as virulent as his Irian Barat campaign. What followed was first demonstrations, volunteering, and demagoguery; next, border raids in Borneo and piracy along the North Borneo coasts and in the Straits of Malacca; then political and economic boycott accompanied by constant threat of full-scale military attack.

With Sukarno manning the controls, the Indonesia–Malaysia, Sukarno–Tengku *konfrontasi* turned alternately hot and cold and constituted a 1963 Southeast Asian crisis second in proportions only to that of Vietnam. Bung Karno was determined, quite obviously, to convert anti-Malaysian *konfrontasi* into a major crisis which would distract the Indonesian people from their hardships and frighten the international world into efforts toward appeasement. He failed, however, to stir up much international support, and he himself was confronted with a dilemma which his own policies further compounded. Indonesia at the moment was flat broke. Indonesia, in fact, was bankrupt, mortgaged, and so far as potential international credit agencies were concerned, it was blacklisted. The Soviet Union was being importunate about installments due on a billion dollars worth of arms. The United States was indignant about the wastage of a few hundred millions of dollars' worth of aid. Without a generously replenished supply of Russian arms or American dollars—and both the Russians and the Americans were proving difficult about being played off against each other—Bung Karno could not count on stopping Malaysia, which might therefore be formed in defiance of his will and with damage to his prestige. Bung Karno thereupon invited the Tengku to a May 31 rendezvous in Tokyo, embraced him, assured him of friendship and brotherhood, urged him to forget the August 31 date for Malaysia, and as the two parted company pressmen and cameramen immortalized their reconciliation.

The Tengku left Tokyo under the impression, apparently, that Sukarno would abandon *konfrontasi;* Sukarno left under the impression that the Tengku would proceed with Malaysia, if at all, only on his, Sukarno's drastically revised conditions, thus putting Malaysia under the Indonesian aegis. President Macapagal of the Philippines, meanwhile, had scripted himself into the rapprochement by proposing a grand confederation of the Philippines, Indonesia, and Malaya. The Borneo states, of which the Philippines had been claiming North Borneo as its own rightful territory, were presumably to come in as separate members. After the Tokyo tête-à-tête, the foreign ministers of the three countries met in Manila. Each for obscure reasons of his own endorsed a modification of Macapagal's proposal which clarified nothing save that it was to be euphoniously rechristened "Maphilindo," in accordance with a suggestion made by Indonesian Foreign Minister Subandrio, a Sukarno-style slogan-maker. Interpretations of Maphilindo were as various and as conflicting as the personalities of the three ministers and their three chiefs of state. Maphilindo was commonly billed, nevertheless, as a loose confederation of

Malaya, the Philippines, and Indonesia, something not unlike what Macapagal seemed to have had in mind, save that the Borneo states might in fact attach to Malaysia. Maphilindo from its very conception and inception embodied less substance than speculation. All three nations kept exhorting each other to resolve their differences in accordance with the "Maphilindo spirit," engaging meanwhile in mutual recriminations about who, at the moment, was violating it.

With *konfrontasi* apparently once again expiring and Maphilindo apparently gestating, the Tengku proceeded with the practical arrangements for delivery of Malaysia. A last minute dispute with Singapore over pro-rating the expenses, a concurrent dispute with Brunei over sharing the oil royalties, and various other incidental complications threatened for a period of weeks to kill the unborn infant. Then suddenly, in London on July 9, almost all of the recently rancorous problems were resolved. The Malayan, the Singapore, and the British representatives to the negotiations were all satisfied; Sarawak and North Borneo would come in; Brunei, for the time being at least, would stay out; the formation of Malaysia at last was a certainty. On July 10, accusing the Tengku of "breaking his promises" by negotiating with the British, Bung Karno cranked up *konfrontasi* all over again.

The Tengku was appalled, but this time less acrimonious than conciliatory. Bung Karno staged monster demonstrations and threatened massive retaliation, but once again, the lack of international applause and the sight of the bare Indonesian treasury sobered even him. The Tengku and the Bung both kept an appointment to meet Macapagal on July 31 in "summit conference" in Manila. Once there, Sukarno made demands which would certainly have frustrated Malaysia, just as he had publicly promised to do. He failed, however, to intimidate the Tengku, and he outmaneuvered himself by seizing upon the Tengku's one concession, only to find out too late that it led downward, not upward, on the political escalator. The Tengku agreed to refer to the United Nations' Secretary General the question of self-determination of the Borneo people in joining Malaysia, self-determination having suddenly become for both Sukarno and Macapagal a crucial issue. U Thant, they assumed, would demand a referendum; a referendum would certainly delay Malaysia long enough for almost anything to happen; Sukarno felt safe in committing himself in advance, as did Macapagal, to acceptance of U Thant's findings. But U Thant, it developed, would undertake merely a quick "assessment," an on-the-spot survey to determine whether the North Borneo elections of 1962 and the Sarawak elections of 1963 had indeed been free and fair and whether Malaysia had indeed been the issue.

The results of the "assessment" being a foregone conclusion, for the elections had been conspicuously free and fair, Sukarno immediately undertook to delay and to sabotage the whole operation. He quarreled with the British, for instance, over how many and what type of Indonesian "observers" would be admitted to the Borneo Colonies during the operation. U Thant's assessors went about their business, nevertheless, despite Indonesian attempts at harassment, and they soon announced that the Borneo elections had been free, fair and pro-Malaysia. Sukarno thereupon rejected the Secretary General's findings and refused to recognize the new nation. When the Tengku promptly broke off diplomatic relations in consequence, Sukarno refueled *konfrontasi* in Djakarta by burning the British Embassy and some fifty other British properties besides, seizing British business concerns, the former Malayan Embassy and other Malaysian-owned properties, and promising yet again and again to "smash" Malaysia for lending itself to the evil British "neocolonialist" plot of "encirclement." Sukarno also cut off all trade relations with Malaysia, thus confronting the Tengku with a difficult and himself with an impossible economic problem, Indonesia's Malaysia trade being critical to Malaysia but absolutely vital to Indonesia.

The Tengku expresses dismay these days at Sukarno's resolute determination to destroy Malaysia and at his rejection of all reasonable advances such as would enable the two Malay rulers and nations not only to coexist but to cooperate. The Tengku is unable to comprehend the psychology of a ruler and of a nation capable of courting self-destruction in order to chastise those who resist interference. The Tengku is not alone in his bewilderment about Sukarno, for the great majority of the Malaysians share it with him. This circumstance should work to the Tengku's, not Sukarno's advantage, should the contest become prolonged, to determine which nation, Indonesia or Malaysia, will succumb first to the hazards implicit for both in Sukarno's *konfrontasi*.

Tengku Abdul Rahman today does not seem very much subdued as a result of his experiences with Sukarno, Lee Kuan Yew, and a miscellaneous lot of other politicians who have become involved in his Malaysia plan. For a Prime Minister, he is still relatively carefree, relatively uninhibited, relatively ingenuous about such matters as trusting either an associate or an opponent other, of course, than Sukarno. He is also relatively serious when he talks of the pleasures of retirement and the advantages of letting responsibility pass to younger, fresher, possibly bolder men. He is perhaps a little more touchy and aloof than before, but not much. He becomes annoyed, for instance, about the common report that he always passes up the paper work and never misses a race meet —he wishes it were true, but it isn't. He still makes much ado about his own carelessness and forgetfulness, but he is beginning to feel that on the basis of the record no one should be misled into thinking him gullible. Highest on the list of those by whom he will not be gulled he places Sukarno.

The Tengku lives a good part of his private life these days in a hilltop mansion overlooking downtown Kuala Lumpur. It is a spacious old British colonial bungalow, now refurbished and air-conditioned. He prefers it to the fine modern villa the government intended originally for him but then assigned to the Deputy Prime Minister. The Tengku lives there with his third wife and their two adopted children, one of them Chinese by race, and a large household of relations and retainers. His first wife, a Siamese–Chinese who died of malaria in 1935, bore him a son and a daughter. The son is now an officer in the Malayan Army. The Tengku's second wife, an Englishwoman, returned to England before the war. Technically, to pursue the matter of his matrimonial affairs a bit further, he has practiced polygamy in that he married his present wife before he and his English wife were divorced in 1946, but as a Muslim he was within his legal rights. He was the subject of a mild sensation in 1953 when he was named corespondent in a London divorce case, and again in 1954 when, on returning to England to lobby for his country's independence, he finally paid up the £700 damages.

The Tengku makes the opportunity several times a week to

play golf, a game at which he might be better if he kept his eyes on the ball and his mind off the conversation. His handicap is twenty-four, and he is showing no improvement. He has set the fashion for Malay officials, many of whom have been rather aloof from Kuala Lumpur society, to appear at the golf club and at other clubs as well. The Tengku fancies swimming, boating, and sports cars, and he finds time also to patronize football, being in fact President of the Malayan Football Association. Most of all, the Tengku fancies the horses. He used to own ponies and to enter them in the races, but he no longer indulges himself to that extent. His tips on the races are highly thought of in sporting circles; on his state visit to Australia a few years back he astonished his hosts by his unerring eye for the winner.

Without neglecting sport, the Tengku manages also to patronize education. Lately he has accepted the post of Chancellor of the University of Malaya, an institution whose swift growth and progress he has greatly encouraged. He is a devout Muslim, going regularly on Fridays to the mosque, and performing the orthodox schedule of private prayers. He is a serious, if not altogether a discriminating student of Malayan history and culture. His own ventures into cultural creativeness consist mainly of writing. He has to his credit two rather thin Malay novels, one a romantic thriller, which was made into a successful moving picture a few years ago, the other a vampire chiller which has still to be published. He also likes to dance and quite disregards criticism— much of it originating in Indonesia, where Sukarno is an avid dancer—that this is an evidence of frivolity. He prefers the Malay *ronggeng,* a dance of sinuous, sometimes rather sophisticated steps in which the partners do not touch but skillfully follow each other's lead through a succession of figures. Under the Tengku's patronage, the *ronggeng* is enjoying a revival, not only in the taxi-dance halls or at the stag parties to which *joget* girls are invited, but also in Kuala Lumpur's upper social circles. The wives of important Malay officials, including the Tengku's own, have been taking lessons in order that they may emerge from the near social eclipse to which Malay tradition has long consigned them.

Despite his years and bulk, Tengku Abdul Rahman displays as astonishing a degree of youthful agility and gaiety at *ronggeng* as he does in politics. The Tengku's almost unfailing effervescence of spirits may prove even more essential to himself and to his nation in the future than in the past. After guiding Malaya successfully and happily through its first few formative years, Tengku Abdul Rahman is clearly pushing his luck in undertaking to do the same for Malaysia. He finds himself now in open conflict with Sukarno, another gentleman apparently favored by fortune, one whose particular luck in recent years has been in personally surviving the ruin he has brought upon his nation. Whether the Tengku's or Bung Karno's brand of luck now holds will serve as an important clue in the destiny of Southeast Asia.

Honest Mac, The *Tao* of Malacañang

"I am . . . a poor man. I was a poor boy. I belong to one of the poorest and wretched [*sic*] families in Pampanga. In my life, I have known all the hardships and sufferings of the poor. In my boyhood, I often knew hunger.

"I remember when I was a boy the many times at noon when we hungry children asked our mother for food. Instead of feeding us she would make us go to sleep so that we would not feel our hunger while she would go from neighbor to neighbor, from relative to relative to ask for a handful of rice which, when given, appeased our hunger at four or five o'clock in the afternoon.

"I remember when as a boy I used to play by myself along the rugged roads of our barrios [villages], wearing torn and shabby clothes, so pauperish in appearance that I could not play with the sons of the rich in the neighborhood and could not even approach the fences of their tall and big houses.

"As a boy and as a young man I knew what it was to live in a nipa [palm thatch] shack and when heavy rain fell at night and leaked through the unpatched nipa roof, we moved our tattered mat from one spot to another for any remaining dry place on the bamboo floor until none was left and sleep was rendered impossible for the rest of the night.

"I remember as a young man striving for an education how I walked three kilometers back and forth from the slums of Tondo where I lived to the state university, and how when it rained after night classes, I would wait for the rain to stop. I would walk that distance under the rain starved, sleepy, shivering, and with the raindrops mixing with the tears on my cheeks, but I stood it all because as a poor boy, like the children of the countless miserable families in our country today, I also dreamed of a better life for myself.

"So I struggled and I worked my way through school, and through the grace of Divine Providence, I finished my schooling and then joined the public service. The records of Congress and the government will show that because I was poor and came from the bosom of the poor, I have always stood as a public official by the rights of the poor as when I successfully fought for the minimum wage law or other legislation to alleviate the plight of the poor."

With this message—his own life story, tirelessly reiterated, plus embellishments that at times added even more misery, more nobility, more bromides and promises of a "New Era" for "the common man"—Diosdado Macapagal won the Filipino voter and the 1961 Philippines election to become the fifth President of the Republic of the Philippines. To odds-giving skeptics he proved that although he and his Liberal Party lacked a well-lubricated machine he had other and unbeatable assets. His political message was only a little better, a little more bathetic than the bare truth. His public, namely, the jeepney- (jeep-jitney), the outrigger-, and the carabao-riding public, not the Cadillac class, was eager for its vote to be won, not bought or coerced. His opponent, President Carlos Garcia, was transparently everything that Macapagal was not and was his own best exhibit for the discreditation of his Nacionalista Party regime.

While "Honest Dadang" (also known as "Honest Mac, the Poor Man's Best Friend") was scripting himself from the platform as though he were Diosdado Alger III, "Don Carlos" was enacting, as usual, the role of the political grandee, the brilliant and ruthless maestro accustomed to winning at politics as he won at chess and with an air of effortless ease. Don Carlos conveyed himself to the electorate in his P5 million "floating villa," the yacht *Lapu Lapu,* or in his P1,500,000 "flying palace," the specially fitted Fokker Friendship jet, or in an air-conditioned Cadillac, often accompanied by his elegant wife and her elegant "kitchen cabinet" of Manila society ladies, exquisite in piña cloth and diamonds. He wooed the voter with carnivals, carrots, clubs, and poetry. After his campaign managers had fixed all of the fixers in a given town and then staged a variety show, Don Carlos discoursed eloquently to the audience on the state of the nation and, yielding graciously to public demand, concluded by sonorously reciting some of his own *balaks* composed in polished Cebuano. This is a stanza from one that was a sure hit with his entourage and his audience:

To the Filipino Woman

Filipino woman, perfumed pride of my race,
Inspiration of the lyre of Rizal, Balagtas, and Ranudo
And fire for the brush of Luna, Hidalgo, and Amorsolo,
You have a body that is a poem of curves
That I crave to give to my famished arms;
You have lips beautifully curved by a vision
That surely is the gateway to Paradise,
Where I would plunder a thousand kisses
Though I might pay away my life in martyrdom.

Honest Dadang ridiculed Don Carlos' *balak* recitals. "This is hardly the time," he said, "to dish out poems in elegant language," not while "the people wallow in misery and want." Honest Dadang, to be sure, had won his own first political victory by engaging during the congressional elections of 1949 in a contest of quick improvisation to versify in the Pampango dialect a political message more potent and elegant than that of his opponent, Amado Yuzon, the "poet laureate of Pampanga," who was also the candidate supported by the Communist guerrillas, the Hukbalahap. He seemed to feel in 1961, however, as did his most ardent partisans, that this time his message was nonlyrical. His own most famous poetic effort, a "Requiem" composed on the death of his great friend and patron, the statesman-philanthropist Don Honorio Ventura, included stanzas which, with minor emendations, he might have applied to himself. The true quality of the original may not have survived translation, but just one brief excerpt would seem to vindicate Macapagal's decision to leave the scanning and the rhyming to Don Carlos, and himself to concentrate upon prosaic autobiography and muckraking:

Our province's chief executive—
He was then three and thirty still;
In San Fernando he did give
A permit to build a sugar mill;
In thousands he was offered shares,
But he declined and told his friends:
"My office is for public affairs,
And shouldn't be used for personal ends."

Idealized realism or tarnished romanticism: to oversimplify vastly, these were the alternatives which the Filipino voter faced in 1961, and he chose Macapagal. The choice, one may argue, was symbolical of a new era for the nation. Official corruption, extravagance, and chicanery have been the postwar norm, and the politician who was not also a knave swiftly joined the 20 per cent of the nation's citizens who were job-hunting. On November 1, 1961, the Filipino voter defied the dopesters, the pollsters, and the gangsters; he repudiated Garcia and acclaimed Macapagal.

The 1961 election, many people thought, marked the end of a fourteen-year-long political bacchanalia and the dawn of that long-awaited new day, the era of Juan de la Cruz, now more nationalistically known as "The New Era" of the *tao*, the "common man." It would be easier for the outside observer to believe so too had it not been for some unhappy facts of history. Back in 1953 the Filipino voter had elected Ramon Magsaysay, the "Man of the People," for much the same reasons and against much the same opposition. "The Guy" did not actually achieve or even clarify much of his program before his tragic death in a plane crash on March 17, 1957. Don Carlos won the November, 1957, election on the same reform platform, only to betray it. Finally, to anticipate by bringing the chronicle of disenchantment up to date, in his first half term in office Macapagal has become snarled up in the same old political imbroglio. All the same, Macapagal is President until 1966, and in addition to the *tao*, he has also—or he has had—gifted and idealistic young adherents such as one Raul S. Manglapus, who has managed to be honest about the Philippines' problems and yet to speak, write, and radiate "Faith in the Filipino."

For all those who shared Raul Manglapus' campaign-period confidence, the career of Diosdado Macapagal is both an inspiration and an admonition. It is the story of the idealized "average" Filipino, poor, honest, industrious, a good man who courageously seeks for himself and for others a good life. It is the story of a man who dares to defy the politician, the bureaucrat, even the old and new rich, because he puts his trust in God and in the common man. It is also the story of a man who plays the political game he excoriates, one who both enjoys it and excels in it, so that he himself has become a most uncommon *tao* indeed.

Tao Diosdado Macapagal was born on September 28, 1910, in Barrio San Nicholas Ist, Lubao, Pampagna Province, one of the more impoverished parts of an impoverished district which was later to be the recruiting center and stronghold of the Hukbalahap movement. He was born at just about the same time and into a family of just about the same circumstances as was Luis Taruc, a Pampangano boy who distinguished himself later as the Hukbalahap leader. Macapagal and Taruc each surmounted formidable obstacles to gain an education and embark upon a profession, but Taruc's career led him to Bilibid Prison and Macapagal's to Malacañang Palace.

Diosdado Macapagal was the second of four children, the second son of one Urbano Macapagal and his wife, Romana Pangan. Urbano Macapagal, the literary son of a composer of ecclesiastical music, was an impoverished poet-peasant who practiced an occasional and desultory bit of agriculture but devoted himself mainly to the composition of zarzuelas, that is, blood-and-thunder Tagalog plays written in verse on the melodramatic Spanish model. Urbano, according to his son and other witnesses, was an affectionate but irresponsible parent whose instincts were those of a Gypsy. He was, in fact, a strolling playwright, one who followed the barrio troupes from fiesta to fiesta, leaving to his wife the onerous routine of raising and feeding the family. Romana, fortunately, was a strong-backed, strong-willed woman, a catechist, a midwife, and a business operator. She was determined that her children should get ahead. She put them through primary school in the barrio, and when it came time for the boys to enter secondary school she rented a nipa hut in the town of San Fernando—

or so, at least, goes the popular version of the story today—and in order to pay expenses raised pigs and took in boarders.

Young Dadang, growing up in San Nicholas and San Fernando, did in fact suffer something fairly close to misery, poverty, and hunger in a ramshackle nipa hut, just as the campaign legend has it. His youthful tribulations make President Magsaysay's boyhood, heretofore the classical Philippines poor-boy-becomes-President story, look almost like life on a hacienda. Still, though Dadang had to herd carabao for his peasant grandfather, he certainly derived the normal Filipino boy's pleasure from relaxing in the sun on their broad backs; although he caught frogs at night in order to supplement the meager family diet, catching frogs and eating frogs' legs is not total drudgery. He suffered the humiliation of not having good school clothes, but he also enjoyed the triumph of winning school distinctions—once, for instance, for a recitation of "Crossing the Bar" in an interschool contest. He was top student in his primary class and a close second in his high school class; not the first because one teacher, he says, marked him on clothes, not brains. He excelled and he knew that he excelled as a school writer, debater, and cadet. In his darker moments he derived satisfaction from contemplation of such inspiring thoughts as "Brighten your corner." Also, he enjoyed billiards, cockfights, and, like his father, fiestas.

Macapagal's education, thanks to his own efforts and his mother's, and the eventual support of a wealthy benefactor, was far superior to that of the ordinary barrio boy. His ambition eventually led him, after he was already well established in his career, to take doctoral degrees both in law (University of Santo Tomas, 1947) and in economics (Santo Tomas, 1957). By that time he had his eye firmly fixed on the Presidency and he was determined to have unimpeachable credentials.

After finishing high school in San Fernando in 1929, young Dadang received an offer of a job as teacher. He declined because he was determined to seek his fortune in the city. In Manila, where he found room and board with relatives in the slums of dankest Tondo, his immediate fortune was a P30-per-month clerical job with the Bureau of Lands (1930–1931). On his meager savings, supplemented by an intermittent allowance from his mother and his grandmother, the latter also a practicing midwife, he paid his tuition in the University of the Philippines and set himself to study law. His first try for a law degree came to an abrupt end in 1931 when he collapsed from malnutrition and had to return to his barrio to recuperate.

Back in the barrio Macapagal was almost diverted into another career, and in the process found himself a colleague, a kinsman, a rival, and a wife. He happened to read a manuscript of his father's and was so taken with the purple poetry and prophetic plot, a poor boy makes good story reimbellished, that he revised it, produced it in collaboration with his father, co-starred in it, and took it on the road for the barrio festivals.

"Bayung Herusalem" (The New Jerusalem) proved to be a smash hit at the fiestas. Macapagal played the hero, sharing feature billing with a beautiful heroine, Purita de la Rosa by name, and a handsome villain, Purita's brother, Rogelio de la Rosa. Purita de la Rosa, whose family included Filipino, Spanish, and Chinese strains, was later to become his wife. They were married about 1936 but she died during the Japanese occupation after bearing him two children. Rogelio de la Rosa went on to become a matinee idol, a motion picture and television star, and a Congressman, one whose theatrical good looks and platform manner win for him virtually the unanimous vote of the feminine sector of his constituency. In 1961 Rogelio de la Rosa entered the presidential campaign as a rival candidate to Garcia and Macapagal; he staged a variety-show campaign which rivaled Garcia's. At the most strategic possible moment, just ten days before the polls opened, Rogelio appeared on a nationwide television hook-up to announce the withdrawal of his own candidacy in favor of Macapagal's—a "paid frame-up," said the opposition.

Dadang himself stuck to the boards through two more zar-zuelas, but he resisted suggestions, including those of Manila film scouts who gave him some bit parts, that he make the theater his career. Instead, he took up writing as a cub reporter for the Manila *Tribune,* and as editor and fiction contributor to the Pampango magazine, *Ing Katimawan.* With the money he thus earned, plus occasional honoraria for composing orations and love letters for his less gifted friends, plus continuing remittances from home, he enrolled again in the University of the Philippines. Again he experienced serious financial difficulties but by immense good luck, as a result of participation in school debates in which both his legal and his theatrical training showed through, he attracted the attention of the famous Pampanga lawyer and philanthropist, Honorio Ventura, who offered to help finance him.

At this point Dadang transferred to his patron's institution, the University of Santo Tomas, where he completed his studies and earned his Bachelor of Laws degree (1936). That same year he took the Philippines bar examinations and placed top on the national list with a score of 89.95 per cent. This distinction quite startled his professors and most of his friends as well, for he had been a self-effacing, average student, too poor to afford the books he needed for his studies, too proud to call attention to himself when he could not excel. He had managed only by chance to gain access, after he had already completed his studies, to a good law library in which, in preparation for the bar examinations, he had crammed steadily for four months, seven days a week, fourteen hours a day. By topping the bar examinations, he virtually ensured his professional and political future, for all Filipino political and civic leaders accept the highest-scoring candidates as qualifying almost automatically, after a few years' internship, for the nation's most distinguished positions.

Shortly after leaving law school, Macapagal entered the well-known Manila American law firm of Ross, Lawrence, Selph, and Carrascoso, starting at a monthly salary of P75. He stayed with the firm for three years, acquiring a wide range of experience. Shortly before the outbreak of the Pacific War, he resigned from the firm in order to teach law at Santo Tomas University and simultaneously to study for an advanced degree. Santo Tomas, of course, was destined soon to operate as a prison camp rather than a university, and Macapagal himself spent the war years inconspicuously in Manila. He had been an enthusiastic cadet officer both in high school and in the university, but he affiliated himself during the war not with the guerrilla troops but with the urban underground. Just how he made his living during this period the record does not show, but his was at least as precarious a living as that of most other Manileños. It was impossible, for instance, for him to secure adequate medical care for his wife, who died on October 27, 1943, soon after giving birth to her second child, a son, who was christened Arturo after General MacArthur.

Soon after the end of the war, Macapagal joined with several other Manila lawyers and established a law firm in which the membership changed but he remained the senior partner. He built a reputation for himself as a formidable courtroom performer, skilled in handling both civil and criminal cases in either English or Spanish. He mixed more and more in political as well as legal circles and resumed, meanwhile, both his teaching and his studies at Santo Tomas. He achieved relative prominence and prosperity, as signified, for instance, by his appointment as Assistant, then Chief of the Legal Division of the Ministry of Foreign Affairs, and by the removal of his law office to the Escolta, Manila's combined Fifth and Madison Avenues, Broadway and Forty-second Street. Gradually he came to devote less and less of his time to teaching and practice, more and more of it to political party activities. It became clear to everyone, as he himself had long since realized, that his real calling was politics.

In 1948 Macapagal was appointed chief Philippines representative to negotiate with the British the Philippines' claim to the Turtle Islands, a sparsely inhabited and heretofore almost forgotten little group of islets lying between the Sulu Archipelago and North Borneo. After first establishing the fact with the rather supercilious British negotiators that the Philippines really meant business, Macapagal managed to gain British acceptance of the Philippines' claim. Then, as representative of his own government at the transfer ceremony, he delivered a fiery speech about Philippines "extension of moral imperialism" as "true disciples" of the "mother countries" (i.e., Spain and the United States) "who have taught us their democracies."

The Turtle Islands attracted Macapagal's attention also to North Borneo and he dug up from the files a half forgotten agreement of the year 1878 between the Sultan of Sulu and the first European settlers, in accordance with which the British were still paying five thousand Straits dollars per year to the Sultan's heirs for occupancy of the territory. He drafted a resolution calling for "restoration" of North Borneo to the Sulu Sultanate, and in 1950 gained unanimous approval for it in the Philippines Congress. The North Borneo claim, it may be noted here, was to be revived in 1962, when President Macapagal yielded, not unwillingly, to pressure from the Sulu heirs, the Manila lawyer who represented them, the Philippines *Free Press,* and the Philippines Congress to make new demands upon the British. He did so just at the time that his partner in the Association of Southeast Asia, Tengku Abdul Rahman, Prime Minister of Malaya, was proposing that North Borneo merge with the proposed new Federation of Malaysia.

Macapagal's Turtle Island triumph was succeeded by appointments as First Secretary of Embassy in Washington (1948), Delegate to the United Nations (1950), and Chairman of the Philippines Delegation to the United Nations General Assembly in Paris (1951). At the Paris session he distinguished himself in verbal encounters with Russia's Vishinsky and Malik, and gained the reputation of being one of the Philippines' most convinced and articulate anti-Communists. Meanwhile, he had also embarked upon a political career at home. He had been called back to the Philippines in 1949 and personally requested by President Quirino to "stop" one Amado Yuzon, Congressman from Pampanga, who was a major embarrassment to the administration, for besides being "poet laureate of Pampanga" and "idol of the masses," Yuzon was also a Hukbalahap spokesman. As already noted above, Macapagal managed by swift and judicious combination of rhyme and reason not only to beat the heretofore unbeatable Huk but to do so by the almost unbelievable margin of 20,000 votes. Once seated in Congress, Macapagal established himself in the eyes of the highly critical Manila press as one of the "ten outstanding Congressmen" of the year during each year of his incumbency and the "best solon" for the period 1954–1957.

Macapagal, like most Filipinos during the mid-50's, fell under the spell of Ramon Magsaysay, the composite contemporary reincarnation of the sixteenth-century warrior, Lapu Lapu, who defied the Spanish conquerors; of the revolutionary, Bonifacio, who in 1896 sounded the Freedom Cry of Balintawak; and of Juan de la Cruz, the patient *tao* rising above poverty, ignorance, and oppression. Ramon Magsaysay, a folk hero whom the Americans anointed and the Filipinos canonized, was a big, handsome, athletic, personally magnetic soldier who rode in an army jeep, wore fatigues, and both talked and acted tough about cleaning up the "rotten mess" which the politicians had created. More the brawny than the brainy type, Magsaysay never wanted or needed any major correction to his 20–20 political vision, which informed him that behind the troubles with the insurgent Hukbalahap lurked not only Communists but also avaricious landlords, corrupt politicians, incompetent bureaucrats, and gangsters, goons, and government goofers. To everyone in the Philippines who had had his fill of the white-sharkskin-suited, cigar-smoking, pork-barreling political fixers and their bejeweled and butterfly-gowned ladies, Ramon Magsaysay symbolized the genuine, decent, aspirant Filipino, demanding and now at last preparing to come into his own.

"Magsaysay Is My Guy," said the slogan makers, and the ordinary public took to "The Guy" as it took to juke boxes, westerns, and television. The 1953 campaign, consequently, generated all the spiritual passion of a political fiesta. Magsaysay ran against the "unspeakable" Quirino, whose administration had shocked even the Latin-Asian sense of decorum regarding the acceptable limits of corruption. "The Guy" swept into office to open Malacañang Palace to a barefoot mob which made Andrew Jackson's White House callers seem genteel, and to a crowd of politicians who revived not only the New Deal and anticipated the New Frontier but also—inevitably in Manila—the Big New Deal and the Wild New East.

Ramon Magsaysay died on March 17, 1957, before his programs had been fully defined, let alone implemented, but the glorified Magsaysay ghost lives in Malacañang Palace today as cotenant with Macapagal. The Magsaysay apocrypha is that of poor-boy-makes-good, and good-man-cleans-up-the-administration, the legend that Macapagal now seeks to attach to himself. In doing so, he runs the double hazard of falsifying the facts and of impersonating a myth. Magsaysay was an inspiring national hero who died before his glory could dim, but he was neither a poor boy nor an efficient administrator. Macapagal has the edge on Magsaysay in having actually been poor, and as an administrator seeming in fact to be good. He has still to show how capable he is of cleaning up government; but he labors under the tremendous competitive handicap that his record as a living reformer must compare with what the Filipinos think Magsaysay's might have been had he survived.

Ramon Magsaysay's childhood, according to the new folklore which is becoming part of the national heritage, was that of an impoverished barrio boy who tended carabao in the rain, ate coarse peasant fare, and gained an education through dogged perseverance; one who forged his way steadily upward and onward to become an industrious mechanic, an irresistibly impetuous suitor to a lovely mestiza, a fearless anti-Japanese guerrilla, then the nation's foremost soldier and its finest President. Through the chinks in the shellac appear the facts that Magsaysay's parents were reasonably well-to-do landowners, and that he owned a Ford in his schoolboy days and gave as much thought to it as to his studies. He became the enterprising operator of a small fleet of buses, and he was indeed an impetuous suitor, a fearless guerrilla, an honest and competent military commander, and a much loved President. What Magsaysay was not was a self-made man at the beginning of his career, or the inspired architect of a new Philippines at the end of it. The Guy was a muscular liberal whose instincts were sound, although his mental processes were uncomplicated; but he was opposed by men who by instinct were crooks and by long practice were political contortionists of Ringling Brothers, Barnum and Bailey caliber.

Magsaysay as a military commander pacified the Hukbalahap, and Magsaysay as President electrified the public; but Magsaysay as Chief Executive never bridged the gap between a national policy objective and its fulfillment. He decreed that corruption would cease, that development would commence, that the government would govern and the people would prosper. To begin with, however, he virtually stalled progress by opening the telegraph offices to any and all complainants, of whom the total number, naturally, corresponded with remarkable exactitude to the total population. He then directed the easily diverted national bureaucracy to suspend other business while it investigated and answered the complaints. Meanwhile, he gave conspicuous reformers their heads in proposing but not in implementing new programs; he sacked conspicuous corruptors, who, being relieved of other responsibility, could then conspire full time against the reformers. He himself, finding desk and paper work uncongenial, pursued whatever problem would keep him on the move.

The discrepancies between Ramon Magsaysay the myth and

Ramon Magsaysay the man reflect no discredit upon the Magsay-say image, which is gradually clarifying as that of a national hero of much greater promise than achievement. It reflects discredit, rather, upon the image makers, who were determined to see in Magsaysay what in fact he was not: the prophet not only with a message, but also with a method to carry it out. Ramón Magsay-say, instead, was all too exactly what they said in their slogans: he was The Guy. He lived and, to adopt the idiom of his own era, he thought with his guts. He did not realize that the Philippines' political mess was one calling not for overnight Herculean labors in an Augean stable but for decades of thought as well as action. Diosdado Macapagal, whose thinking is less visceral, although his critics regard it also as less vigorous, started out by being far more fully aware of the nature and the dimensions of his problem. But Macapagal, in trying to fill Magsaysay's size 11 boots, is forced by political pressures to adopt Magsaysay's stance of instantaneous and combative positivism. Whereas Magsaysay was given to fits of depression at contemplating the results of his plans, Macapagal seems more given to cynical adjustment.

Diosdado Macapagal was never particularly close to Magsaysay, even though he himself, as the model "solon," was one of the shining ornaments of the period. Neither was he particularly close to the assorted brain-trusters, image makers, and fair or fast deal-ers, all of whom sought to use Magsaysay for their own purposes, some of these purposes highly laudable. Macapagal, rather, was a loner, and he gained long and valuable experience as a top-drawer loner during the Garcia era.

Diosdado Macapagal entered the big-time political show in 1957, when he ran for Vice-President on the Liberal Party ticket. Even in 1957, Macapagal aspired to run for the Presidency. The Liberals were impressed with his competence but not with his political or financial pull, and they tried to play it smart. They ran Yulo, a sugar baron and party power for President, and Macapagal for Vice-President. When Yulo lost and Macapagal won, they reasoned, as did the Nacionalistas, that the public voted for Macapagal mainly in protest against the Nacionalistas' vice-presidential candidate, the conspicuously unpopular José Laurel. In the Philippines the President and the Vice-President win as individuals, not as a team, so in 1958 the Liberal Vice-President

Macapagal assumed office together with the Nacionalista President Garcia. Macapagal's victory was in fact highly impressive, for he won 116,940 more votes than did Garcia himself.

President Garcia, who admired success even in an adversary, warmly congratulated his unwelcome administrative partner, then set about showing the young upstart his place. Garcia denied Macapagal a cabinet post, even though the Vice-President traditionally expects to be Foreign Secretary. He assigned him a dingy office in an inaccessible quarter of Malacañang Palace where the air conditioning was unreliable. He placed at his disposal a battered old Cadillac which broke down repeatedly in official processions and had to be pushed. The harbor tug, Garcia decreed, was more appropriate to vice-presidential seafaring needs than the presidential yacht, the *Lapu Lapu,* and the commercial airlines would serve his purposes as well as the presidential Fokker *Friendship.*

Macapagal accepted relegation from responsibility as an opportunity to launch his 1961 campaign in 1957. He busied himself with political tours of the provinces, where he never failed to make it clear that he had nothing whatsoever to do with the Garcia administration and its appalling record of scandals. In case not just rustic voters but Manila politicians as well were listening, he went to some pains to review over and over again the items on his own record which would make him a logical choice for the Presidency. He had to his credit, he kept pointing out, the sponsorship of the minimum-wage law and of the five-day government week, plus various pieces of legislation providing benefits for the barrios—roads, health services, credits, and local legislative authority, to mention the most important.

Macapagal, the Manila President-makers thought, was very good, but not by any means good enough. His obvious honesty, sobriety, and sincerity would pull votes to the party. But he was no Magsaysay, and the politicians would settle for no less. Macapagal, the Manila pundits said, had no message. To point with pride to the record would impress the literate, but the literate piled up no majorities. "Poor boy makes good" was old hat. "Throw the rascals out" had a little more political chic but not much. What they wanted was a political Messiah capable of moving the masses to ecstasy and the rival politicians to frenzy.

Macapagal, they kept reiterating, was weak, neutral, negative, colorless. He projected no image. He lacked charisma.

Nevertheless, when the professional politicians of the Liberal Party and the inspired young amateurs of the Grand Alliance came together in the United Opposition to support a candidate who could stop Garcia, only Macapagal was not surprised when the choice fell on him. During the exhilarating campaign, while the bands played "Happy Days Are Here Again," "Honest Mac, the Poor Man's Best Friend" not only told his strive-and-succeed story to the tireless *tao,* but he consorted happily, indeed at times gaily, with the very politicians whose esteem for him had been notably tepid. There was Emmanuel Pelaez, for instance, the pragmatic and on the whole humanistically motivated wheeler and dealer, the vice presidential candidate, who, less than two years after being elected, broke openly with his chief and began pouring contempt upon him as another Garcia. There was also Raul Manglapus, celebrated variously as the Philippines' "youngest solon," its "oldest teenager," the Opposition's fastest-thinking and talking spokesman for the Magsaysay political ideal, whose post-election attitudes toward Macapagal have become increasingly ambivalent. There was also, of course, Arsenio Lacson, ex-pugilist-columnist turned Mayor of Manila (d. 1962), who broke with Macapagal almost immediately after the elections to the accompaniment of remarks better left unquoted in favor of a more printable epigram he produced during the campaign: "Macapagal," said "Old Arsenic," "is like a woman without sex appeal; I provide the falsies."

Macapagal, as it turned out, did very nicely without applying to Lacson for advice on new lingerie, political or otherwise. He wore his rather rumpled old long-sleeved sports shirts when the fashion was the elaborately embroidered *barong tagalog,* or smuggled American banlon. He greased his hair slick and parted it in the middle, when the fashion was the crew cut or the Kennedy rumple. He tramped the barrio roads despite mud or dust; he shook every hand he could reach until his palm and his fingers blistered; he kissed babies and hugged old women; he rode out-riggers, waded through floods, perched on the steps of buses, bucketed about in an old plane, and was several times almost given up for lost by land, sea, or air. Over a period of months he told and retold his life story until his eyes were glazed and his voice shrill, and often, by 2:00 A.M., in the rain and among the mosquitoes, both Honest Mac and the patient *tao* were too fatigued to listen. He seemed peculiarly obtuse, thought even his adherents, about the surer, easier devices of radio and television —at least until election eve, when he staged a six-hour radio-TV "heart-to-heart talkathon."

Against such cloddish competition, even though word began drifting in from the provinces that even Magsaysay had never been like this, Garcia declined to run very hard or very fast. In strict point of fact, Garcia was in such poor health that he sometimes had virtually to be carried, and he probably would not have entered the contest at all against any other candidate. Still, Garcia was so confident that he could beat Macapagal that when the returns were in and Macapagal had 3,554,840 votes to his own 2,902,966, he refused to concede defeat. He demanded a recount and it was not until two full years later that he allowed his demand to lapse.

As of January 1, 1962, Macapagal assumed office, and became the new tenant of Malacañang. He was the first authentic peasant boy in Philippines history ever to occupy the splendid palace, now many times remodeled and re-embellished since the days when it had been the seat of the Spanish Governors General. He moved in with his wife and three of his four children (two of them by his second marriage), to find that the patrician Garcias had spent all but P18 of the household funds meant to last through the next six months, that the rugs and drapes and upholstery were dirty, and that in every way the wily Don Carlos could contrive, not only the palace but the whole administration was booby-trapped. President Garcia's last official act had been to swear in some twenty "midnight appointees," anti-Macapagal politicians who were being rewarded with choice patronage positions, such as that of president of the National Bank, appointments which the new incumbent quite naturally had expected to have at his own disposal.

As of January 1, Diosdado Macapagal began to exhibit a new personality, or, as he himself prefers to put it, to disclose more fully the old. His controlling philosophy of life, he now acknowledged, was to refrain from manifesting his full competence and confidence until he was in a position more to attract than to repel by so doing, and clearly he thought his time had arrived. Diosdado Macapagal, the President, suddenly began to bring the long-flickering Macapagal image into rather sharper focus. He radiated self-assurance, indeed complacency, even a degree of arrogance. He revised his little personal homilies on "strive and succeed" themes into political adages which sounded like "feint, then duck, then strike." He took swift, decisive, dramatic action, sometimes in small but quite significant matters. He prohibited anyone from having business dealings with any members of his family, charged ex-President Garcia's brother with corruption, and advertised the *Lapu Lapu* for sale. (It remains unsold but not unused.) He also took action in major matters. He announced a new Five Year Plan which he himself had authored. (It is the revised version of his doctoral thesis.) He also decontrolled the currency, nullified Garcia's "midnight appointments," and launched a vast Emergency Employment Administration reminiscent of both the worst and the best of the WPA. In the second year of his administration he championed a Philippines land reform program, not quite the sweeping measures to emancipate the peasant which were already a century overdue, but a courageous start.

President Macapagal also began what he called a campaign against vested interests but what his opponents called a rash of vendettas. He reiterated his campaign promise that he would not run for re-election but would stand or fall on the record of a single term. At the same time, he laid the groundwork for a "Draft Mac" ground swell. Repudiating Garcia's Filipino First policy, he reintensified the Philippines pro-Western, anti-Communist policy, but at the same time he canceled a state visit to the United States in order to bring the American Congress to heel about a long promised final war-damages payment of $73 million. As a further lesson to Washington, he shifted the Philippines Independence Day from July 4 to July 12 in order to commemorate not the 1946 transfer of sovereignty by the United States, but the 1896 declaration of independence from Spain. Presently he affronted the Americans, the British, the Thais, and others as well by laying claim to British North Borneo (June 22, 1962) and thus shaking Malaysia, ASA (Philippines-Thai-Malayan economic and social cooperation program), and SEATO solidarity. The North Borneo claim soon threw Macapagal into company with Indonesia's "anticommunistphobia" Sukarno, who also for his own reasons opposed Malaysia. This Macapagal-Sukarno partnership may work drastic changes in Southeast Asia —scarcely, however, one change which Macapagal professes to hope for, i.e., Sukarno's conversion into an amenable and anti-Communist neighbor.

President Macapagal is now deeply involved in championing the highly dubious Philippines claim to sovereignty over North Borneo and the 99 per cent unfeasible Macapagal formula, "Maphilindo," for resolving by one fine diplomatic *démarche* the triangular Philippines-Malaysia-Indonesia imbroglio over former British Borneo. This personal commitment constitutes one of the less reassuring indicators of his reading of his Magsaysay testament. Macapagal claims North Borneo on the basis of the translation into English of one Malay word (was it "lease" or was it "cession"?) in an 1878 agreement between the Sultan of Sulu and an Austrian baron who subsequently sold his rights to a British company. The original Malay-language copy of the document has disappeared, but Macapagal supports his claim with a series of ingenious—his critics say ingenuous—legalistic arguments. The obvious facts are that the original Sulu claim itself was shaky and the Macapagal arguments are specious. The Philippines never until 1962 asserted its succession to the Sulu rights or defined its own territorial limits to include North Borneo. Quite a lot of history, furthermore, has washed through the Sulu Sea since 1878, none of it disposing the people of North Borneo to look with favor upon the Philippines as a prospective motherland or mortgagor.

Macapagal's legalistic arguments against the formation of Malaysia yielded precedence after a time to a double-header anti-colonial, anti-Communist argument calculated to gain support from almost any quarters. Not only North Borneo, Macapagal said, but Sarawak as well was submitting to British "neocolonialistic" pressure to join Malaysia, and the new Federation of Malaysia itself, obviously an unnatural and unstable creation, was an invitation to Communist subversion which could spread through Borneo into the Philippines. Macapagal's resolution to the whole problem was for the Philippines, Indonesia, and Malaysia to come together into a "loose confederation" to be called "Maphilindo," a name coined by Indonesia's Foreign Minister Subandrio. All disagreements could then be resolved, he said, through brotherly consultation, and "Malay triplets" separated at birth by cruel colonial foster parents would at last be "reunited" to share their common heritage and achieve their common destiny.

Macapagal's euphoric dream of Maphilindo—the great foreign-policy achievement of his administration, he has called it—soon proved a very coltish chimera indeed. Indonesia's Bung Karno endorsed Maphilindo but then proceeded again and again to crank up his own policy of *konfrontasi,* his belligerent attempt first to "frustrate," then to "smash" Malaysia. Macapagal nevertheless condones and supports Sukarno, accuses the British, appeals to the Tengku, and persists in staking his reputation in foreign policy upon a project which his Foreign Secretary describes, with pride rather than misgiving, as an "inspired improvisation."

President Macapagal, according to his critics, who seemed very soon after his induction into office to grow at least as numerous and as outspoken as the critics of Garcia, has been experimenting with quite a lot of more or less inspired improvisations. He has swiftly converted himself into the political maestro and devotes himself today to living both dramatically and dangerously, not in the pattern of Garcia but in the composite pattern of Quezon, Roxas, and Magsaysay. He combines something of Quezon's theatricalism, Roxas' adroitness, Magsaysay's bluntness, plus his own as yet indefinable nuances. He proved his polished political finesse to friends and enemies alike by picking off, one after another and even covey by covey, many of the leading opposition politicians, persuading them to desert the Nacionalistas and join the Liberal ranks, with the result that the Liberals, who started out with control of neither the House nor the Senate, gained control of both. With more or less subtlety, Macapagal made the inducement fit the case—here a reminder that patronage was strictly for the Liberals, there an intimation, in the course of investigation of whatever scandal was current, that repentance and Liberal Party affiliation might lend relative immunity to personal exposure; even forthright invitation to jump aboard his bandwagon.

Honest Mac, the Poor Man's Best Friend, so recently regarded as the political rabbit, had metamorphosed himself. The features were not yet sharply defined, but certainly they were not those of a rabbit. A Lacson quip of the 1953 campaign, that the voter had his choice between The Guy (Magsaysay), The Gab (Romulo), and The Thing (Quirino), might have been, but was not, updated to read that the 1961 voter, in trying to destroy The Grab had created The Thimg. Just what The Thimg was, no one could yet be sure, neither the ardent supporters who hoped it was a savior nor the opponents who feared it was a dictator, for friends and enemies seemed to switch roles and outlooks almost as easily as politicians switched parties.

Even in this abnormally kaleidoscopic Philippines political ruckus, a few roles seem to have found their reluctant players. One is that of scapegoat. The brothers Lopez, the Iloilo "sugar barons," share it. Another is that of red herring. Harry Stonehill, an "American carpetbagger," is it. Few weep for the Lopezes, either Senator Fernando or tycoon Eugenio, or for Harry Stonehill, all of whose millions, if not whose reputations, are virtually intact. On the other hand, quite a few believe that many other Philippines millionaires are at least as ruthlessly acquisitive as the Lopez family, and that among them are those residents of Forbes Park, Manila's luxury suburb, who put money into the Liberal Party campaign (as the Lopez family somehow neglected to do) and have now displaced the Lopez clique in Malacañang society. And even more believe that Harry Stonehill, however culpable he may have been, was slugged with headlines to distract attention from political maneuvers and that he was hustled out of the country very fast indeed, just when he was beginning to mention interesting names and figures.

The facts of the Lopez and the Stonehill cases are for some determined antiquarian a decade hence to disinter, for Philippines scandals, probes, and trials displace each other much too swiftly in Congress, court, and press for public interest in any one or two of them to be indefinitely sustained. Basically, however, in the Lopez case the administration pinpointed the Lopez interests as those primarily responsible for much of the political and economic skulduggery of recent years. It set about depriving the Lopez brothers of their alleged control over Congress, via the Nacionalista Party, their "monopoly"—achieved through government loans—over MERALCO (Manila Electrical Company, purchased in 1961 from American interests), and much, much more besides. In the Stonehill case, the government in early 1962 moved to arrest, investigate, try, and deport one Harry Stonehill, a World War II military officer who turned big-time financial and industrial operator. Stonehill's business empire was worth many tens of millions and his political connections shared in the profits. The Stonehill case was abruptly dropped just before public announcement was to have been made of the names of high government officials allegedly implicated with him, and Stonehill, who had been fighting deportation, suddenly requested it and was allowed to depart at his own immediate convenience. But the case did not stay dropped.

On July 20, 1963, for instance, former Secretary of Justice, José W. Diokno, who had been peremptorily sacked by Macapagal in 1962, went on a nationwide radio-TV hookup to make a sensational disclosure of alleged documents "implicating," among other administration notables, even President Macapagal himself in the Stonehill scandals. Current Secretary of Justice Salvador Mariño next day made an equally electrifying counterexposé of documents implicating, among many, many others, even Vice-President Pelaez. Pelaez thereupon resigned his post as Foreign Secretary, retaining, however, his elective post as Vice-President, and took to the platform to defend himself and to denounce Macapagal's "treacherous" and "dictatorial practices." President Macapagal himself remained silent, but the administration presently produced "evidence" that one "Golden Arm" José Ignacio, a convicted forger, had been sought out in jail by representatives of the political opposition and persuaded to practice his art on documents whose descriptions corresponded to some of those in the Stonehill file, especially those naming Macapagal. Throughout late 1963, the Stonehill case was still gaining both fresh momentum and imaginatively contrived dimensions of further confusion. Whenever it slipped even a few points in the political Hooper rating, new "exposés" relating to the Lopez case could be counted on to hit newspaper row, radio-TV, the halls of Congress, and Malacañang.

Diosdado Macapagal today is obviously enjoying his job, and he is just as obviously convinced that he is doing it well and that no one could do it better. He exhibits the self-confidence which

Magsaysay sometimes seemed to lack, but little of the warmth and exuberance in which Magsaysay abounded. He has relatively few intimate friends, and with his political colleagues he maintains an attitude which combines reserve with watchfulness, although for the benefit of the photographers and the public he can put on a show of camaraderie along with the best.

President Macapagal seems to have settled, happily on the whole, into life in Malacañang Palace, a gilded cage into which every politician, every political reporter and columnist peers daily, indeed almost hourly, then hustles off to the nearest coffee shop to compare notes with his colleagues and rivals before starting or passing on the latest spate of rumor. When rumors are too remote from, or for that matter too close to the truth—as, for instance, the extravagant cost of his state visit to Madrid and Rome in 1962—Macapagal lets irritation provoke him into a sharp display of temper. For the most part he seems reconciled to being almost permanently on call to politicians, press, and public. He works long, hard hours, still insisting upon drafting important papers for himself. He practices, he says, a system of "command responsibility" whereby he delegates large blocks of authority, while in fact maintaining himself ready at any point to intervene and to sack. He has proved himself ready on very brief notice indeed to jettison even his State Secretaries—Secretary of Justice Diokno, for instance, and most recently, Secretary of Foreign Affairs Pelaez. As Vice-President, Pelaez remains a favorite son of the Grand Alliance, a clique of Liberal Party intellectuals, which may have been the decisive force in the 1961 elections and could prove so again.

For relaxation from his job, President Macapagal depends upon westerns or detective novels, movies, and television. He shows little interest in sports, although he has just begun to take up golf. The palace golf links, like its swimming pool, are much quieter these days than they were during the Garcia era. When he feels the need to get away from it all, he occasionally holidays on a remote island, but he seems to find a political barnstorming tour of the provinces rather more to his taste. He still claims to feel most at ease not in the palace but in the barrio, and his trips into the hinterland (via Garcia's Fokker *Friendship,* since rechristened in champagne by Señora Macapagal as *The Common Man*) quite possibly help Macapagal himself as well as his nationwide constituency to maintain the illusion.

The President's family has made the adjustment to Malacañang with little sign of tension. Evangelina (Eva) Macapagal, the President's second wife, whom he married after the war when he was an impoverished widower with two children, was formerly a career woman, in fact a medical doctor. She proves a valuable political asset, since she is fluent in at least six Philippines languages, besides Spanish and English, and is at ease in any society. She made the transition to housewife when the family occupied a modest Manila suburban home, one which belonged to her own well-to-do family. There she usd to do much of the cooking and housework and to maintain open house for the droves of visitors whom every Manila politician expects to receive, to entertain, to feed, and to provide with jobs. She has now taken the palace-keeping arrangements firmly in hand, improving the standards of decorating, cooking, dusting, and gardening, about which the Garcias were notably lax. The palace storerooms have yielded some historic and antique furnishings which she has now restored to prominent display. Under her supervision the carpenters have taken out or put in quite a few partitions which may or may not serve any better than numerous previous remodelings have done, to make the palace a home.

Mrs. Macapagal has resigned herself to the *marienda* (high tea) which is likely to occur two or three times daily and seven days a week, if not in the palace, then at some public function which the President's wife must grace. She manages to keep the children from becoming objectionable celebrities, no mean feat in view of the avidity of the Philippines press and the teenage set for the juvenile personality cult. The President's elder daughter, Cielo, is already an adult, married and living in a home of her own and the mother of two children. The elder son, Arturo, a handsome young man of twenty-one, studying at San Beda College, is just beginning to cut a swathe in Manila society. Eva Macapagal's two children, a daughter of fifteen and a son, Diosdado, Jr., age eleven, seem precociously bright. They are being brought up, according to report, to adhere to their father's standards, most revealingly summarized in his own rhetorical idiom:

"I have sat at the sumptuous tables of power, but I have not run away with the silverware. "

The Filipinos, like the Americans, are a nation of myth-makers and myth-breakers and they have the Spanish tradition of iconolatry as well as that of American iconoclasm to guide them. They now have a gigantic mass-media network with an insatiable and uninhibited appetite for romantic or sensational materials. There is already being created for the Macapagal family, therefore, both a pretty, polished stereotype, and an ugly, infamous counterpart, and it is becoming increasingly difficult to distinguish the elements of truth. Their home life, according to common report, remains as idyllic as in the fairly recent days when Eva Macapagal did her own marketing and her husband carried the basket. The language of the home is Spanish and the favorite family game is billiards. The preferred family diet is extremely simple, the President himself having a taste for *sinigang* and *paksiw* and also, at any time of day or night, incredible as it may seem, for American canned salmon. The President does not smoke, he drinks only at social affairs and then very moderately, and Mrs. Macapagal counts her calories. They are plain, simple people, unspoiled by sudden prominence. They would seem to be the idealized *tao*. But the reverse of the myth is also becoming current.

President Macapagal, say an increasing number of highly articulate critics, should not forget that he is in fact the common man he claims to be, and should be on his guard against delusions of grandeur. His official biographers, they say, are being encouraged to trace the peasant Macapagals back to the aristocratic Macayabundilis, the remote female ancestor being reputedly a Tagalog princess, the male the son of a Philippines sultan who was descended, somewhat circuitously, to be sure, from Philip of Macedonia. This new genealogy, they point out, may serve to counteract one of the unhappier developments of the last presidential campaign, when the Nacionalistas compounded and disseminated "black propaganda" connecting the Liberal candidate with three "black Macapagals" of infamous memory. But vindication of the presidential name is one thing and myth-making is another. Macapagal's critics are becoming more and more insistent that the meek and humble candidate has developed into the power-mad incumbent, given increasingly not only to unprincipled political machinations but, as may be even worse, to fits of temper, acts of pique, and disturbing indications of egocentricity. According to the standard of measurement which is possibly as good as any in the Philippines, namely, how long it takes for charges not only of betrayal but of corruption to become current, the New Era of the *Tao* with "Honest Mac" as its hero did last one full year. It was not until early 1963 that President Diosdado Macapagal and his family were made targets of attack on charges of having begun to enrich themselves at the public expense. Allegations were then made by an opposition "solon" that Macapagal's daughter Cielo was dealing in smuggled goods and his brother, Angel "Star" Macapagal, running a gambling joint. These allegations were disproved, but others arose, and then suddenly in midyear Honest Mac himself was listed as a Stonehill beneficiary. After that one miraculous year of purity (1962), the New Era of the *Tao* began to look more and more like the long-familiar era of anything goes or at least anything is worth trying. Charges of megalomania and paranoia, for instance, have now become routine.

Whether the alleged maladversions are "anomalies" (factually but not legally substantiated charges) or "canards" (political red herrings), to resort to the standard Philippines political and journalistic vocabulary, President Diosdado Macapagal has by now demonstrated conclusively that he is not above politics, as no one can ever be, least of all in the Philippines. The question which remains unanswered is whether he can stay well ahead of the other politicians. He has managed in the course of his first half term to get some relatively hopeful national development programs under way. In doing so he has had to outmanipulate opponents who seek now, naturally, to outmanipulate him. The only means by which he can keep his programs going is by himself keeping a lap or two ahead of some of the fleetest political sprinters Southeast Asia has yet produced. Honest Mac is still running, talking, and thinking hard. His tough *tao* muscles do not seem to have gone soft in Malacañang.

High Priest of the
Human Person

Ngo Dinh Diem, late President of the Republic of Vietnam, was a good man, possibly even a great one, yet he died little loved and less mourned, and his tragedy, instead of inspiring pity and fear, arouses the ignoble emotions of relief mixed with apprehension. Ngo Dinh Diem was one more victim of the irony of history, which sets an improbable man in an impossible situation where his very virtues eventually become the vices which destroy him. Yet the tragedy of Ngo Dinh Diem did not induce the true sense of catharsis which proceeds from the perception that human dignity defies disaster. It brought, rather, the grim realization that the disaster could have been—and quite possibly will yet become—immeasurably worse, and that in the twentieth-century world the man of high intelligence and pure ideals may be ill-equipped for the role of truly noble tragic victim, or even of popular national hero.

The story of Ngo Dinh Diem can easily be distorted to fit the long-familiar thesis that power corrupts and absolute power corrupts absolutely. In 1955, after the defeat of the French and Ho Chi Minh's triumph at Dien Bien Phu, Ngo Dinh Diem emerged as the clear-eyed, uncompromised and uncompromising anti-Communist hero. Under his one-man rule, his nation emerged as the battered but still battling survivor of international confusion and conspiracy. By 1963, however, South Vietnam was so nearly unviable as to be regarded even by the enemies who coveted it as a millstone around the necks of its possessors. Ngo Dinh Diem had become rigidly and self-righteously authoritarian, intolerant of advice or of criticism, so persuaded of the exclusive validity of his own insight as to court personal and national disintegration by denying the relevancy of any other.

Diem's was not the usual pattern of autointoxication with the privileges of power. If it had been, he might have proved at once a worse and a better man, one capable of inspiring the idealistic disciple and of inciting the inflammable rabble. He never effectively consolidated power in his own hands; he defaulted in exercise of what power he had; and he renounced only the shadow of it even to his hated "strong-man" brother. During much of his career as President, he exhibited hesitation, procrastination, and obfuscation in pursuit of policies so virtuous as to be platonic. His rule was on the whole far more repressive than oppressive. People were purged, imprisoned, and persecuted, to be sure, but not with the degree of ruthlessness which characterizes many other police states. Almost everybody, however, including Diem himself, was frustrated. The Diem regime simply did not allow for action, not even, until the moment of its collapse, for the wildly destructive sort of action which might earlier and artificially have shored it up. Diem's story, therefore, is an example of paramount authority inducing callousness rather than cancer, not so much then of power which corrupts but of impotence which paralyzes.

In Vietnam, nearly everybody bungled—not only Ngo Dinh Diem and his equally self-righteous family, including his brother and adviser, Ngo Dinh Nhu, and his brother's beautiful, puritanical wife, Mme. Nhu. Even the Communists failed to seize many of their opportunities. Diem himself had not only Communists and family to cope with, but also colonialists, royalists, gangsters, fanatics, and Americans, everyone vigorously stirring a Vietnamese broth which became positively toxic. A man of brains, guts, and faith, Diem became more and more convinced that these attributes alone, even if rarely accompanied by acts, were enough to ensure his own and his nation's survival.

President Diem, living under heavy guard in his second best Gia-Long palace after having been bombed out of Independence Palace by his own air force, was confronted in his later days with implacable personal enemies just outside the gate and Communist guerrillas in the suburbs. He had isolated himself from the general public even to the extent of ordering the removal of the huge, fluorescent-lighted portraits of himself which once gazed down loftily from public buildings. From the moment he rose at 6:30 A.M. to attend mass in his private chapel until the moment he retired at 11:00 P.M. with the latest stack of state papers carefully read and reread—but still unsigned—he drove himself almost relentlessly. He might take time out for a siesta but he no longer allowed himself the relaxation and exercise of walks through the city streets or horseback rides in the palace grounds, and besides it was much too dangerous. He held interminable conferences with ministers of state, army commanders, ambassadors, and mere underlings, conferences which generally turned out to be torrential self-exculpating monologues, punctuated by reiterations of "N'est-ce pas?", to which the visitor was expected to answer always "Mais oui." So hypersensitive had he become to criticism that even a noncommittal reply to a casual observation seemed to him to be an affront. For President Ngo Dinh Diem, more by far than for any other Southeast Asian leader, power had become a burden, but one which he would neither take up nor yet lay down.

For the rest, President Diem was a man of minor vices and major virtues. His only excesses were smoking, reading, meditating, and talking. He ate only tolerably well, albeit rather heavily, whether of Vienamese or French cuisine. He drank in moderation, mainly wine but sometimes whiskey. He chain-smoked, preferring American cigarettes. Otherwise his tastes and his habits approached the ascetic. He was an undeviating bachelor. Although he was fascinated by gadgets such as cameras and transistors, his personal possessions and his private quarters were spare almost to the point of monasticism. By nature he was kind, generous, and considerate, save, of course, when it came to dealing with a political opponent. A man of great intellectual accomplishment in Vietnamese, Chinese, French, and English, he had a history of unswerving adherence to his convictions, most of them laudable and some of them saintly. He was thoroughly versed in the principles of Chinese Confucianism and conservatism, French Catholicism and rationalism, American democracy and egalitarianism, Vietnamese nationalism and revolution. Combining the characteristics of the mandarin, the priest, the bureaucrat, and the freethinker, President Ngo Dinh Diem packed into his rotund, roseate person even more incompatibles than do most of his distinguished contemporaries in Southeast Asia. He seems less baffling as a personality than many others mainly because in his very complex background it is relatively easy to find a plausible motivation for the most startling aberration.

Ngo Dinh Diem was born on January 3, 1901, in the imperial capital of Hue, the third son of Ngo Dinh Kha, minister and counselor of the Emperor Thanh-Thai. Although he himself never married, Diem was pre-eminently a family man. He was brought up in the midst of a fiercely proud and clannish family by which, both by fate and by choice, he was always surrounded. Since the members of his own family were the only persons who ever enjoyed both his affection and full confidence, and since all of them shared in some degree his own special abilities and disabilities, it is essential to the Diem story to dwell upon the Ngo family background.

The Ngos have been for centuries one of the distinguished families of Vietnam, "Ngo" being, of course, the surname, and the President, properly speaking, being President Ngo Dinh Diem or President Ngo, not President Diem—although he became resigned to being so known to the international world. The Ngo family inherited the Chinese mandarin and the Vietnamese Catholic traditions, the sons regarding the mandarinate as their natural career even though their ancestors had been converted to Catholicism by some of the early French missionaries. The conversion dates back, perhaps, to the seventeenth century, when the French Bishop of Adran helped to restore a Vietnamese emperor to his throne and then helped him to rule the country.

Of the members of his clan of his own generation, Ngo Dinh Kha was by far the most illustrious, and his career was a remarkable preview to that of his son, Ngo Dinh Diem. Ngo Dinh Kha was born into a Vietnam which, as usual, was torn by civil disorders, some of them involving elements of anti-Catholic persecution. In his early youth he was sent by his parents to study in Catholic mission schools abroad, first in Portuguese Macao, later in British Penang. On his return to Vietnam he entered a seminary to study for the priesthood, continuing meanwhile intensive studies of Chinese classics and setting himself also to master the

French language. Ngo Dinh Kha decided presently against taking holy orders and devoted himself instead to education. He established a private school in Hue, the first in Vietnam which combined Western with Eastern studies. His intention was to work simultaneously for the modernization of the nation and for the preservation of its ancient culture, at a time when French influences were becoming steadily more widespread. Among his pupils were the young princes of the royal court, and from teaching, Ngo Dinh Kha made the transition by rapid stages to serving as a court official. He rose swiftly to the position of Grand Chamberlain and became, in effect, the intermediary between the French and the throne. Both the French and the royal family reposed great confidence in him, and had he chosen to profit from his position he could have become a man of immense wealth and influence. He chose instead to lead a modest life. When the French created a crisis by deposing the emperor and putting his young son on the throne, Ngo Dinh Kha resigned his court position in protest (1907). He retired to his country home in the village of Phu Cam, now an integral part of Hue, and there he devoted himself to his studies, to the education of his six sons, and to the life of the gentleman farmer.

Ngo Dinh Diem, therefore, had always before him his father's example—that of the devout scholar who decided against entering the Church but retained always a deep attraction to the priesthood; that also of the high official who preferred to withdraw rather than to compromise. Ngo Dinh Kha died in 1923 without ever having emerged from his long retirement. His widow still survives, now a venerable matriarch of 92. In recent years, before the great family tragedy of 1963, she had presided proudly over family reunions at which there appeared the leading figures of the nation. One son, the Provincial Governor (Ngo Dinh Khoi, d. 1945) was missing, but the others made every effort to participate: the President, the Archbishop (Ngo Dinh Thuc), the Ambassador (Ngo Dinh Luyen), the Political Adviser (Ngo Dinh Nhu), and the "unofficial agent" (Ngo Dinh Can).

Growing up in a family destined for such awesome accomplishment, Ngo Dinh Diem was conditioned to excel, to know that he excelled, and to be intolerant of mediocrity. In his early youth he learned something also of the splendor, arrogance, and decadence of the imperial court. There he was the companion of young princes, including the future Emperor Bao-Dai, whose intellectual accomplishments he dwarfed. As a very young child he accompanied his father on the rounds of the Citadel—the moated and walled Imperial City. There he witnessed the splendid rites and ceremonies which made life in Hue resemble life in Peking. Hue, the Citadel, and the court were already anachronisms, to be sure, but to the Ngo family they represented dignity and stability.

Ngo Dinh Diem's way of life changed drastically but not altogether for the worse when his father retired from the court to lead a life of contemplation, meanwhile, Rousseau-like, tending the fruit trees and the flowers and even, according to the legend, doing a little planting of rice. Diem himself led the life of a glorified peasant boy. His home was austere and his fare was simple by contrast with the past, but his daily routine was that of the carefully reared child who tramped through the rice fields, to be sure, but mostly on his way to school, with the Imperial City walls serving as a backdrop to the rustic foreground. He attended Pellerin School in Hue and won just about every prize that was offered, including those in French language. He also studied the Chinese classics, with his father to review him and check him not only on the form but also the nuances. Occasionally he and his equally gifted brothers actually visited the rice fields at planting or harvesting time. The apocrypha have not yet clarified on one salient point—whether they did more rice farming or more riding by canal boat to and from the fields while their father played the flute and recited poetry.

Diem's education was more systematic and purposeful than it sounds. For a few years he studied with a view to entering the priesthood, and at one time in his youth actually entered the novitiate but soon changed his mind. According to some reports he found the Church too restrictive to his talents; according to another, however, he found it too easy an answer to the problem of self-discipline. At any rate, after studying first for the priesthood, he studied later for the mandarinate, that is, an administrative career in government. The training at that time being a French colonial overlay upon the traditional Indochinese system, he entered the French-operated School for Law and Administration in Hanoi. He was graduated first in his class and his career prospects, naturally, were auspicious.

Ngo Dinh Diem, a Catholic mandarin like his father, and a young man of extraordinary attainment in languages and literature, was no effete intellectual devoted only to his books. He was also physically strong and vigorous—a skilled horseman, a sure marksman, an enthusiastic hunter. He learned riding at an early age, according to the legend, by prevailing upon a young cavalry officer to teach him despite his father's express prohibition. Thanks to his father's predilection for taking his sons drifting about the countryside to observe with both aesthetic and scientific interest the phenomena of nature, the young Diem was also something of an amateur naturalist. The one element apparently left out of his nature and his experience was any overpowering attraction to or for the young ladies. It is said he once entertained rather a brief and tepid admiration for a pretty girl. Before he could get around to making up his mind, let alone speaking it, she had entered a convent.

The young Diem earned quite early and maintained later a reputation for being given to alternating shows of temper and of extremely stern self-discipline, moods of participation and of withdrawal, phases of elation and despair over his own achievements. Always, however, except in the curious history of his relations with the Church, he was unswerving in his pursuit of whatever objective he had set himself. His true calling, many observers now believe, might indeed have been the priesthood.

On qualifying for the mandarinate (1921), Ngo Dinh Diem was appointed to an administrative post in the provinces. Almost at once he gained the reputation for being tireless, honest, and efficient, a combination of qualities so extremely rare in the decadent mandarinate of the period that he caused more astonishment than resentment among his colleagues. While other administrators remained in their offices and made themselves accessible only to *fonctionnaires* and *propriétaires,* Ngo Dinh Diem spent his days on horseback or in the public places or on the agricultural lands, actually studying his province, meeting his people, and counseling them on their problems. It was a practice which he later tried to adopt on the national level until for security reasons it became impossible. His young associates, who consulted a soothsayer to tell them what he already knew, announced that of the whole lot of them, he was the one who was headed for greater things.

No one was much surprised, therefore, when at the age of twenty-eight Diem became Governor of Phan Thiet Province. The French, among others, however, were surprised when he began not only to talk but to act with regard to certain very delicate matters. One was land reform, and it was generally French-owned land which was involved. Another was Communism, this being the period when Communist agents first became active in Indochina, and Diem argued for combating them not just by arrest, but by reindoctrination and rehabilitation.

The French, observing Diem's capabilities, and some perhaps fearing them, counseled the young Emperor Bao-Dai to call him to Hue and there to appoint him Minister of the Interior, to be responsible for implementing some administrative reforms then being contemplated. Diem, then aged thirty-two, accepted the appointment with massive misgivings and provisos. When both the French and the emperor, who was little more enthusiastic than the French about his proposals, not only declined to institute genuinely meaningful reforms or modernizations of government but attempted to exploit his own prestige for the benefit of the regime, Ngo Dinh Diem resigned in protest. The French and the emperor thereupon competed to deprive him of such dignities as academic degrees and government decorations, all of which he was apparently quite content to relinquish. From that time onward Diem put no faith in anything which either the French or the emperor promised to do, either for himself or for the nation. He went into a period of retirement which lasted for twenty-one years, and nothing the French, the Japanese, Bao-Dai, or presently Ho Chi Minh offered could lure him out of it.

Between 1933 and 1954, that is, between his thirty-second and his fifty-third year, Ngo Dinh Diem seemed less like a man than a myth. Diem, it was said, was the one Vietnamese who had proved himself a competent, incorruptible administrator, a totally dedicated nationalist, a match for the royal court, the French, and the Communists. Ngo Dinh Diem had only one rival in prestige, a man who himself seemed, during the first half of that period, less like a myth than a wraith, and later, to the Western world at least, less a wraith than a monster. He was Ho Chi Minh, the nationalist-Communist-conspirator, a national revolutionary and international fugitive, commonly rumored more dead than alive. If it were not to be Ho Chi Minh who brought order to Vietnam, many people thought, then it must be Ngo Dinh Diem.

Virtually nothing that Ngo Dinh Diem did or did not do—and he actually did very little—seemed to the uninitiated outsider to lend much substance to the legend. It was a widely held belief, nevertheless, one with which the French had to cope, also Bao-Dai, also the Japanese, Ho Chi Minh, and presently, after 1954, the Americans. At one time or another they made overtures to Diem, and Diem at times responded, but never very vigorously until 1954. By his very inaction, it seemed, he kept his reputation unblemished while others were losing theirs. The earliest of the Vietnamese nationalists, anti-French royalists who lived in exile abroad—Prince Cuong-Dê in Japan and his followers elsewhere—conspired and declined and lapsed into futility. Bao-Dai played emperor, abdicated, played adviser to Ho Chi Minh, fled to Hong Kong, and then played emperor again. He exhibited a schizophrenic attraction to the Citadel in Hue, the hunting preserves in the highlands, the Rue Pigalle in Paris, the Rue Catinat in Saigon, and the Côte d'Azur, where, since 1954, he has quietly and luxuriously relapsed into oblivion. Ho Chi Minh for years fueled the national and international debate whether he was more patriot or more Communist. Even the enigmatic Ho Chi Minh, however, could not maintain the mystery indefinitely and at last he showed his hand—tightly gripped in Mao Tse-tung's. Ngo Dinh Diem remained unchanged, always the one last great hope.

About Diem's life during the 1933–1945 period very little is publicly known and his intimates say that there is in fact very little to know. Most of the time he lived in the family home at Phu Cam, a modestly handsome establishment extensively rebuilt by his elder brother, Ngo Dinh Khoi, a provincial governor of distinguished record. He devoted himself to reading and writing, riding and walking, religious meditation and political discussion. He was watched, naturally, by the French Sûreté. He did little to reward their interest. During the Japanese occupation, he was watched also by the Kempeitai. Toward the end of the war, the French were contemplating exiling him to Laos, the Japanese were

contemplating nobody knew quite what, and Bao-Dai was angling for him to become Prime Minister in a Japanese-sponsored
puppet state. The French and the Japanese, meanwhile, were plotting and staging coups against each other. Diem was tipped off
that someone was about to snatch him up. Just before the unknown agents pounced, Diem vanished. A few months later the
Ngo Dinh Khoi home from which he had vanished was seized
by Ho Chi Minh's Communists. The house was burned and
Diem's personal library of some 10,000 volumes went up in the
flames. His brother, Ngo Dinh Khoi, and his brother's son, were
either burned or buried alive or shot. On that point the accounts
vary, but Diem always held the Communists accountable for
their murder.

When the Pacific War came to an end, Diem was in hiding in
Saigon, living in a rented room with his brother, Ngo Dinh
Luyen. When he heard reports from the north that Emperor
Bao-Dai was about to abdicate and that Ho Chi Minh was about
to form a government, he set out for Hue, determined to dissuade
Bao-Dai. Although he knew Ho Chi Minh only by reputation, he
was already persuaded that Ho was no nationalist patriot, as many
others asserted, but rather a doctrinaire international Communist.
He disliked Bao-Dai and what Bao-Dai stood for—complaisant
accommodation to the French. He felt, nevertheless, that only by
maintaining the legitimate regime and working through it was
there any chance of orderly achievement of true Vietnamese independence.

The whole of Vietnam was in chaos at the time that Diem
made his trip northward by car and by train. At Tuy-Hoa, in
September, he fell into the hands of the Communist insurgents.
During the next few weeks the Communists at times threatened
him, at times wooed him. They shifted him about capriciously
from one miserable place of detention to another. At times they
seemed to forget who and where he was, at other times to be on
the point of murdering or executing him. Then they shipped him
off into the remote highlands and left him pretty much to himself in a squalid mountain village. There he shared the poverty,
the hunger, and the disease of the inhabitants, several times being
on the point of death from fever or malnutrition. He shared also,
however, in the daily life of the villagers. He found a friend,

teacher, and physician in one venerable mountaineer whose mystical books he studied with a philosopher's detachment, gaining, miraculously, in physical and mental health as he did so. At last he received word that he was summoned to Hanoi at the personal command of Ho Chi Minh.

After another arduous and dangerous journey, Diem arrived in Hanoi just at the time that Ho Chi Minh was contemplating a deal with the French and was looking, according to Diem, for a puppet figure whom he could set up as a responsible minister and use as scapegoat. Diem had no intention of obliging. He had learned, furthermore, in the course of his detention, that his elder brother, Ngo Dinh Khoi, to whom even more than any of the others of his family he was deeply attached, had been murdered by the Communists, that Khoi's son had been murdered along with him, and that other members of the family had been subjected to intimidation. The news had reconfirmed Diem in his uncompromising opposition to Communists and to communism. Murder, pillage, rape, and treachery, he was convinced, were integral elements of Communist policy, which was in all respects incompatible with his own brand of nationalism.

Once in Hanoi, Ngo Dinh Diem was delivered at once to the splendid mansion which had once been the residence of the French Governor and was now the home of Ho Chi Minh. Although he was dressed like a refugee and still looked much the worse for his illness and his journey, he was received by the household staff as an honored guest for whom every amenity he had missed for months was at once provided—soap and hot water, clean clothing and a good bed, whatever he cared to order from the kitchen or the storeroom. He had an overnight interval in which to refresh himself, and the following day he met his host. In the elegantly furnished drawing room, Ngo Dinh Diem and Ho Chi Minh, Vietnam's two great leaders, met each other for the first time, and, each speaking in polished French, they enacted a scene which might have been scripted by Racine.

Ho Chi Minh was at once subtle and stagy. He was a man of calculated mystery, a fragile wisp of a figure, emanating friendliness, intelligence, sincerity, somehow even ruggedness both of sinew and of spirit, a living contradiction to all the recurrent reports that he was in fact devious, demoniac, or, for that matter, dead. He invited Ngo Dinh Diem to join him in government, urging a ministerial position upon him as a patriotic duty, intimating delicately that it was also good life insurance. Ngo Dinh Diem was cold and rigid, not the suppliant but the accuser; as always, he was pedantic even when most impassioned. He repudiated communism at some length, both in theory and in practice. He accused Ho Chi Minh of "murder" and rejected his explanation that Ngo Dinh Khoi's death had been "a mistake." He then walked out of the interview and out of the house to vanish into the crowds of refugees and soldiers in the city of Hanoi, and much later, after a long illness, to turn up again in Saigon.

The next few years were chaotic and tragic for the whole nation. The French were fighting the Vietnamese nationalists of many but of few clear descriptions. Ho Chi Minh's Communists, Bao-Dai's royalists, and Saigon's opportunists and fatalists were engaged in confused but lethal rivalries. Ngo Dinh Diem avoided commitment to anybody, even to the little clique of noncollaborating, noncombatant nationalists whom he attracted to himself until one by one they drifted away because he had nothing positive or hopeful to offer. Several times he traveled back and forth between Hong Kong and Saigon, attempting to persuade Bao-Dai, who periodically absented himself for strategic and personal reasons, to make at least preliminary moves directed toward true Vietnamese independence. Bao-Dai, however, always settled with the French for prestige and comfort rather than power, and since the prestige was obviously shallow, Ngo Dinh Diem declined Bao-Dai's invitation to share it with him by serving as Prime Minister. Ngo Dinh Diem became most outspokenly critical just when the French and Bao-Dai made the least futile of many unpromising moves—the acknowledgment on June 5, 1948, of the limited "independence" within the French Union of the State of Vietnam. This, said Ngo Dinh Diem, was puppetry and not independence, which, of course, was exactly what Ho Chi Minh said too.

By early 1950, Ngo Dinh Diem had begun seriously to fear for his own physical safety in Vietnam. The French Sûreté, perhaps, was planning to arrest him. Ho Chi Minh's Communists were staging acts of terrorism, one of which might at any moment be aimed against him. The Cao-Dai and the Hoa-Hao—exotic sects which blended Eastern and Western religious mysticism with military adventurism—had been making overtures toward him and their advances might become violent. The Binh-Xuyên, a society of gangsters, pirates, and thugs, to whom Bao-Dai rented the Saigon police to "protect" the vice operators, was known to have compiled rather an extensive liquidation list on which someone might well have entered Diem's name.

Ngo Dinh Diem's brother, Bishop (later Archbishop) Ngo Dinh Thuc, was planning a trip to Rome for the Holy Year (1950). Ngo Dinh Diem decided to go along. The two brothers traveled via the Philippines, Japan, and the United States, the Bishop concentrating upon visits to the clergy, Ngo Dinh Diem spending at least as much time with the politicians. In Japan, for instance, he visited the forlorn and almost forgotten Prince Cuong-Dê. In the United States, where they were guests of the Department of State, the brothers made the grand tour. They then proceeded to Europe, where the Bishop elected to remain in Rome while Ngo Dinh Diem moved on to Spain, Switzerland, and then to France, irresistibly drawn toward Paris.

In Paris, rather than moving in with Ngo Dinh Luyen, who was then living with his family in the suburbs, Ngo Dinh Diem set himself up a small, cheerless hotel room. His quarters very soon began to rival the Quai d'Orsay as a clearing house for visitors concerned more or less deeply and directly with developments in Vietnam. There he listened—as was not later his custom—thought, waited, and disappointed everybody, including the French Sûreté. Ngo Dinh Diem took counsel with himself by walking long, lonely hours, early in the morning and late at night, and to the incredulity of his Sûreté shadowers, he ended up always at a church.

When Ngo Dinh Diem tired of Paris, he returned to the United States. He retired to the Maryknoll Seminaries in Ossining, New York and Lakewood, N.J., and settled into a way of life which was half monastic, half propagandistic. He made lobbying expeditions to Washington and New York, religious and academic expeditions to various other American cities, talking with politicians, reporters, professors, and churchmen, always preaching the Vietnamese nationalist cause. He gained considerable admiration—from Cardinal Spellman and Congressman

Walter Judd, among others—but little effective support for his lonely crusade.

In advocating complete and immediate independence as the only solution to the Vietnamese problem, Diem had to combat the prevailing American impression that Vietnam had already achieved independence and that the withdrawal of the French and their troops would be an invitation to the Communists. Diem's arguments served mainly to improve his command of English. The failure of his mission may be one reason why he later avoided the use of the language, even though his spoken English was adequate and his written English was positively literary. His travels also served to introduce him to American community life, including a mild taste for, and what rapidly became a surfeit of hamburgers, baseball, and golf.

After about a year in the United States, Ngo Dinh Diem returned to Europe, profoundly discouraged about prospects for a new American policy toward Vietnam. He took up residence in Saint-André-lès-Bruges, the Benedictine monastery near Bruges, and remained there for a few months. The swift and disastrous course of events in Vietnam then determined him once again to go to France, where he could be in close touch with the Vietnamese community. At the time of the Dien Bien Phu calamity, Ngo Dinh Diem was living quietly in Paris. He was ready and willing when the French and Bao-Dai, and even more particularly the Americans—whose involvement had by this time become almost total—having tried everything and everyone else, at last made the decision of despair and turned unconditionally to him.

Diem attached his own conditions, which included a guarantee of genuine independence from the French, promise of noninterference from Bao-Dai, virtual dictatorial powers for himself, and open-end support from the United States. In a few days of busy negotiation in Paris and on the Côte d'Azur, where Bao-Dai was in residence, Ngo Dinh Diem accepted one-man responsibility for Vietnam. He then boarded an Air France plane for the totally demoralized city of Saigon. There, on June 26, 1954, he was greeted at the airport by some stiff, disapproving French colonial officials, a few jaded reporters, a little band of mainly accidental bystanders, and all of his own family who were able to turn out for the occasion.

Prime Minister Ngo Dinh Diem waited almost two weeks to appoint his cabinet and much longer to activate it. As soon as he could get possession from the reluctant French, which was not until late August, he virtually sealed himself off in the palace. He devoted himself, it seemed, not to planning or taking any official action, but to screening lists of names to decide who was trustworthy. His conclusion, it seems, was that virtually nobody qualified for his confidence except the members of his own family. The outside world having devised and implemented the Geneva agreements, by reason of which Vietnam was partitioned between Ho Chi Minh and Ngo Dinh Diem, a flood of refugees had started pouring from Ho's sector to Diem's, and Communist military triumph had bred an appetite for still greater triumph to be achieved, obviously, at Diem's expense.

When Ngo Dinh Diem returned to Saigon, virtually nobody thought he could last out the year. Soon after his return people began to doubt whether he could last out the month. His most recent experience in administration had been twenty years in the past, under conditions which were scarcely comparable. For the last four years he had not even been resident in Vietnam, and now on his return he was surrounded by professional troublemakers who were conspiring against him just as they conspired against everyone else.

General Nguyen Van Hinh, the Chief of Staff of the demoralized and mutinous Vietnamese armies, was a tool of the French, with aspirations of his own toward the palace. "General" Le Van Vien, Chief of the Binh-Xuyên society of gangsters, had just paid Bao-Dai a $1,000,000 honorarium and planned to reimburse himself from the opium, gambling, and vice dens, relying upon the cooperation of the Chief of Police, General Lai Van Sang, whose expensive loyalty he commanded. General Tran Van Soai, leader of the armies of the paramilitary Hoa-Hao religious sect, intended to carve out a military satrapy or two of his own, and his long-haired guerrilla disciple, Ba Cut, intended to usurp them. The pope of the competing Cao-Dai sect ruled Tay Ninh, just 100 kilometers from Saigon, as if it were a military fief, invoking, among others, Jeanne d'Arc and a legendary Vietnamese nationalist as his patrons, but not Ngo Dinh Diem.

The city of Saigon was a shiny-surfaced shambles in which

French food, wine, perfume, and prostitutes were readily available at a price. The countryside about it was a no man's land, where French colonial troops scarcely maintained the pretense of discipline. The life of the peasants had been for so long disrupted by war that great tracts of once rich land had passed from cultivation. The urban population was mainly parasitic upon the military and accustomed to terror almost to the point of indifference. Saigon and Vietnam were in state of economic collapse, which meant that a relief operation of disaster proportions was in order —yet tens, soon hundreds of thousands of refugees were crowding in from the North.

In the midst of this debacle, Ngo Dinh Diem for many weeks made almost no move which could be detected by the naked eye. He studied his problems endlessly but suspended decision on all of them. He listened to Vietnamese, French, and American importunities, but he gave no one any satisfaction. The French, who had been disposed at first to sabotage him, decided presently that they could merely write him off. The Americans, publicly committed to giving him full assistance, were privately dismayed that he did nothing, proposed nothing, and accepted nothing which they could vigorously support. As it turned out, however, Ngo Dinh Diem had in fact made a few strategic moves. Mainly he had spotted a few people whom he felt he could trust to some degree in positions where they could be effective.

Three months after assuming what looked like powerless power, Ngo Dinh Diem at last began to act—or to be forced into action. Then, after long deploring his inertia, many of the Americans, the French, and even many of the Vietnamese deplored his impetuosity, for he made quick decisions which resulted in the constant threat and at times in the actuality of violent conflict within Saigon's city limits as well as in the countryside. Most of his advisers counseled prudence, compromise, and gradual change, and Diem disregarded them.

General Nguyen Van Hinh had openly been preparing for a coup, and troops moved, in fact, on the palace. Ngo Dinh Diem telephoned a few military officers in whom he placed some reliance. He gave them orders to move against the general and, if necessary, to shoot. The coup fizzled out, the General fled to Paris, and miraculously, in late November, 1954, Diem found himself in command, or at any rate almost in command of the army. He continued personally to command it thereafter, applying the control strategy he happened to devise back in 1954. He put his more trusted—but not necessarily the more efficient—officers in the more responsible positions, rarely coordinating their units or letting them achieve coordination on their own; relying, rather, upon direct orders to individual commanders and units. He achieved, said his critics with increasing vigor and proof, not a military force but a military diffusion, an army which perhaps could not overthrow him but one which certainly could not fight.

Once he had the army more or less under his command, Ngo Dinh Diem turned his attention to the police. He sacked the pro-Bao-Dai Chief of Police (Nov. 29, 1954) and a few months later took on the Binh-Xuyên syndicate. First he closed Le Grand Monde gambling hall (January 15, 1955), then the Dai-Kim-Do (Hall of Mirrors) fancy house, meanwhile fighting battles with the gangster forces in the streets of Saigon, disregarding Bao-Dai's orders, cabled from the Côte d'Azur, to cease and desist. He defied, in fact, all of Bao-Dai's claims to authority. In a national referendum (October 23, 1955) he offered the population its choice of himself, or Bao-Dai. Big campaign posters pictured Bao-Dai as a bloated plutocrat, clutching at women and money bags. By a vote of 5,721,735 to 63,017, the public chose Ngo Dinh Diem. It was not one of the more democratic contests in Southeast Asian history, but more so than any subsequent Vietnamese election, since there was nothing actually to prevent Bao-Dai from campaigning. Diem thereupon proclaimed the Republic of Vietnam (October 26, 1955) and ran off elections for a Constituent Assembly (March 4, 1956). To the Assembly he presented a draft constitution which the members found little reason to alter or even to debate before they accepted it (October 26, 1956) and tidily elected Diem as President.

The year 1956 was Diem's year of triumph and glory. In 1954, sheer desperation had finally moved him to action. Unexpected success gave him confidence, and by 1956 he felt strong enough to challenge the last of his organized opponents in South Vietnam—the paramilitary religious sects—as well as the Communists in the North. He had already prepared, in fact, for a showdown with the sects. He had seduced their leaders with bribes—as much as $1 to $3 million each to the major figures—and had encouraged suspicion and feuding among both leaders and followers. When the sects proved recalcitrant about disbanding their armies or merging them into the national forces, Diem ordered a military campaign against them and managed, sect by sect and leader by leader, to pick them off. On March 2, 1956, he received the surrender of the Hoa-Hao commander, although it was not until midyear that government troops tracked down and guillotined Ba Cut, who had meanwhile perpetrated numerous outrages. By then the Cao-Dai had already given up and its pope had gone into exile in Cambodia.

The climactic date in 1956, however, was July 20, the deadline set by the participants in the Geneva Conference for a nationwide referendum on the reunification of North and South Vietnam. Diem had never accepted the Geneva agreements. As for a referendum, he argued that North Vietnam would never permit a free vote (nor, as everyone was aware, would South Vietnam). He refused to be victimized by Communist voting tactics or to be intimidated by Communist bluster. Western participants in the Vietnam crises agreed with most if not all of Diem's arguments against a referendum, but they feared the reaction of the Communist world if the Geneva agreements were violated. The event vindicated Ngo Dinh Diem. He ignored the July 20 'deadline, and the Communist world fulminated but did not fight.

By 1956 Diem had become accustomed to being proven right, and from 1957 onward it was virtually impossible to argue with him that he might in some instances be wrong. At half a dozen points in 1955 and 1956, the Americans in Saigon had been quite prepared to wash him out, and he knew it. They deplored the rashness of his decisions and they were appalled by the apparently needless death and destruction which resulted from fighting in Saigon and its environs during the government clashes with the Binh-Xuyên and the sects. They deplored also his reliance for advice upon the Ngo family clique. Since that advice had proved both more expedient to accept, and more dramatic in its results than would have been any advice of the Americans, animosity between the Ngos and the American officials was impossible either to avoid or to conceal.

The Ngos and the Americans, however, were stuck with each

other. No matter how good a face either party to the arrangement might put upon it at any given time, the problem of adjustment was one which became progressively more difficult. Diem could not long survive in Vietnam without massive American assistance. Unless Diem survived and ruled, South Vietnam seemed certain to fall to the Communists. The longer he survived, however, the more difficult it became to persuade him to avoil the build-up of violent, Communist-exploited resentment toward his authoritarian policies. Diem's very triumphs of 1955 and 1956 in many ways conditioned the disasters of the years 1962 and 1963.

By late 1956, President Ngo Dinh Diem seemed—with massive American assistance—to have achieved some major successes. Constitutional democratic government, at least insofar as the formalities were concerned, was getting under way. The nation's army of some 100,000 men, even though badly trained and badly organized and still subject to some rather questionable French technical assistance, had restored a reasonable degree of order in the countryside and was itself reasonably amenable to discipline. South Vietnam had managed to absorb, not easily or well but well enough to avoid large-scale disorders, nearly a million refugees from the North. The government had made a start toward land reform—redistribution of the huge French holdings among the peasant operators, and reclamation of land abandoned in the course of the war against the French. The Vietnamese economy was turning out rice, rubber, and other essential products in quantities that led to expectations that prewar levels might soon be restored. American-financed imports were pouring in so fast that city shops were well stocked even with luxury goods and country stores suffered no critical shortages. Schools and hospitals were back in operation.

To most outward appearances, South Vietnam was not only pulling itself together again but moving in the direction of modern development. Closer analysis of the situation, however, led to disquieting conclusions. In other areas than the political and the military, President Ngo Dinh Diem had not himself decided, ordered, or promoted much of the change, and both the political and the military arrangements were very shaky. Still, he had not actually prevented healthful development. He had accepted American aid so comprehensive that it meant providing the logistics and picking up the check for a program of disaster relief, run just like any other such program on a wildly inefficient crash basis. The United States paid for the imports; it transported, fed, and clothed the refugees; it equipped the military; and it backed the democratic innovations. At every stage, however, Americans found President Ngo Dinh Diem extraordinarily touchy to deal with, even when all they wanted him to do was to sign some receipts so that the money could continue to flow. They found they had always to deal personally with Diem or with his family, for the President flatly refused to delegate authority.

Apparent Vietnamese progress thus turned out, on close inspection, to be mainly emergency rehabilitation. Vietnamese democracy proved to be mainly a formality, a one-man or rather a one-family show. South Vietnam's development was more than Burma or Indonesia were achieving, but it added up to considerably less than a sound new basis for nationhood. South Vietnam, the critics began to say, was a Diemocracy. They might as appropriately have described it as a Diempotism or a Ngologarchy.

President Ngo Dinh Diem rationalized his regime on the basis of a political philosophy called "Personalism." This doctrine, said Ngo Dinh Nhu, who bore primary responsibility both for its formulation and its promulgation, was based upon the "inviolability of the human personality." The "human person," the apologia ran, achieves its truest self-realization and simultaneously the greatest national good by acceptance of rigorous self-discipline, in application of which, said the critics of Personalism, the state (meaning the Ngos) stood ready to see that the human person did not waver. Personalism was never very satisfactorily explained even in the course of Ngo Dinh Nhu's lengthy indoctrination sessions for civil servants, who "volunteered" unanimously to join the "nonpolitical" Personalist Labor Party. If only for that reason, Personalism gained a bad name even among insiders, many of whom regarded it as mere state-supervised incantation of self-improvement slogans, a kind of neo- or Nhu-Couéism.

No authorized gospel of Personalism was ever published, and it is now superfluous to attempt to compile one. A few citations and a little exegesis may suffice, nevertheless, to show what it was thought to be, or rather, why people did not really know quite what to think. The Constitution of the Republic of Vietnam presumably revealed the dogma. Article 4 of the Constitution reads: "The State recognizes and guarantees the fundamental rights of the human person in his individual capacity and in his capacity as a member of the community." According to Article 5: "Every citizen has duties toward the Fatherland, the community, and fellow citizens in the pursuit of the harmonious and complete development of his personality and that of others." Article 9 elaborates a bit further: "Every citizen has the right of life, liberty, and the security and integrity of his person." By 1963 some 30-50,000 political detainees had erred, presumably, in failing to achieve the "harmonious and complete development" of their personalities or those of others in accordance with their "duties toward the Fatherland."

In all fairness to the Ngos, Personalism represented to them not an immediate but an eventual goal. The very special circumstances of Vietnamese society today, combined with the very special inheritance from the past and aspiration for the future, dictated Personalism's exploration rather than its practice. The nation, they pointed out, was bisected at Geneva, and until it was reunited, the national personality and, inevitably, the human personality would be split. It was just emerging from the Confucian past into the Personalist future under the leadership of a President who knew best, they insisted, what was good for the state at its current stage of development. So long as his rule was enlightened, the people would enjoy sufficient freedom to develop their own capacity for enlightenment. Had it not been enlightened, man or nature would already have overthrown it.

President Ngo Dinh Diem's was the triple assumption, it seems, of the Confucian scholar, the devout Roman Catholic, and the French intellectual aristocrat. Each of the three adheres in his own way to the theory that virtue in the ruler will inspire virtue in the subject, and conversely, that lapse in virtue in the ruler will result in his own downfall and the elevation of some new ruler designed by divinity, nature, or reason to take his place. Diem's Personalism, consequently, was at least as much a question of morality as of politics. Indeed, it was even more metaphysical than moral. The basic issue in the modern world, President Diem frequently declared, was the spirit versus materialism. The basis for Vietnam's political life, he therefore advised the National Constituent

Assembly, "can only be a *spiritualist one:* such a line that the human person follows in his innermost reality as in his community life, in his transcendent vocation as in his free pursuit of intellectual, moral and spiritual perfection." The President, presumably, was thinking not in English or even in Vietnamese when he compounded this explanation, but in eighteenth-century French and classical Chinese. He soared into astral spaces where few could find their way. He himself would have pointed out, however, that it was not necessary for the ordinary people to read the road signs, only to follow him. The difficulty was that he did not lead. He merely stood—or sat—still.

President Diem's Personalism, comprehensibly, was not a popular philosophy suitable for galvanizing the masses. President Diem himself was no demagogue, and he enjoyed his own oratory no more than did his auditors. He appeared on the public platform infrequently and reluctantly. His speeches lacked punch and his delivery lacked sparkle. The best that could be said for him as an orator was that his public discourses were superior to his private monologues, if only in point of brevity.

President Diem's allergy to public speaking was in fact an allergy to the public. By heroic effort, he forced himself in the very early days of his regime, just as he had during his period of provincial administration in the 1930's, warmly to meet and greet the laborer and the peasant, even to tolerate old ladies and fondle little children. By nature, however, he was given to patrician detachment and to paternalistic, even pedantic exhortation. He displayed what was for him an excess of exuberance and animation when he smiled, waved, and moved on. In the early days, to be sure, he seemed actually to want to move about outside of the Palace and outside of Saigon, and he showed genuine courage in ignoring a couple of early assassination attempts. He would much have preferred, however, to travel incognito in order to avoid public receptions. He came to welcome bodyguards lining the road like a picket fence to shield his person—not, however, out of fear but out of intense reserve.

The reticence which Diem showed on public occasions did not manifest itself in private relations, however, for he kept his associates, other than his family, in constant fear of upbraiding. Since he assigned his subordinates little real responsibility, there was little they could do to earn his praise. Since much, in fact most of the routine business was left undone—even the mere filing of papers so that eventually they could be found again—there were frequent occasions for explosion. President Diem could be most thoughtful and considerate in small personal matters, such as solicitude for misfortune, but in official relationships he treated his associates like especially obtuse bureaucratic *fonctionnaires,* which, in fact, most of them were. In public relationships he preferred the father role but tried to play it *in absentia.*

The Ngo family, consequently, took over many of the public and private functions of the Presidency. The President himself, if he entertained any misgivings about this arrangement, exhibited also relief. Archbishop Ngo Dinh Thuc, Ambassador Ngo Dinh Nuyen, and Ngo Dinh Can each played an important role. The Archbishop was in fact the arbiter of South Vietnam's important Roman Catholic community of 1,500,000 out of the nation's 14 million population. The ambassador was more influential in foreign affairs than was the Foreign Minister. Ngo Dinh Can's role was less easily definable unless, as most people in Saigon thought, he was the behind-the-scenes political boss of the strategic northern province. The archbishop, the ambassador, and the "boss" were far less conspicuous, however, than the Political Adviser, Ngo Dinh Nhu, and the political adviser's wife, the fascinating and infuriating Mme. Nhu, nee Tran Lê Xuan.

Ngo Dinh Nhu and his wife, who served as the President's official hostess, came more and more to fill the role which Diem himself in effect renounced—that of the political activist. They earned for themselves little except opprobrium, which was the more bitter because Diem's adherents and admirers for years clung to the belief that Diem himself was capable of positive and constructive action but that his family inhibited him. Ngo Dinh Nhu, an archivist by training, was a man of keen intellect, but he was scornful of his associates and positively contemptuous of the public. He became first the intermediary through whom most of Diem's official contacts were channeled. Then, gradually, he became the decisive force in directing those agencies of state about which President Diem, who recoiled from action but conceded that in certain areas action was unavoidable, was content to know least and to trust most, at any rate insofar as day-to-day routine was concerned and so long as his brother reassured him that all was under control. Ngo Dinh Nhu took over the supervision of the political parties, the police, and more and more as years went by, the military. Mme. Nhu, a minute and exquisite creature of *femme fatale* aspect but also a lady of intense drive and ambition, took over the role of feminist political and social whip. She made herself the power within the National Assembly and made her militant women's organizations a symbol of the nation's will to modernize.

Ngo Dinh Nhu swiftly acquired the reputation of being the Gestapo-style master mind ruthlessly plotting the destruction of his enemies. Mme. Nhu gained the reputation of piling up treasure for herself not only in a prim little feminist heaven but in Swiss banks and Paris real estate as well. The impression spread, and the Nhus did nothing to correct it, that whatever went on in Vietnam, Little Brother—and also Little Sister—was watching.

To both the Nhus there adhered an aura of venom and old brocade. They both sounded almost as vicious, whether they spoke out, as they often did, about their Communist enemies or about their anti-Communist allies. They equated criticism with communism, and communism with the destruction of the Diem regime. Nevertheless, they had about them the quality of the aristocrat, pampered and petulant, to be sure, but also supremely self-assured. Their hauteur was the more irritating because Nhu was indeed competent far beyond the Vietnamese administrative norm, and his wife was indeed frail, fragile, and fragrant, albeit in the manner of the exotic jungle orchid which proves on close inspection to be carnivorous. Both of them, even in the midst of the noisiest personal vituperation, indulged in a good deal of staginess, as if they were ageless mandarins smiling serenely in comprehension of the transient trials of an age whose marvels they enjoyed without committing themselves to its banalities, attending, it seemed, not to the political din about them but to inner gongs and cymbals.

Ngo Dinh Nhu openly devoted himself to the behind-the scenes manipulation which made the National Revolutionary Movement in fact the paramount political party, and the Can-Lao Nhan-Vi Cach-Manh-Dang (the Personalist Labor Party) an elite cadre system for policing the National Revolutionary Movement and what slender splinters broke off from it. He made no secret of the fact that he organized things so effectively that unless there was some accidental slip, only the approved candidates managed to run, let alone to win in the elections. The Can-Lao itself constituted a nationwide body not only of propagandists but of informers. The ordinary and the special police, both of them well trained as a result of American technical assistance and of intuitive Vietnamese know-how, constituted an auxiliary arm of Nhu's office, maintaining surveillance over the Can-Lao and everything and everyone else. The army, navy, and air force, extensively equipped and trained by means of American aid and French technical assistance, developed separate little hierarchies of their own and Nhu ably assisted his brother Diem in keeping them divided against each other, eventually in bringing them more and more within his own area of manipulation. Brother Nhu had time also to propagate the Personalist philosophy, which stressed self-realization through self-renunciation of anything except the status quo.

Mme. Nhu, meanwhile, lent animation to the somnolent National Assembly, but only by lobbying through legislation which virtually nobody wished to support but virtually nobody dared openly oppose. Her "Family Law" and similar measures proscribed divorce, adultery, prostitution, gambling, dancing, prize fights, beauty contests, the singing of popular Western music, and comparable hazards to home life. In closing down the "twist-easies" and outlawing not only genuine immorality but even mild impropriety, she alienated large segments of the Vietnamese population which favored the traditional practice of polygamy, or at least of easy divorce, and the modern fashions in gaiety. Saigon, in consequence, was converted from the Paris to the Boston of the East, a joyless town not only for American GI's, but also for the Vietnamese.

Mme. Nhu held that "dancing with death"—as the soldiers were doing at the front—should be enough. She exercised great vigilance, furthermore, to make sure that any Vietnamese to whom a passport was issued for travel abroad should be a good representative not so much of Vietnam as of the Diem regime; also, it was constantly rumored, but never proven, that everyone to whom important export-import licenses were issued should be a generous contributor. Her greatest public triumph was the marshaling of the Women's Solidarity League, a massive feminist movement with paramilitary aspects. The members of the Women's Solidarity League did not actually wear sashes embroidered with slogans, but some of them expected to have to tie them on almost any day, once the marching, singing, and target-shooting began to go stale.

Little loved even by the Women's Solidarity League, Mme. Nhu was even less beloved by Saigon's American community, which regarded her as an unhappy combination of Mme. Chiang, Carrie Nation, and Lucretia Borgia and frequently said so. Mme. Nhu herself was never at a loss for words with which to reply. She took such frequent and public cognizance of her own unpopularity, especially among the Americans, that she could issue a communiqué in rebuttal without even pausing to redraft it, her Hong Kong convent English being quite adequate to the strain. The following is a specimen of her earlier style, before she added the refinements of face-to-face television confrontation of American audiences:

> . . . I am against the people of any nationality, who, instead of helping us in this critical time of our history allow themselves to be intoxicated by our enemy or its lackeys, abuse our hospitality to plot against us, to sow division in our ranks or, more simply, who like to submerge us in sanctimonious and pretentiously paternalistic sermons. As I have said in my most recent public speech: 'Through naive pretensions and lack of solidarity, they are often bent on denying the Vietnamese their successes or reason for success, finding it easier to blame them whenever setbacks or causes for setbacks occur, at times pushing perversity so far as to faithfully mouth the enemy's propaganda or to offer to the enemy itself the propaganda platform which it desires.'

Notwithstanding widespread dissatisfaction in Vietnam with the Ngo family regime, the situation up until about 1960, whether or not much credit accrued to the Ngos, was one in which improvements were visible and promise of further improvement seemed possible of fulfillment. The peasants were becoming property owners and standards both of production and of consumption were rising. Although the Communist Viet-Cong terror continued intermittently in the countryside and new agricultural settlements were badly administered, nevertheless, as compared with conditions in the early 1950's the nation was well off. The city of Saigon, even though it had been deluged with refugees, had managed to settle and absorb them, not comfortably, but on the whole more profitably than anyone could have anticipated. With the arrival of trained and skilled manpower from the industrialized North, Saigon was beginning even to experience a mild industrial revolution. The armed services were beginning to jell, social services were expanding, and the nation's educated elite was gaining something of a sense of accomplishment. With continued American aid, rapidly increasing numbers of Vietnamese were not only being trained for all the services of a modern state but were actually being placed in positions of dignity and potential responsibility. Nevertheless, the very degree of unexpected success, first in preserving the nation from the extinction which seemed almost inevitable in 1954, and second, in rehabilitating it to a degree which seemed unlikely even in 1956, generated on the part of the Vietnamese a hope that the pace of progress might accelerate, and on the part of the Communist Viet-Minh a fear that it had already gone much too far. President Ngo Dinh Diem proved unable to cope with either the hope or the fear.

The really serious symptoms of fresh trouble began to appear in mid-1959, and by mid-1960 all the alarms were ringing. In August, 1959, the government ran off carefully rigged elections for the National Assembly. All went smoothly, on the surface at least, except that in Saigon two nonapproved candidates not only ran and won but piled up impressive majorities. One was Dr. Phan Quang Dan, the most outspoken by far of the critics of the government. A medical doctor trained in France and the United States, Dr. Dan was a popular figure by reason of his charitable work among the Saigon poor and his articulate expression of the views of the intellectual elite. When the time came for the Parliament to assemble, Dr. Dan and the other winning opposition candidate were prevented on "technical grounds" from assuming their seats, and Dr. Dan himself was later (November 1960) imprisoned. The election-time demonstration that some small degree of democratic freedom had begun to assert itself was canceled out by the government's postelection reprisals, and the long latent bitterness within the intellectual elite came clearly to the surface.

On April 26, 1960, eighteen of the nation's most distinguished leaders published a manifesto in which they traced the rise of authoritarianism in Vietnam and called upon President Diem to make reforms. By this time, however, the conflict between the President and the intellectual elite had become irreconcilable. His answer was not reform but a series of arrests and imprisonments, and a flagrantly manipulated election (August 9, 1961) in which he himself was re-elected for a five-year term by 5,900,000 out of 7,230,000 ballots.

Concurrent with and in fact contributory to the rising discontent on the part of the educated classes with the Ngo regime was a recurrence of serious unrest in the countryside. Beginning in the latter half of 1959 came reports, at first discounted by the government, of increased activities on the part of the Viet-Cong guerrillas and increasing cooperation with the guerrillas on the part of a discontented and terrorized peasantry. The Ngo Dinh Diem government proved incapable of planning or even authorizing the sort of military moves which might have checked disorders before they became really widespread. The President tried to keep the military subject to his personal control and what was more, he kept the troops concentrated in fixed installations, as had the French before him, rather than creating a really mobile force which could protect the villagers. The Viet-Cong infiltrated more and more guerrillas from the North and recruited more and more local peasants to join them. Once again, as in the early 1950's, it became difficult to distinguish peasant from guerrilla. The government troops, which rarely fraternized, were disposed to shoot first, distinguish later. The peasants' resentment toward the military was immensely aggravated by the fact that the government was attempting to concentrate them into new settlements, then called *"agrovilles,"* where neither housing nor other facilities were adequate, and to interfere arbitrarily with their movements to and from their fields. Throughout 1960 the incidence of disorders in the countryside rose sharply. Responsible military officers felt that the situation called for new and drastic measures. President Ngo Dinh Diem refused either to accept advice or to give new orders. The result was an attempted military coup.

On November 11, 1960, President Ngo Dinh Diem awoke to find his palace surrounded by troops and himself confronted with demands for sweeping reforms, namely, abandonment of dictatorial methods, better organization of government, elimination of corruption, curtailment of Ngo family influence, a bolder policy for the military, more effective measures against the Communists, and much more besides. The President negotiated with the coup leaders by telephone; he negotiated also by telephone with military officers outside Saigon. While loyal troops began to move on the city, Diem stalled off the coup leaders with promises. The coup evaporated within thirty-six hours, as did the promises. Important segments of the military, however, now felt not only disgruntled but betrayed. The next manifestation of anti-Ngo feeling was more violent but even less successful. Two air force pilots on February 27, 1962, bombed the Presidential Palace. The President and his family retreated hastily into the bunkers, Mme. Nhu, incidentally, suffering injuries when she fell down the palace stairs. The palace was almost destroyed but the regime survived, and so did intense and widespread hatred for it.

During the latter part of 1961, the United States government went through a period of agonizing reappraisal with regard to President Ngo Dinh Diem and the Republic of Vietnam. It dispatched General Maxwell Taylor to make one last great effort to persuade President Diem that massive American support was contingent upon massive Vietnamese reforms. Although he made a few public gestures of agreement, President Ngo Dinh Diem remained unpersuaded. The United States, however, had persuaded itself in the interim that it had in fact no choice but to lend its support. It seemed to be a case of backing President Diem, regardless of reform, or of forfeiting Vietnam outright to the Communists—the sort of dilemma on which American policy has foundered before and since. The years 1962 and 1963, consequently, were years of reintensification of American effort. By mid-1963, American outlay of funds had increased to about $1.5 million per day; American troops, 15,000 of them as compared with about 1,000 two years earlier, were directly committed to combat and were experiencing heavy casualties. Americans had become deeply involved in a new program to create "fortified hamlets," new and militant versions of the former *"agrovilles,"* little rustic strongholds where in theory at least, the troops protected the villagers and were prepared to fly, swim, or march against any infiltrating enemy.

President Diem gave his formal approval to a far more active and widespread effort to resist the Viet-Cong guerrillas, but still he declined to give the orders which might have galvanized either troops or people into action. Ngo Dinh Nhu, meanwhile, according to his critics, made the "fortified hamlet" program his own weapon for political regimentation rather than military campaigning, and pushed it much too fast and much too far for it to be very solidly based. As for the ordinary Vietnamese, the feeling was that Diem was losing and the Viet-Cong was winning what the Vietnamese, like other propagandists, call the "struggle for the minds and the hearts of the people." This feeling commonly induced a spirit of hopeless cynicism, occasionally a spirit of "Let's go down fighting," which by mid-1963 was perhaps the most constructive attitude to be found in the nation. A few demonstrable military successes and a few political reforms, said American military advisers, among others, might do a lot to alter the national psychology for the better, but virtually nobody, unless he was speaking to boost morale, was very sanguine about prospects.

By early 1963 even the Ngos were aware that change was inevitable, although they were seriously in error in their estimate of what the situation required. "The present regime is a rotten one to be overthrown from the base," Ngo Dinh Nhu announced, and virtually nobody would have disagreed with him had he said "to be reconstituted from the top." The fault, according to Nhu, lay with the "rotten cadres," presumably his own party agents, a thesis which even his enemies could in large part accept. Nhu's own proposal for reform, however, was that the cadres be even more intensively indoctrinated in the philosophy of Personalism and that their efforts be directed toward even more rapid expansion of the "fortified hamlets." But the hamlets, said his critics, were already a Nhu political enterprise, and besides, Nhu himself, they said, was making secret advances to Ho Chi Minh, in the hope of negotiating a "neutralist" settlement.

Quite suddenly and unexpectedly in May, 1963, the drive for reform did in fact set in and on the broadest possible base—that of the Buddhist religious community which makes up the great majority of Vietnam's population. Buddhist adherents in Hue demonstrated in protest when the government ordered them to fly only national flags, not Buddhist flags, at a religious ceremony. The government used force against the demonstrators in Hue and against sympathy demonstrators elsewhere. There then occurred, almost spontaneously, it seemed, a series of fantastic and fanatical acts of defiance of the regime: the fiery self-immolation of Buddhist monks who made funeral pyres of themselves in the streets of Saigon. The Ngos accused the Buddhists of lending themselves to Communist plots to overthrow the regime, and Mme. Nhu made a chilling crack about a "Buddhist barbecue." The Buddhists accused the Catholic Ngos of anti-Buddhist discrimination. Neither communism nor Buddhism nor Catholicism was in fact the issue; it was the Diem regime, which virtually everybody now found intolerable.

The denouement was delayed beyond the expectancy of almost anyone except the Ngo family members, who had long since retreated into a world of their own devising. The Buddhist immolations and the efforts on the part of Ngo Dinh Nhu and his wife to disparage or to deny their significance led to nationwide and world-wide protest. The grisly publicity was revealing not only of Vietnamese fanaticism but of Ngo family obtuseness to anyone's tragedy, including its own.

Despite new top-level, on-the-spot investigations and official expressions of reassurance, the United States government presently found itself unable any longer to maintain the pretense of confidence in Diem or in Diem's Vietnam. It announced the suspension of essential aid, then refrained from any further endorsement of Diem or his policies and awaited the coup which it thereby tacitly encouraged.

Then, while the United Nations dispatched a commission to inquire into the Buddhist troubles, Mme. Nhu launched herself upon the international world as a fury of accusation and vengeance. From coast to coast in the United States she denounced American policy and its agents and insisted that the Diem regime needed only material support, without any accompanying advice or interference, in order to defeat the Communists. Her father, Tran Van Chuong, who had resigned his post as ambassador to Washington in protest against Diem's refusal to negotiate with the Buddhists, went on a nationwide lecture tour to refute her.

Meanwhile, back in Saigon, the generals and the colonels could neither read one another's minds nor make up their own. The coup which virtually everyone, including the military, expected momentarily remained week after week unstaged. Ngo Dinh Diem began to seem vindicated in his own appraisal that he could continue almost indefinitely to be both right and President. On November 1, 1963, it happened. A junta of a dozen generals mounted an armed attack upon the armed defenders of the Gia-Long Palace, all the while negotiating by telephone with President Diem and his brother, calling upon them to resign and surrender. The attack began at 1:30 P.M. During the evening the junta held its fire to allow Diem one last chance to make up his mind. Sometime during the late evening or early nighttime hours the brothers escaped from the palace, reportedly disguised as Catholic priests, and made their way to a Chinese merchant's home in Saigon's twin city of Cholon, where they spent the night. Next morning, the troops renewed the attack, captured the palace, and ransacked it in a vain search for the fugitives.

President Ngo Dinh Diem and Ngo Dinh Nhu were then in a Catholic church in Cholon, where they were recognized. At about 9:00 A.M. they were taken into custody by armed soldiers. Shortly thereafter they were shot, the exact circumstances of their death being as yet undisclosed. The news of the coup and of the deaths and of the military regime, instead of stunning the city and the nation, electrified them. Possibly the most shocking aspect of the whole shocking sequence was the overt public rejoicing at the downfall of a fundamentally virtuous man and the advent of a clique of military unknowns.

President Ngo Dinh Diem, who now lies buried alongside his brother in a secret grave somewhere in Saigon, died a prophet without honor either in his own country or abroad. He had saved his nation in 1955 from the disaster of revolutionary warfare which was leading to a Communist take-over, yet in 1963 it seemed that only his own death could save it yet once again from exactly the same danger. Diem's death, however, like his life, may have solved none of Vietnam's problems, not even his own. For all his faults and his failures and all the hatred he ultimately attracted, Diem was basically a good and honest man who dedicated himself wholeheartedly to his country. The mystery remains as to exactly

what he could in fact have done—what his successors must do—
to make Vietnam the sort of country in which a man like Diem
can live in peace.

History perhaps will be less harsh in its judgment of President
Ngo Dinh Diem than have been his recent critics, just as it will
be less laudatory than were those who saw in him in 1955 and
1956 a firm and an enlightened ruler. Diem's tragic flaw was that
of the proud and stubborn intellectual who sees too many relevant
factors in a situation to determine very readily to his own satisfaction which is the salient one; but having once so determined,
scorns to adjust his judgment or his conduct to the demands of
those who disagree.

Diem was generally cold and aloof and rigid. Occasionally and
in company with a few relatively trusted associates he showed,
however, that he could be outgoing, good humored, and witty, but
even then he was often asserting his own attainments. His intimates report, for instance, that he was a master mimic. He could
simulate any of the local French notables with the precise intona-
tion of the "eh" or the "mais oui," accompanied by the exact smile
or shrug. His renditions of American ambassadors added nuances
which were not to be found in the original, but the effect was
artistic if not exact. President Ngo Dinh Diem, some people
thought, might one day mimic himself, and that would be the day
of his own and of Vietnam's true awakening. That day, of course,
never came.

President Ngo Dinh Diem, age sixty-two, his tubby figure
wrapped in a double-breasted suit or bulging the long gown of a
Vietnamese mandarin, his minute hands constantly maneuvering
a cigarette, his toed-out feet carrying him with surprising agility
about the French period furniture he favored, was a demiheroic
figure in the semitragic sense that his motives were good, his
efforts were tireless, and his principles were long incorruptible.
His lifelong devotion to a cause had blinded him to the fact that
since first he embarked upon it, he himself, the cause, and the
world had changed almost beyond recognition.

H.R.H. Prince Comrade

"The Prince is indulgent, courteous, cheerful, good to the lowly, and extremely truthful. That is how he has gained the love of his people and the esteem of a great many foreigners.

"And let us not forget that he is a music composer—(several of his works were performed abroad)—that he is a good horseman, and that he leads a simple life. . . .

"This biography would not be complete, if, besides being introduced as a diplomat, the Prince were not introduced also as a soldier. A former pupil of the 'Cavalry and Armor School' (École de la Cavalerie et de l'Armée Blindée) at Saumur, the Prince is a 'Général de Corps d'Armée' of the Khmer Forces which he himself led several times to battle when, as King, he was also commander-in-chief."

To those who know him, this reassembled vignette of Cambodia's Prince Sihanouk is probably no more arresting than others which have been essayed by less definitive writers. It comes from an official handout, and since the Prince inspires if he does not indeed compose and deliver a very high percentage of Cambodia's official prose, it may safely be assumed that this characterization reflects the royal self-image. It complements the public image and at the same time contradicts it, both the Cambodian stereotype, that is, of "le père de l'indépendence" and the Western stereotype of the mercurial Marxist playboy-prince-politician. The "good to the lowly" bit, for instance, sounds more like the royal patron than the public servant or the princely plebeian. "Extremely truthful" would strike even a Sihanouk-phile as hyperbole, best amended, perhaps, to "torrentially outspoken." As for the simple life, almost everybody knows about iced champagne at 10:00 A.M. in the throne room. And almost nobody, whether he relies upon *Paris-Match* or the *New York Times,* is at all likely to forget that the prince is a musician—to be indelicate about it, a saxophonist.

Prince Sihanouk, in brief, condenses into his compact, convex person contradictions enough to make it almost equally plausible to call him, as various people do, Samdech Sachachivin (Prince Companion, or Prince Comrade), Snooks, Monseigneur, Son Altesse Royale, or a second Sukarno. Soldier-diplomat, horseman-musician, neutralist-nationalist, socialist-monarchist, ex-king, current Chief of State, and many, many (technically, only seven) times Prime Minister, Prince Sihanouk has elected, unfortunately, in writing his autobiography, if such it is, to omit or drastically to abbreviate some highly significant episodes. He has turned out one of the most meager documents in what seems likely one day to become the twenty-foot shelf of his selected works.

During the days of their friendship, Sam Sary, a onetime colleague now branded a traitor and lurking in exile in Bangkok, produced a modestly monumental volume, *La Grande Figure de Norodom Sihanouk,* which enshrines a heroic statue, to which there adhere only a few shreds of fact. Less privileged biographers, when they have attempted inquiry into the Prince's public and private life, have come up with relatively little in the way of anecdote or even legend, save about the Prince's playboy phase. They have devoted themselves mainly, therefore, to recounting political events plus speculation on whether Son Altesse is out of his depth.

Prince Sihanouk did not actually emerge as a distinct individual until the age of about thirty, when suddenly he appeared as a floodlighted international figure. He seemed then and he seems now either extraordinarily mature or extraordinarily immature for his years. There is no real consensus, at least outside Cambodia, and even inside the nation observers have been known to switch back and forth from the one opinion to the other.

Cambodia itself is one of the emerging nations whose just aspirations almost everybody endorses the more sympathetically for not knowing quite what they are or where it is. Even the unusually well-informed foreigner is likely to bound Cambodia by naming Laos, the Congo, Pago Pago, and Ruritania. Laos, to be sure, did still at last checkup precariously adjoin to the north, but the other neighbors are Thailand and South Vietnam, with which, in addition to boundaries and history, Cambodia shares little except quarrels.

The story of the coming to age of discretion or indiscretion of Prince Sihanouk is distinctively the story of Cambodia as well. It begins, necessarily, as all royal tales must, with the royal forebears. Most conveniently for purposes of this account, it begins in the mid-nineteenth century with King Norodom, who played off the French against the Thais and lost to both but gained a kingdom. King Norodom traced his ancestry, somewhat obscurely, back to the medieval Khmer monarchs who built and ruled the empire of Angkor and then in the end ruined it by their excesses in war, religion, and court ceremonial, including the cost of upkeep on personality-cult temples too numerous and grandiose for the state to support. King Norodom came to the throne in 1862, just about one decade after Europeans rediscovered the ruins of Angkor and the less scholarly of them, all unaware that the Spanish and the Portuguese had "discovered" Angkor and some of its history back in the late sixteenth century, gave rise to the legend of a great civilization that had vanished into the jungle as mysteriously as it had appeared.

King Norodom himself perhaps could not and certainly did not enlighten the newcomers. His library consisted of about 100 unread volumes packed into a couple of boxes buried deep in the royal treasury. His memory was overburdened by the necessity to recall the names of the two hundred dancing girls who then were or were soon to become his wives, it being a ceremonial chore of the kings to wed or bed the whole female Cambodian corps de ballet.

King Norodom had other distractions as well. He had not as yet actually been crowned, and he was worried that he might never be. It all depended upon King Mongkut of Siam, a whimsical monarch who had custody of the Cambodian royal regalia, without physical possession of which no Cambodian ruler could legitimize his reign. King Norodom had just returned from exile in Siam, where he had had to leave the regalia as pledge of a fealty which neither he nor his Siamese royal cousin put much stock in. The problem was, how to lay hold of the crown without taking some rather distasteful oaths and posting some new security.

The French did not simplify the king's problem. At just this time they were eying Cambodia with both archaeology (Angkor) and empire in mind. They dispatched a frigate and a certain redoubtable M. Doudart de Lagrée. The French took up residence in a temple compound near the palace and began proffering copious advice which a newly arrived Siamese ambassador as assiduously countermanded. King Norodom, yielding one day to the French and the next day to the Siamese, signed whatever agreement either demanded, intent only upon his crown. At one point he started off impetuously for the Siamese border, hoping to be crowned there, but when the French fired off a few admonitory cannon shots he panicked and turned back. He ended up under French protection without Siamese sympathy but wearing nevertheless, thanks to French intervention in Bangkok, the royal crown, the jeweled sword, and the golden slippers. The crown, significantly, was handed to him by M. de Lagrée, whose official successors, the colonial Governors-General restored to Cambodia at expense of Siam certain rather extensive border provinces which he had misplaced along with the court treasure.

Once he had actually fitted on his crown, King Norodom reigned for forty years, almost the complete Oriental despot. His absolutism was modified only slightly by French insistence upon a modicum of modernization, which, in turn, lent wealth and luster to what would otherwise have been not merely an obscure but a dingy court. The king delighted in the enhancement both of his possessions and of his authority. One day, on his request, the French even installed a little laboratory in the palace in which to gold-plate his knickknacks. On another occasion he invited a French surgeon to display his kit of tools and then, out of irrepressible curiosity, ordered a court official to volunteer for an impromptu operation for removal of an extra thumb which the official would much have preferred to retain.

King Norodom, who was not very popular with anyone to begin with, gradually became known as the Great King Norodom, under whom the kingdom was restored to much of its ancient prestige and glory. Its regional rivals, then as now, the Thais and the Vietnamese, were confounded and in fact infuriated. From the Cambodian point of view, this compounded the triumph. King Norodom's reign being linked not only with the spread of Cambodian but of French power and influence, Cambodia enjoys a tradition almost unique in Southeast Asia: it saw colonialism revive rather than dismember or anesthetize a proud and ancient kingdom.

King Norodom's half-brother, Sisowath, succeeded to the throne. King Sisowath had been brought up as a hostage in Siam, then trained as an apprentice ruler by the French. In the course of his reign (1904–1927), Cambodia began really to modernize. Acceding to the advice of the French, and accepting French functionaries throughout the administration, King Sisowath both promulgated and permitted to be enforced many modern regulations concerning administration of justice, collection of revenue, ownership of land, and other matters equally significant. King Sisowath, however, like King Norodom, was less engrossed in the details than in the perquisites of ruling. Dancing girls, whom he personally escorted to the Colonial Exposition in Paris, an exercise rather like carrying dolls to Dresden, profusely ornamented the royal palace. The population was happily lethargic. Imports of champagne doubled and redoubled. The rare non-French visitors envied the French residents this picturesque and placid kingdom.

King Sisowath's son, Monivong, tried to follow in his father's footsteps, which so frequently and tipsily led to the harem, but unfortunately King Monivong lacked *élan*. He had started his adult life, it is true, as an army officer in France, but he ended it in a deplorable state of dissipation. During his later years even the royal family regarded him as too disreputable to keep on view in Phnom-Penh and let the French sequester him in the provinces.

King Monivong's son, Prince Monireth, a more serious and professional soldier, who hurried to France to volunteer when World War II broke out, deplored his father's feudal mentality and seemed to be in earnest when he talked about modern progress. He also seemed to be in earnest when he suggested French colonial reforms. The French, therefore, decided that the time had come to right a former wrong whereby the Sisowath cadet line, rather than the Norodom "direct" line of the royal family, had inherited the throne upon the death of the Great King Norodom. They mentioned young Prince Norodom Sihanouk, whose father was a Norodom and whose mother was a Sisowath, as a kingly candidate whose qualifications should not be overlooked. The royal council, naturally, found the qualifications eminently satisfactory and agreed unanimously to designate him as the successor.

Prince Norodom Sihanouk was at that time an eighteen-year-old schoolboy preparing for the *baccalauréat de rhétorique* in Saigon. He is the son of Prince Norodom Suramarit and Princess Monivong Kossamak—their only son, although his father later had other children by another wife. During his youth his parents had been unassuming members of royalty, neither very rich nor very prominent, their home in Phnom-Penh being unpalatial, their manner of living modest. The Prince was a proficient flutist, the Princess a skilled dancer, and their most engrossing interest seemed to be the royal ballet.

Young Prince Sihanouk had been sent to an ordinary day school in Phnom-Penh, one in which the instruction was in French and the curriculum was calculated to make him much more aware of French kings and queens and flora and fauna than those of his own country. After completing elementary-level schooling at the École François Baudouin, he was sent to Saigon, where secondary schooling was better than anything Phnom-Penh had to offer. In Saigon he was enrolled in the Lycée Chasseloup Laubat, and lived in the school compound as a boarding student. As his guardian, his parents chose a personal friend of theirs, a minor French customs official. His parents were always determined, says Prince Sihanouk today, that he should grow up as an ordinary boy, accustomed to the life of the ordinary people, not as a pampered princeling.

Prince Sihanouk's school record was good but not distinguished. He was never actually graduated, and he is still sensitive about his lack of a secondary, let alone a university degree. He had to discontinue his studies when he returned to Phnom-Penh to be enthroned. His teachers and his schoolmates remember him as handsome, alert, bright, and active, fond of sports and quick at his studies, not just another prince, but not especially outstanding either. The French regarded him as malleable, a young man who would cut a good figure as king but not try to cut them out from any of their prerogatives. For quite a few years that was exactly what they thought they had, but then during the early years, so far as the French were concerned, it scarcely mattered. Those were the years of the Japanese occupation.

Prince Sihanouk came to the throne on April 26, 1941, some ten months after the fall of France. The Japanese had assumed military control of Cambodia, with the rest of French Indochina, but they had left the colonial French in charge of the administration. They were just at this point about to force Cambodia (May 9, 1941) to yield to Siam the border provinces which France had restored to the nation.

For Cambodia these were troubled times, and the immediate circumstances of Prince Sihanouk's coronation were scarcely propitious. The French Governor General, Admiral Decoux, who was to hand the crown to Norodom Sihanouk just as M. Doudart de Lagrée had handed it to Norodom, was delayed in Hanoi by bad weather.

Prince Norodom Sihanouk waited anxiously that morning in the royal palace, decked out in the resplendent regalia and looking handsomer than any of the male dancers in the royal ballet, lacking only the crown to be king. The court astrologers had designated the stroke of 11:00 A.M. as the auspicious moment. It was not until 9:50 that a plane flew low over the palace and the court knew that the Governor General was actually on his way. At 10:30, exactly on schedule, Admiral Decoux, who had scarcely paused even to comb his hair at the Residency, entered the throne hall. The ceremony went off without further impediment, as did the subsequent cremation of King Monivong and the interment of his ashes in the royal pagoda at Oudong. Had the coronation itself been delayed, the consequences, from the point of view of the ordinary Cambodian, would have been unthinkable.

For the duration of the Japanese occupation, King Norodom Sihanouk virtually disappeared within the royal palace. The palace, to be sure, was a small royal village behind high walls that stretched half a mile along the river front. It included extensive residential quarters in addition to the throne hall, the entertainment pavilion, the Silver Pagoda, the treasury, even a miniature chateau, ornamented with wrought iron, which had been a gift of Louis Napoleon. Most of the palace buildings were relatively new, designed and built by the French in traditional Thai-Cambodian style but constructed of concrete and furnished in red plush.

Like many royal courts, the Cambodian palace was a nest of intrigue. At the center of the intrigue was frequently to be found the Princess Mother, now the Queen Mother—known to the French as another Catherine de' Medici. On being introduced into the palace, she proved to be possessed of extraordinary will power, business acumen, and dynastic ambition. The royal family includes a total of almost two hundred princes who are eligible, according to the law of the royal household, to become candidates for a vacant throne. The palace, therefore, has a politics of its own, obscure to the general public, but full of zest for the initiate.

King Norodom Sihanouk occupied himself during the Japanese period with mastering the extremely complicated protocol and ceremonial of the court. His diversions were informally matrimonial. The court genealogists do not confide in the outsider, but it appears that the King, without going through the formality of a court wedding, began to marry and to beget offspring. He had two wives and two children by mid-1945. Up until the present time he has had at least six wives, with only one of whom he has gone so far as to appear in a marriage ceremony. None of the wives has been designated queen, presumably for failure to meet the rigid dynastic qualifications. The King's first recognized wife was a member of the royal ballet. The second mothered his eldest son, Prince Norodom Yuvanath (b. Oct. 17, 1943), a virile and handsome youth who lives with the accustomed dynastic abandon. His father recently and publicly pronounced Prince Yuvanath a menace to the morals of young ladies of high families, then married him off in some haste, but put Phnom-Penh matrons on stand-by alert, nevertheless, with regard to the virtue of their daughters.

The Japanese occupation came to an end in Cambodia with far less explosive but no less far-reaching consequences than was the case in Vietnam or even in Laos. In Cambodia, as elsewhere in Indochina, in March, 1945, the French attempted a badly planned little anti-Japanese insurrection. The Japanese smashed the attempt and dissolved the French administration. The King, prompted by the Japanese, thereupon declared Cambodia's independence.

Through the period of Japanese collapse and Allied, i.e., British, occupation, King Sihanouk ruled over a technically independent but chaotic little kingdom. The French, on their return, soon persuaded him that independence was a mirage and that Cambodia's best hope for the future lay in renewal of its traditional ties with France. On January 1, 1946, therefore, the King and the French signed a *modus vivendi* in accordance with which France acknowledged Cambodia's aspiration to independence, Cambodia acknowledged France's resumption of administrative responsibility, and traditional relations, it might appear, were restored. The King's decision, however, was far from popular. Then and later, even when he was himself reversing it, he felt impelled also to justify it, the more vigorously as criticism mounted. He became particularly impassioned about suggestions that he should have cooperated not with the French but with the armed insurrectionists who were at large in Cambodia, as in Vietnam and in Laos. "Patronner les bandes de pirates," wrote the King, "ouvrir nos frontières aux vietnamiens Vietminh, pour que, au nom de la lutte contre les Français, ils massacrassent le petit peuple, pour qu'ils brûlassent nos ponts, nos maisons, nos temples, nos écoles, nos infirmeries, nos auberges, nos hôtels, nos villes, était-ce une solution patriotique et acceptable pour un roi digne de ce nom?"

King Sihanouk hoped, rather ingenuously, it seems in retrospect, to lead Cambodia gradually toward a greater and greater measure of independence, enjoying meanwhile the loyal support and the good will of the old-time French colonialists, of the new Cambodian nationalists, and of the slowly awakening masses, plus the sympathetic approval of the outside world. This idyll shattered abruptly, for the Khmer Issarak (Free Khmer) insurrectionists chose to fight, the politicians to conspire, the French to intrigue, the masses to respond to agitation rather than to paternalism, and the international world proved sensitive mainly to crisis.

Considering the limitations of his training and experience, King Sihanouk learned fast and proved to be remarkably self-reconstructible. It is difficult to believe that he really analyzed his problem—although he did so later on—for he seemed to be guided exclusively by intuition. He was caught up in a nationalist revolution, one of the irrepressible nationalist revolutions of Southeast Asia which in Cambodia more than in almost any other country, except perhaps Laos, seemed suddenly and spontaneously self-generating. As is the nature of revolutions, the Cambodian one aimed at the destruction of the established order, which meant not only French colonialism but the Cambodian monarchy as well.

Instead of putting up an increasingly angry and futile resistance, King Sihanouk transformed himself into a royal revolutionary, using the monarchy itself as an instrument of drastic change. He used the French, meanwhile, to put down the more violent of his opponents, and the revolutionary extremists to put pressure upon the French to make concessions. From the revolutionary point of view, he made serious blunders, but it must be considered that he was pioneering quite a new sort of revolutionary leadership, that of the man in position of authority seeking to maintain himself. Other Southeast Asian revolutionaries, Sukarno, for instance, moved into this phase at a much later point, and when they did so, they took some tips from Sihanouk.

King Sihanouk's greatest initial handicap was that he was a king. When he got into full stride as a revolutionary leader, Son Altesse Royale abdicated the throne and became Samdech Sahachivin (Prince Comrade), head of his own Cambodian Nationalist Community of 100,000 Sahachivins (a name coined for the members of his new mass movement). He managed thus to retain all the luster of royalty while adding to it the happy glow of commonality.

From the very beginning, however, King Sihanouk had many circumstances working in his favor. He enjoyed the ultimate luxury of a Southeast Asian nationalist leader, in that the colonial masters were very much preoccupied elsewhere, specifically in Saigon and Hanoi and presently Dien Bien Phu. The other major setbacks which the French experienced in Indochina disposed them to be conciliatory in Phnom-Penh. Almost any Frenchman, given his choice of yielding to the King or fighting the insurgents, which was the choice King Sihanouk offered them, preferred the former. The Cambodian nation, furthermore, for all its susceptibility to the agitators, had not for a millennium been in a hurry, and it graciously allowed itself yet another decade.

King Sihanouk, consequently, had leisure in which to learn. What he learned most thoroughly was that whatever his troubles, he could handle them best not by being placatory, but by being highhanded. The transition from Son Altesse Royale to Samdech Sahachivin, therefore, was a transition from political and revolutionary neophyte to ultranationalist zealot. The amiable, amenable monarch became the fiery, intractable maverick. He made a career of goading the French, the Khmer Issarak, the politicians, including the Communists and the royalists and the protean intellectuals; also the Americans, the Russians, and Chinese, and always, of course, those hereditary ogres, the larcenous, villainous, murderous Thais and Vietnamese.

King Sihanouk's collaboration with the French earned him many Cambodian enemies, from whom, more than from his French and his Cambodian colleagues, he gained his political education. The first was Son Ngoc Thanh, now in exile, the number-one tenant in Sihanouk's rather thickly populated stable of *bêtes noires.*

Son Ngoc Thanh, a bold and articulate gentleman a few years ago but a mere nonentity today, is often, to Sihanouk's great outrage, called "le père de l'indépendence." As founder and editor in the prewar years of the nation's first indigenous-language newspaper, he was the pioneer Cambodian gadfly of the French. He was also, of course, an anticolonialist and an antiimperialist, and he gained the reputation of being a Marxist. At the very beginning of the war he organized a futile but troublesome little anti-French insurrection, relying upon the Japanese for aid which was mysteriously withheld. He found it advisable soon afterwards to leave the country, and chose Tokyo as his destination. There he joined the Japanese army and rose to the rank of captain.

When the Japanese acknowledged Cambodia's independence in early 1945, they fetched Son Ngoc Thanh back to help King Norodom Sihanouk run the nation. Son Ngoc Thanh became Foreign Minister (June 1, 1945), which meant that he became a special Japanese agent. Two months later, at the time of Japan's surrender, he staged a little power coup in the course of which he put the King and his parents under palace arrest and made himself Prime Minister. Before the Allies had had a chance to ship in occupation troops, Son Ngoc Thanh had run off a national plebiscite in which the population reaffirmed the nation's independence.

Son Ngoc Thanh, the French decided, must go. The British

commander of the incoming occupation troops arrested him and in October, 1945, shipped him off to Saigon. There he was tried as a war criminal, convicted, and sentenced to twenty years' hard labor and twenty years' restricted residence. On the King's intervention, however, his sentence was remanded and he was exiled to France. There, although he was allowed a small pension and the company of his family, he was kept under close surveillance by the French police. On his request, the King again intervened and succeeded in getting him both more money and greater freedom of movement. A few years later, the King persuaded the French to allow him to return to Cambodia. Sihanouk's solicitude for an exile's welfare, as he himself has quite frequently pointed out, went far beyond the call of a monarch's duty to his subject, and his reward was not mere ingratitude but outright treason.

In October, 1951, Son Ngoc Thanh returned to Cambodia to be greeted by the Phnom-Penh public with a hero's welcome. Soon he was back in business as a newspaper editor, attacking the French—and also the King for collaboration with the French. Presently he vanished from Phnom-Penh to rematerialize in the provinces as leader of the Khmer Issarak insurgents. By reorganizing and redeploying the jungle guerrillas and later by propagandizing from Bangkok or Saigon, Son Ngoc Thanh made himself and the Khmer Issarak movement a constant exacerbation to King Sihanouk's highly sensitive nervous and political system.

One of Son Ngoc Thanh's associates was Dap Chhuon, former corporal in the Khmer armed services, self-promoted to "general" of his own Khmer Issarak guerrilla contingent. In 1950 Dap Chhuon repented and then accepted one of King Sihanouk's recurrent amnesty offers. Soon after being treated to a joyous welcome back into the bosom of the motherland, however, Dap Chhuon proceeded to carve out what amounted to a private military satrapy in the strategic border province of Siemreap, which King Sihanouk visited thereafter only on sufferance. When Dap Chhuon so overreached himself as to plot a coup, in connivance, naturally, with Son Ngoc Thanh, the King resorted to denunciation, invasion, elimination, and moving professions of sorrow.

Since Sihanouk is by nature deeply emotional, he was no doubt shocked by Dap Chhuon's perfidy, as by Son Ngoc Thanh's, and even more so, considerably later on, by that of still a third and even closer associate, one Sam Sary. A brilliant and witty sophisticate, a favorite of the French and of the Americans, Sihanouk's one time right-hand man in Phnom-Penh and later his ambassador to the Court of St. James's, Sam Sary fell from grace when he became too openly implicated in scandals. Most scandalous of all, because widely publicized abroad, was a deplorable London episode in which Ambassador Sam Sary was accused in court of flogging a Cambodian "servant girl." Later, after he had been cashiered as ambassador, Sam Sary was implicated—together with Son Ngoc Thanh, naturally—in the coup attempts which Sihanouk has regularly discovered and reported, generally with embellishments regarding alien (Thai, Vietnamese, American) complicity.

King Sihanouk's political education, as in the case of his experiences with the Son-Dap-Sam Sary trio, was often an excruciatingly painful process. It included experimentation with the practice in Cambodia of French-style parliamentary government. The results were approximately what any knowledgeable political scientist would retrospectively predict.

The King himself presented the nation (May 6, 1947) with a beautifully drafted Constitution than which even the French was not more lucid, logical, and complex. He then authorized national elections for a Constituent Assembly to study and approve it and invested the Democratic Party, which won 54 out of 74 seats, with authority to form a government. But the Constituent Assembly debated practically everything except the proposed constitution; the government ministers found intrigue, corruption, and nepotism far more congenial than administration; and the public began to expect, on the basis of experience, recurrent waves of demonstrations, assassinations, and bomb-throwings.

On becoming convinced that he could not get along with the Constituent Assembly, King Sihanouk dismissed it (September 18, 1949), only to discover that he could not get along without it either. Hopefully, he held elections for a new Parliament (1951), which proved, however, no less disputatious and conspiratorial than the former Constituent Assembly. In the interim, he had negotiated an "Independence Treaty" with the French (November 8, 1949), in accordance with which Cambodia, like Vietnam and Laos, became an "independent" member of a "French Union." A "triumph," decreed the King, and the arrangement was much applauded in France and in the United States but not in Cambodia. A "sellout," said the Cambodian politicians, the Khmer Issarak, and a large contingent of the new Sihanouk-recruited, French-trained Cambodian Army, whose smartly groomed young officers marched off to join the guerrillas.

King Sihanouk kept trying, nevertheless, to make a go of parliamentary democracy and of evolutionary independence. In mid-1952, however, when disorders threatened really to get out of hand, he decided he had had enough. He arrested relays of suspected subversives, declared martial law, and dissolved the National Assembly (January 13, 1953). Ceasing to make either a virtue or a necessity of democratic procedures, he announced that he was taking full power into his own hands and that at the end of a three-year trial period he would leave it to the nation to give its verdict as to how satisfactorily he had discharged his responsibilities. Then, while everyone waited breathlessly for his next move, he departed for the south of France.

King Sihanouk, the international press rather indelicately suggested, and "well-informed" diplomatic circles seemed to concur, was not only an unpredictable but an irresponsible monarch. Leading French publications engaged in spirited competition to publish stories in which there was a minimum of fact, mainly about saxophone jam sessions, palace-produced mad-scientist movies, dancing girls, speedboat racing, elephant and tiger hunting—all true; and a maximum of speculation, mainly about another Bao-Dai or Farouk.

To the great disappointment of the reporters who went to the Riviera to cover the events, King Sihanouk was neither sun-bathing, skin-diving, water-skiing, judging beauty contests, nor playing roulette. He was sitting in the study of his rather modest villa at La Napoule in the Alpes Maritimes composing two rather lengthy letters to M. Auriol, President of France. In them he argued, with all of the intellectual ingenuity and literary felicity of a French academician, that as King of Cambodia he could outmaneuver and defeat the Khmer Issarak and the other dissidents only if he himself exacted from the French the true national independence which everybody professed to favor. Peaceful negotiation and future cooperation, he pointed out, would be at least as advantageous to the French as to himself.

The King's arguments were rather too elaborate for the French readily to refute or even to reply to. President Auriol had him to lunch at the Élysée Palace, talked banalities, and bucked the letter onward and downward into the oblivion of the French bureaucracy. King Sihanouk, who had moved first into a villa at Fontainebleau and then into the Hôtel Crillon in Paris in anticipation of a long visit, packed his bags and departed precipitately for unannounced destinations. He left it to his representative in Paris, Prince Monireth, to explain to the skeptical French, who counseled "prudence" since "it was a matter of the crown," that he had no idea at all, really, what was on the King's mind. Reports soon came from Montreal, where the King issued a public statement; from Washington, where he paid a fruitless call on "M. Foster Dulles, who never understood;" from New York, where he gave an interview to a *New York Times* reporter; and from Tokyo, where he issued another public statement. What the King had on his mind, it turned out, was an international publicity campaign to win world public opinion for what he called a "Crusade for Independence."

King Sihanouk checked in briefly at Phnom-Penh to find out how the French were reacting and then took off into self-imposed exile which constituted an ultimatum: he would not return to Phnom-Penh until he had achieved independence. For his place of exile and propaganda headquarters he chose Bangkok, where his forebears had recurrently found either sanctuary or confinement, depending upon the circumstances of the moment. To his very great dismay, he found that the Thais were both embarrassed and uncordial.

Prime Minister Pibul, who had previously supported the Khmer Issarak exiles and propagandists but had recently cut off funds, supplies, and facilities when he became suspicious of their Communist connections, was not yet ready openly to support the King. He informed him, in fact, that although he might remain in Thailand he could not establish a government-in-exile or a propaganda office. He even advised him not to take up residence in his own embassy but rather to live in a hotel, where—at least according to King Sihanouk's account—other Thai officials intimated it would be inappropriate for them to visit him. The King of Thailand, who had palaces to spare, placed none of them at King Sihanouk's disposal and seemed personally aloof even at the palace jam sessions to which he invited his royal visitor as guest artist.

Never slow either to take or to drop a hint, King Sihanouk decided not to loiter in Bangkok. He checked in on June 15 and out on June 20. That brief and chilly visit has led to a long series of unneighborly exchanges between Sihanouk and the Thais regarding the true quality of Thai friendship and hospitality, and of Cambodian gratitude.

From Bangkok King Sihanouk removed himself to Battambang, the capital of the Cambodian province which, as part of the post-World War II settlement, the Thais had recently and indignantly been constrained to restore to Cambodia. From Battambang he bombarded the French and the world with propaganda. The choice for Cambodia and for the French and the Western world, said King Sihanouk, although never in so few words, was between himself and the Communists. The Communists themselves were soon to amplify his warning with artillery barrages at Dien Bien Phu (mid-March 1954).

The French chose Sihanouk. After a few more crises over French intent to turn over actual as well as theoretical control of such incidental functions as security, justice, and finance, King Sihanouk on November 8, 1953, returned to Phnom-Penh, now at last king of a truly independent Cambodia. It was just twelve years since he had accepted the crown from Admiral Decoux, just ten months since he launched himself on his royal and nationalist crusade.

November 9, 1953, the day that King Sihanouk at last laid hold of the nationalist grail, was still two years and two months short of the three-year time limit he had set himself to prove his royal mettle. In the interval he tilted with various enemies. By proxy, at the time of the post-Dien Bien Phu Indochina settlement at Geneva, he met Ho Chi Minh and Ho's allies. King Sihanouk had instructed his delegation to accept no limitation upon Cambodian independence. Subsequent Cambodian firmness stalled the conference when the Soviet Union insisted upon recognition of a Khmer Issarak "regroupment area" (like the Pathet Lao area in

Laos), also upon the imposition of conditions to Cambodian acceptance of military assistance (again, like the case of Laos). At the last possible moment (July 21, 1954), the Russians, not the Cambodians, backed down.

During and after the Geneva Conference, King Sihanouk met direct Viet-Minh challenge within Cambodia itself, Viet-Minh Communist troops having infiltrated certain Cambodian territories. Calling upon the nation to resist, the King personally took to the field, where he actually commanded the troops in a few brief engagements. In Cambodia, as in Geneva, show of determination and refusal to compromise resulted in dramatic victories. Cambodia accepted no limitation upon its sovereignty, the Khmer Issarak-cum-Viet-Minh insurrection almost died out, and Cambodia, unlike Vietnam and Laos, has enjoyed peace and security ever since.

By early 1955, as the time approached for King Sihanouk to fulfill his promise to submit his record to the nation for its endorsement, there could be very little doubt as to the verdict. In the referendum of February 7, 1955, the vote was 925,812 to 1,834 in approval of his policies. It was a vote of confidence so overwhelming, in fact, as to invite incredulity.

The King was indeed popular, but not that popular, as other events immediately proved. On February 19, 1955, he disclosed some of the provisions of a new constitution which he proposed soon to promulgate. The disclosure precipitated a political uproar. The King's proposals, said both his domestic and his international critics, were undemocratic. They would result, for instance, in disenfranchisement of all those judged, rightly or wrongly, to have been implicated in the Khmer Issarak movement. There would be no political parties as such, and the cabinet would be independent of the new Legislative Assembly. There were other objections as well, but before the opposition had time vigorously to formulate them, the King made a move which shook even those who thought he could no longer really startle them. On March 2, 1955, he abdicated the throne.

Pausing only long enough to install his father and his mother as his own successors, and to deny that he intended at any future date to reassert his own claim, ex-King Sihanouk, now once again Prince Sihanouk, departed Cambodia on a journey to India. There he formulated to Pandit Nehru the reasons for his decision. "He had to build up a really democratic government," said the former King in his own third-person report of the interview, "and put an end to the oppression of the people by a privileged few . . . as a monarch, he would have been a prisoner of a rigid system that would have prevented him from acting efficiently . . . he gave up his throne to serve the people better."

Like his subsequent resignations and threats of resignation from the Prime Ministership, Sihanouk's abdication seemed to many observers more like petulant reaction to criticism than well-considered strategy. Nevertheless, abdication constitutes in almost anybody's vocabulary a rather more definite commitment than does resignation, and even at the time of his father's death in 1960, Sihanouk did not long waver in his determination not to resume the crown.

Today Prince Sihanouk is formally designated as Chief of State, while the Queen Mother reigns but does not rule. The succession to the throne remains a subject of constant speculation, even though the Prince has of late named one of his sons, now a schoolboy in Peking as his political if not necessarily his royal successor.

For Prince Sihanouk himself, the monarchy, together with socialism and neutralism, remains one of the three props of the Cambodian state. As he may or may not actually have anticipated back in 1955, he himself continues to enjoy all the privilege and prestige of the crown without being vulnerable to the criticism that when he grows eloquent about the monarchy as the major stabilizing factor in the nation, he is growing eloquent about himself.

Prince Sihanouk's pilgrimage to India after his abdication, like his expedition to the Riviera in late 1952, looked considerably less purposeful than in fact it turned out to be. The Prince was preparing in 1955 to enter a new era, but first he wanted to look around, starting with India, the new Asian colossus. Over the years, Prince Sihanouk has switched on again, off again as an admirer of Nehru. He switched off, for instance, back in 1952, when Nehru seemed ready to lend an ear to Son Ngoc Thanh, on again after Nehru gave his warm endorsement to his Crusade for Freedom in 1954, and half off again in 1955. He began his 1955 visit in a state of starry-eyed adulation. He ended it in wide-eyed surprise that in India, as in Cambodia, parliamentary democracy had not brought quite the happy socialistic results that had been anticipated. Prince Sihanouk's opinion of Nehru and of India has been dropping ever since. On subsequent visits to India he has been particularly vexed by the mixture of ignorance and patronage he detects in Indian views on Cambodia.

Soon after his visit to Delhi, Prince Sihanouk headed his own delegation to the Afro-Asian Conference in Bandung (April, 1955). There he consorted not only with Nehru, but with Sukarno, U Nu, and Chou En-lai. If India contributed to his disillusionment with parliamentary democracy and to his inclination to seek other devices to promote socialism, Bandung convinced him of the uses of neutralism and coexistence. Bandung also reinforced for him the lesson he himself had learned during his own Crusade for Freedom about the political uses of domestic and international histrionics. He returned to Cambodia, therefore, to launch his Sangkum—the Cambodian People's Socialist Community—a showy, busy, noisy mass movement. The Sangkum aims at eliminating political factionalism, rallying the nation to support monarchy, socialism, and neutralism, and attracting to Cambodia the international attention which inevitably focuses upon furore.

Early the following year, Prince Sihanouk set out on a series of highly publicized international tours of the sort which many Southeast Asian leaders seem to regard as indispensable to personal and national prestige. He visited Manila, where he was offended and gave offense when such matters as SEATO, anticommunism, and democratic self-government came up. He visited Tokyo, where things went better, and Peking, where things went very well indeed. The Chinese accorded him all the attention and ceremony they usually reserve for leaders of much bigger, greater nations than Cambodia, and they escalated the ovation on his subsequent visits. For Mao, Chou, Li, and other Chinese leaders, the Prince developed an infatuation which coexists easily enough, it seems, with his suspicion of world communism and his contempt for the domestic product.

Prince Sihanouk's subsequent travels might seem a bit extravagant had they not turned out to be spectacularly profitable. He visited Warsaw, Madrid, Vienna, Prague, Moscow, and Belgrade in 1957; Peking again in 1958; Djakarta, Cairo, Belgrade, New Delhi, and Rangoon in 1959; Czechoslovakia, the Soviet Union, Outer Mongolia, and again China in 1960; and since then he has maintained both speed and mileage. He has also, of course, repeatedly visited the United States, and he never misses an opportunity to drop in on the French. Almost everywhere he goes, joint declarations of undying friendship and understanding have been reinforced by proffers of aid. Cambodia has netted approximately $350,000,000 in American aid, starting in 1950. The Prince points out that on a per capita basis both Vietnam and Laos have done quite a lot better. In late 1963, however, for reasons which are still obscure, he asked for the termination of American aid of all descriptions. Meanwhile, he had graciously accepted $100,000,000 or more from France, the Soviet Union, China, Poland, Czechoslovakia, Japan, and other donors. Western nations have seemed in the past to give all the more eagerly for being accused of bad faith, but then so too have the Communist nations. Sihanouk's travels have seemed in some respects like wildcatting for oil, save that the risk capital was much more modest.

Ever since 1955, in the intervals between travels, Prince Sihanouk has worked hard at making his newly independent nation of Cambodia a Southeast Asian showpiece. He has placed major reliance on the cooperation of the Sangkum in vitalizing or bypassing the formidable Cambodian bureaucracy, and until very recently at least, on the competition of the outside world in providing aid.

The Sangkum, or Sankgum Reastre Niyum, to give it its full name, sprang virtually full grown from the brain of Prince Sihanouk back in 1955, when he dubbed each of his 100,000 disciples Sahachivin (Comrade), himself assumed the title Samdech Sahachivin (Prince Comrade), and set everybody to work stirring up the voters. The Sangkum Sahachivins swept the September, 1955, elections by winning 82.5 per cent of the total ballots, a "too complete" victory by which Samdech Sahachivin confessed himself "somewhat embarrassed," although subsequent victories have been on the order of 99.9 per cent. The Sangkum immediately began to sprout totalitarian-looking tentacles—youth corps, women's corps, cadre training centers, voluntary labor battalions, and the like.

Cambodian government today centers not on the National Assembly, which still meets occasionally, nor upon the cabinet, which
functions indifferently, but upon the Sangkum National Council
and the Sangkum National Conference. In this latter body, a con-
vention-cum-carnival convened regularly in Phnom-Penh, every
Sahachivin can have his say, but Samdech Sahachivin always has
quite an edge in total wordage. Samdech Sahachivin, as Chief
of State, frequent Prime Minister, and Sangkum president, is
quadruply potent. Should any minor dissent arise, he promptly
resigns, or threatens to resign, one or another of his posts until
the dissidents have acknowledged their errors. Resignation constitutes, thus, not just a contrived crisis but a clinching argument.

The Sangkum does not operate unopposed, but Prince Sihanouk
has achieved a remarkable degree of success in bringing the opposition into the Sangkum itself and in placing opposition leaders
in positions where he can more successfully heckle them than
they him. The most formidable opposition centers on the Pra-
cheachon (People's Party), which includes Son Ngoc Thanh's
disciples, and a group of young intellectuals not long since returned from studies in Paris where they gravitated inevitably to
the Left Bank and the left wing. When the disgruntled intellectuals recently attacked the Prince himself in press and parliament,
Sihanouk at first responded by expressions of sorrowful dismay at
their rude conduct, and then, when they failed to repent, by appointing some of them to top jobs where he could watch and
criticize them. He appointed Hou Yuon, for instance, one of the
most gifted and articulate of the group, as Minister of Finance
and later as Minister of Planning, making him responsible for
such important establishments as some new Chinese-gift factories.
He allowed Hou Yuon to surround himself with men of his own
choice and to introduce young blood into some of the other ministries as well, all of which were badly in need of rejuvenation.

Let them learn for themselves, Prince Sihanouk said in effect,
that it isn't so easy to run a government. He then made sure that
they missed none of their lessons. The new Chinese-aid factories,
for instance, proved to be operating at a loss, and the prince
openly laid the blame not on the Chinese but on the new Cambodian managers—the young intellectuals themselves. The Prir
also disclosed that some of the "jeunes rouges" had managed in

quite a remarkably short space of time to acquire a taste for Mercedes-Benz sedans, resort villas, and night club entertainment, and that their wives sparkled with newly purchased gems. Prince Sihanouk returns value received for the confidence the Sangkum reposes in him. Unfailingly he has a stirring message. More and more frequently in the last several years it has been a message of progress and prosperity in Cambodia. In late 1963, however, with the rejection of American aid, it became a new message of austerity and privation. His performance is always embellished with a lively account of the perils which he himself, Cambodia, and the Sangkum have just encountered. Often the perils originate with the capitalist "exploiters," commonly the Americans, who, for their own ulterior motives, have wickedly bestowed or refused to bestow aid, and meanwhile have conspired with Cambodia's enemies, thus forcing him to invite Communist China to supply him with military support. Sometimes it is the Communist "monsters," who are determined to destroy the Cambodian monarchy along with the Laotian, and when they do this, his, Sihanouk's throat will be the first to be slit. Sometimes it is Cambodian "traitors"—Son Ngoc Thanh and Sam Sary and the Khmer Serai (the current name of the Cambodian underground which supports them)—and the Thai or Vietnamese "warmongers" who give his enemies aid and shelter.

The downfall on November 1, 1963, of President Ngo Dinh Diem in South Vietnam and the obscure but ominous events of the year 1963 in Laos, combined with many other indications of Southeast Asian wobbliness and the increasingly ambivalent attitude of the Western world toward deeper involvement, induced in Prince Sihanouk a characteristic reaction. On November 19, 1963, he requested the termination of American military and economic aid programs, alleging as his immediate reason "American complicity" in a suddenly discovered assassination plot aimed against himself. Together with the Americans he implicated the Vietnamese, the Thailanders, and the Khmer Serai. Then dramatically he refuted foreign speculation that he would turn openly and immediately to Communist China to compensate for American withdrawal. He turned instead to France, General de Gaulle having already announced that he was prepared to resume the

Frenchman's burden in the Far East, this time, it seemed, on the basis of achieving a rapprochement with Ho Chi Minh.

Besides reposing his trust in De Gaulle, Prince Sihanouk placed it also in the Geneva Conference powers, whom he invited to reconvene in Indonesia or in Burma to guarantee both Cambodian and Vietnamese neutrality—in fact, neutrality anywhere. Meanwhile, however, he did not neglect to sound the domestic alarms, that rejection of the American dollar meant renunciation not only of such luxuries as champagne and Mercedes-Benz cars and real estate booms, but even of the basic commodities and of the foreign-exchange props on which the Cambodian economy had been resting for years. He also announced the nationalization of all import-export business firms as of January 1, 1964, and of all banking as of July 1, 1964, measures calculated presumably to offset the adverse effects of the cancellation of American aid.

Almost everybody admitted that Prince Sihanouk was completely correct in his appraisal that the Cambodian economy had become dangerously dependent upon American and other foreign aid, and that the time had come to take corrective measures. The Prince's combination of shock therapy in cutting the American life line, quick stimulus by nationalization of business concerns, and self-tranquilization in seeking guaranteed neutrality might or might not constitute compatible treatments. Nobody, probably not even Prince Sihanouk himself, knew whether this time he would reverse himself tomorrow. American-aid personnel began making the necessary moves to terminate all projects by January 1, 1964, and to be out of the country very soon thereafter, some of them still anticipating of course, a last-minute reprieve.

Then suddenly a new furore sprang up when Prince Sihanouk's government radio announcers, in rejoicing publicly over the deaths of Marshal Sarit of Thailand and President Ngo Dinh Diem of Vietnam, made disguised but unmistakable reference in the same jubilant tone to the death of President Kennedy. The United States government requested an explanation, the Prince objected to the request, other complications arose, and by year's end American-Cambodian relations seemed stretched to the breaking point. The whole unhappy sequence of events was perhaps just part of some obscure strategy which would eventually become clear, and indeed Sihanouk began at once to intimate that he did not expect the Americans to take him quite so literally about termination of aid. On the basis of his past record, it would seem that the Prince can reverse himself just as suddenly and as often as may seem to him to be necessary to ensure his own and Cambodia's survival. The real question, then, was whether he still retained his once sure sense of timing, a question which only time itself could answer.

The special flavor of Prince Sihanouk's furious forensics, and something of the reason for them, comes out best not in his outbursts against the United States, which returns a soft answer, but in his diplomatic exchanges in the past with the late Prime Minister Sarit. Thailand, the Prince said not long ago, was a "vulture" waiting to gorge itself upon "carrion" which he, Sihanouk, did not propose to provide. Prime Minister Sarit replied, in effect, that one day he might "cut off the head" of this pretentious upstart and "bathe his feet" in the blood—a monumental insult, since in Thai-Cambodian lore, the head is sacred, the feet are profane, and *lèse-majesté* could therefore proceed no further. Prince Sihanouk in turn appealed to his sons to exculpate him from filial blame should he, on being subjected to such massive provocation, attack Thailand and "wipe out the Thai race." Such a threat, Sarit answered, was rather "like a pig challenging a lion." The day might come, he added, when Thailand would lose patience with "the unstable, shifting, and whimsical fits of Cambodia's leader." Other Thai spokesmen elaborated upon the theme that Sihanouk's "allegations denote such vulgarity and incoherence they sound more like utterances coming from an inmate of a psychopathic ward."

Prince Sihanouk then shifted to other, equally familiar tactics. The Thais, he said, had infiltrated Cambodia with armed troops, adding, however, the new embellishment that American personnel had accompanied them. The Thais, angry at the moment not only with Sihanouk but also with the United States, which was adopting a softer policy on Laos than Thailand recommended, alleged in their turn that Sihanouk was in league with the Chinese to invade Thailand and that the United States was arming him.

Prince Sihanouk's exchanges with Vietnam's Ngo Dinh Diem were somewhat less vituperative, only, perhaps, because Diem lacked Sarit's flair for invective. The Prince, nevertheless, was given to counting more or less imaginary border incidents and threatening that after just one, two, three more—watch out! Cambodian relations with both South Vietnam and Thailand, consequently, are always bad and frequently broken.

The Sangkum, in response to the exhortations to promote national development which generally accompany Prince Sihanouk's imprecations about international conspiracy, has managed in the last few years to go to work on an impressive number of new schools, roads, bridges, temples, clinics, sports fields, parks, offices, homes, in fact just about anything buildable. These *"réalisations"* are scattered throughout the nation according to a master plan so complex and changeable that even the Sangkum has long since almost given up the pretense of a plan. Parts of Cambodia today, especially the capital city, are being so swiftly and totally transformed that a visitor returning after a few years' absence may feel that he has skipped a century and wonder whether the Cambodians have too. The consequences are still as obscure as the plan, save that they are likely to be momentous, especially if cancellation of American aid results in sudden loss or reversal of momentum.

The *réalisations* which stand out in sharpest relief at the moment from the general Cambodian topography must be enumerated seriatim to have anything like the impact they make upon the on-the-spot observer: a $10 million French-gift seaport, christened, naturally, Sihanoukville; a $2.5 million French-gift airport; a $34 million, 132-mile American-gift "Khmer-American Friendship Highway" connecting, now that faulty original construction work has been expensively repaired, the airport and the seaport; an $8 million, 1000-bed Russian-gift hospital; $15 million worth of Communist Chinese-gift factories—one each for textiles, cement, paper, and plywood; an American-gift 100-bed hospital for bonzes (no price tag); a French-gift 163-bed general hospital (no price tag); and the French-gift Lycée Descartes, for 500 students.

Among major *réalisations* not yet completely realized are these: the Sangkum's own vast new *lycée,* an American primary and secondary school (English language) for 900 students; a Russian-gift technical school for 500 students; an American-gift technical school for 700 students, and an American arts and trades school for

1,600 students. With regard to these redundant technical schools: the Americans bid, the Russians bid too; both bids were accepted; the Russians have the better site and the showier layout, right next door to the Sangkum's *lycée*—but then the Russians were hooked a few years ago with an undesirable site for their hospital. The above enumeration does not by any means exhaust the list.

The Poles have supplied equipment for a hospital in the provinces; the Czechs are busy with factories; the Japanese are building a splendid new bridge across the Tonlé Sap; the Americans have had their hands and their money in almost everything, including normal schools, irrigation schemes, public health, and general uplift. They have even pumped a few million cubic yards of silt into the onetime lakes and swamps of the city of Phnom-Penh to allow private individuals, who have become no poorer as result of all this influx of international aid money, to run up mile after mile of new three- to fourteen-story buildings and thousands of suburban villas. The city of Phnom-Penh, consequently, is now transformed into Southeast Asia's most Continental-looking city—Continental in the sense that its new areas resemble those of Rome and Paris and Madrid more than they do those of Bangkok, say, or Manila.

The Americans, the Russians, the Chinese, and other foreigners have accounted for so many of the really big, showy *réalisations* that Prince Sihanouk has felt impelled to argue that Cambodia moves ahead because it aids itself. He points to the innumerable new temples, schools, clinics, and the like which are often overlooked even by the Cambodians. He points also to the tremendous voluntary labor projects whereby Cambodia is building up an elaborate railway network, not very straight or solid new lines, perhaps, and not even lines that are economically very feasible, but a new railway system nonetheless, one which keeps running off oratorically at least in all directions, even up into the forbidding geographical and political terrain of Laos.

Quite apparently, Prince Sihanouk has elected not just to deplore international tensions but to exploit them. As a neutralist he attempts not only to adjust between and among the pressures but to adjust them to suit his purposes. His controlling purpose, he constantly reiterates, is to develop Cambodia and to preserve its independence. He has repeatedly singled out communism as the real national menace, but one which can be held off only by accepting its advances and then, probably, not for long. He has stated again and again that Communist China will inevitably extend its control throughout Southeast Asia and that he seeks mainly to delay its advance in Cambodia. Meanwhile he will use the international Communists, he argues with calculated perversity which bewilders Communists, non-Communists, and anti-Communists alike, to build up the strength by which he will combat them.

Prince Sihanouk keeps one eye and one ear always on nearby Laos, where, he says, "the die is cast" for communism, a nearby object lesson of what could happen to Cambodia; and no one can argue very convincingly that it won't. Cambodia, he says, must become a Southeast Asian Switzerland, its neutrality guaranteed by the international world, or failing that, by reliance upon Communist Chinese military alliance. The United States, he has said in the past and he may, of course, reiterate in the future, must make a bigger and bigger commitment in Cambodia. He admits, however, that he more than half expects the United States and for that matter the French to pull up and get out fast when a showdown with China threatens. French assistance all along has been more welcome than American, especially in the area of cultural cooperation. No Frenchman, indeed, retains a higher regard than Prince Sihanouk for French language, food, and comfort, to all of which the continuing French presence in Cambodia richly contributes in the maintenance of standards. But then France, quite obviously, is a financial and a technical as well as a cultural resource these days and no longer a colonial menace, although it takes a most extraordinary anticolonial nationalist to assume a stance of such Gaelic rationality.

International observers have frequently described Prince Sihanouk's foreign policy as an amateur stunt of walking a tightrope. In actual fact it is more a virtuoso professional performance of juggling Roman candles while spinning by his teeth from a flying trapeze. When the Prince takes the show on the road billed as a state visit, he collects his own admission at scalpers' prices. It is an almost irresistible modern political equivalent of the old time minstrel-medicine show, to which he adds extra refinements. When the songs and dances and acrobatics are over, the Prince invites the audience itself to poultice the wounds which it has inflicted, he says, whether by its gross inattention or by its badly timed applause.

When he is not urging himself on into calculated display of outrage, Prince Sihanouk is possessed of an air of innocent merriment so infectious that even the Thais and the Vietnamese occasionally wonder whether they may not have wronged him. The Prince is possibly the most relaxed, uninhibited, undauntable, inexhaustibly energetic political hedonist since the Italian Renaissance. At the age of forty-two he looks all of twenty-seven, and out of every twenty-four hours he seems to extract the absolute maximum of action and enjoyment. What may look and sound like pandemonium is often sheer exuberance.

Prince Sihanouk seems to have set himself deliberately to demonstrate that vitality did not depart from the Khmer people some seven hundred years ago, as some of the French used to argue. It was merely welled up for release today. If the ultimate achievement of the ancient Khmers was Angkor-Thom, with four serene but enigmatic stone faces gazing from each tower toward the four points of the compass, the Prince has given to each of the faces its proper voice. He has beamed one toward China, one toward the Soviet Union, one toward the West, and one toward his own homeland—the heartland of Southeast Asia and the nemesis of Thailand and South Vietnam.

These days Prince Sihanouk lives not in the Grand Palace, where the Queen Mother holds court and he himself appears on state occasions, but in a modern villa in suburban Phnom-Penh. It is an air-conditioned frenzy of contemporary design backed up close to a heavily-trafficked new highway but opening onto gardens shaded by palms. He lives there with his fifth and favorite wife, Princess Monique. In 1951 Mlle. Monique was the winner of a Rights of Man Day beauty contest in a Phnom-Penh *lycée* when the Prince happened in to bestow the prizes. Today Princess Monique is a very chic young royal matron whose classically perfect Khmer beauty is by no means impaired by Italian nuances— her father was an Italian businessman in Phnom-Penh.

By Princess Monique the Prince has had two sons, one of whom —the present heir apparent to the throne—is being educated in Peking, the other in Moscow. Still another of the Prince's sons, by a different wife, is also studying in Peking. The three are named as wards of Chou En-lai and Nikita Khrushchev. Two other sons have been attending a *lycée* in Marseilles, one of them being on the point of proceeding to Paris to continue his studies there. The Prince has sent none of his offspring to the United States, but he has been heard to remark that discipline is a problem and that no American President has offered to assume custody. The custody of a young Cambodian prince is not, indeed, a responsibility lightly to be taken on.

Prince Sihanouk, of course, has other wives and other children. The present semiofficial tally is six of the former and thirteen of the latter, but the score is adjustable, depending upon certain rather complicated technicalities. The wives include one Laotian princess and one Cambodian ballet dancer—the mother of the ravishing young princess who is now *danseuse étoile* of the royal ballet. La Princesse Bopha Devi, as stunning a beauty as the Khmer civilization has yet produced, is a feature attraction of the Prince's state visits abroad.

His suburban villa serves the Prince as a base from which to operate for a daily program which would seem formidable even to a matinee idol. He sets out at an early morning hour by one of his favorite conveyances, either his helicopter, *l'Alouette*, or his "Ford décapotable." To quote the inspired French-language press of Phnom-Penh, which rarely varies or omits its clichés in the full front-page report it gives to his activities, "Samdech Sahachivin" or "Monseigneur" then makes a "tournée" of "réalisations." The program always features "une immense foule," "un accueil spontané et chaleureux," "une inauguration," and as the pièce de résistance, Monseigneur's "allocution," otherwise described as "une improvisation captivante et spirituelle" which unfailingly occasions "des tonnerres d'applaudissements alternant avec des acclamations de toutes sortes." Presently there is "un repas délicieux" then generally "une manifestation sportive" in which "la rédoubtable formation de Monseigneur" in volleyball, basketball, or football "écrase impitoyablement" any opposition, while Monseigneur is himself "très applaudi" for scoring as many as forty-five "panniers." On these occasions, "l'équipe féminine du Palais," captained by Princess Monique, deals not quite so "impitoyablement" but no less conclusively with the local ladies.

Even fine French rhetoric cannot quite render the sheer rapture of the crowds and of Prince Sihanouk himself when *l'Alouette* comes whirling in, with the Prince strewing down upon his admirers "coupons de tissus"—costume-length samples of the output of the new Chinese textile mill, utilitarian cotton drill in an assortment of rather poisonous but nonetheless welcome colors. As the Prince alights, the roar of excitement subsides into a murmur of delight. The crowds press in just to touch his hand, sometimes so importunately that the Prince is jostled as he moves toward the "tribune d'honneur," waving almost timidly, smiling almost shyly, but radiating joy that such adulation should be exclusively for him. In delivering his "allocution," Prince Sihanouk is sometimes so carried away by emotion that he actually spins and whirls, and the crowds, which he calls upon repeatedly for approval, never fail to respond with joyous shouts. The Prince then takes his departure, pressing "des dons en espèce," that is, wads of banknotes, into the hands of almost anyone who has a *réalisation* on or in view. The ensuing dramatic effect of his take-off strongly suggests belief that *l'Alouette,* rather than merely transporting, is in fact translating him.

In addition to officiating almost daily at "inaugurations" of his *réalisations,* Prince Sihanouk presides over a periodic public audience to which carefully screened suppliants are admitted to petition him to redress their ills. Disabled veterans, dispossessed widows, betrayed wives, unemployed husbands, impecunious students—the more complicated their miseries, the more attentive is the Prince, who weeps with or for the wretched, laughs with or at the clowns, and never, never lets himself be upstaged by either. These audiences, which are the sensation, naturally, of Radio Cambodia, warrant an international Oscar for sheer artistic concentration of the hilarious along with the lachrymose.

At forty-two Prince Sihanouk is physically as well as intellectually much more vigorous than he was twenty years ago. He has long been an expert horseman, and he is also a marksman and fencer. In recent years he has developed a passion for team sports and has embarked upon a highly successful one-man campaign to make his whole nation sports-conscious. Everywhere in Cambodia today, in school grounds, in public parks, and in private gardens there are appearing basketball and volleyball courts and other sports facilities, and everywhere, among a formerly rather somnolent people, sport is the rage. The Prince himself is a dead-eye shot at basketball, a sure killer at volleyball, a fleet and nimble runner in soccer. He grows indignant if anyone suggests that the number of points which he himself scores is in any way connected with the fact that traditionally it has been a capital offense physically to obstruct royalty.

Just as he engages in sports, so the Prince also engages indefatigably in voluntary labor. He sets an example followed—if at times reluctantly—by the bureaucrats of Phnom-Penh and even by the diplomats. Peeling down to his underwear, he swings a pick and passes the earth-laden baskets along with the happy, singing throng building a new road or a new railway embankment. The job could be done better and more cheaply, of course, by wheeling in the bulldozers, but at loss of the inspiring exercise and spectacle of the volunteer labor squads.

In every line of Cambodian endeavor, including the mass media on which to a very great extent he relies, Prince Sihanouk now sets the national mood and pace. He takes special pride in his *allocutions,* delivered in French or Cambodian at top speed and at great length in rather a piercing voice. These are reported verbatim in the daily press, but only the French version receives the royal seal of approval, which is rather a pity, since it often loses in excitement what it gains in polish. The *allocutions,* frequently compiled and republished, now constitute a formidable bulk of current history and literature which only the more intrepid readers manage to keep up with, although any diligent diplomat, scholar, or politician must make the effort.

After having so thoroughly and so often explained himself in his *allocutions,* Prince Sihanouk sometimes becomes impatient with visitors who query him on points which he believes he has long since clarified. Should anyone venture to point out the contradictions, the Prince patiently explains that he is in fact just a very simple man with a very simple message. The one objective to which he has dedicated his life is to preserve Cambodia in peace and happiness. Monarchy, socialism, and neutralism are the three devices he has long been advocating, with additional emphasis of late upon Buddhism and what he terms "Buddhist national socialism."

Cambodia today is a thriving little oasis of relative peace and contentment where monarchy, socialism, neutralism, and Buddhism successfully coexist and Prince Sihanouk flourishes. If high winds blow through the betel palms, and if they carry a good deal of dust from new building operations into the eyes of the startled spectators, ex-King Sihanouk, now the Prince Comrade, would not have it otherwise.

One Captain and a Plethora of Princes

Captain Kong Lê, Prince Souvanna Phouma, and Prince Souphanouvong, in conjunction with miscellaneous other Laotian princes and soldiers, peasants and politicians, demonstrating youths and cremated corpses, have served at least one widely approved purpose. Ever since the 1954 Geneva Agreement which created the new Laos and the endless Laos crisis, they have occasioned highly paid employment for whole relays of diplomats, reporters, peacemakers, and troublemakers. Much of that employment, to be sure, consists of trying to puzzle out in the Laos of the moment exactly who is who, and where, and why.

Even for more knowledgeable connoisseurs of crisis than the television audience, the members of this Laotian cast of characters achieve the distinction of being virtually indistinguishable as individuals. Among the denizens of a remote mountain kingdom which few save opium smugglers and Communist infiltrators could point to with confidence on an unlabeled map, the lead characters in the marathon Laotian crisis are peculiarly difficult, even with the use of a telescopic lens, to bring sharply into focus. The Captain's name, however, being easy to spell, pronounce, and remember, and his original status being neither that of king, prince, general, nor indolent carefree tribesman, Kong Lê may serve as an anchor among his peers and betters of the hitherto obscure Laotian celebrities.

Captain Kong Lê's late monarch, "good old" King Sisavang Vong (reigned 1904–1959), is dead at seventy-four and his royal remains have been cremated in a sandalwood urn atop a vast funeral pyre in his royal city of Luang Prabang, in a feudal ceremony which occurred while his political capital of Vientiane and much of the countryside as well were burning with bright revolutionary flame. The "young" Paris-educated King Savang Vatthana, age 57, who appears to have atrophied intellectually while awaiting the succession, now sits on a very thorny throne newly upholstered by yet another patchwork Geneva agreement.

The "Red" Prince Souphanouvong, the "neutralist" or "Pink" Prince Souvanna Phouma, the "strong" or "White" "anti-Communist" General Phoumi Nosavan—not to be confused with the "strong" or "White" "anti-Communist" ex-Prime Minister Phoui Sananikone—all of these truly extraordinary gentlemen still compete for international attention with General (ex-Captain) Kong Lê, the "mad," "angry" and now "disillusioned" "tool" of "Uncle" Ho Chi Minh and "Leader" Mao Tse-tung.

The "fighting" reformist, corrupt ex-Prime Minister Sasorith Don Katay is dead and his fortune from American-aid funds is largely dissipated. The Oxford-educated revolutionary "hero" Prince Phetsarath is also dead and his empty title, Viceroy of the Realm, has lapsed. The almost equally empty office of Inspector-General of the Realm is still occupied, in semi-absentia, by the "jolly" "warrior" "White" "Anti-Communist" Prince General Boun Oum, now gradually slowing down and drying out. The sinister Marxist "librarian" and "gunsmith," onetime Minister of Information, later Foreign Minister Quinim Phlosena has been assassinated. The dashing Communist guerrilla Colonel Sinkapo, sporting a Cossack greatcoat and boots, enjoys fortune and favor on the Plaine des Jarres or perhaps, at the moment, in Hanoi or Peking. A mysterious Corsican, Signor X, still runs an opium syndicate in Vientiane with a fleet of private planes to fly his popular product to unnameable destinations.

Tens of thousands of bonzes doze blissfully in the temples, while peasants farm, fishermen fish, tribesmen hunt, guerrillas fight, and foreign correspondents interview all of them for human interest stories which seldom fail to sell. The Young King, the Pink Prince, the Red Prince, the Jolly Prince, and the White General shift about from Vientiane to Luang Prabang to Washington, Moscow, Peking, Hanoi, Rangoon, Paris, and Geneva, but the Disillusioned General Kong Lê sticks mainly to the

Plaine des Jarres, where he now looks over his shoulder expecting a knife in the back.

The only way even to begin to make any sense out of this mélange of political mayhemists is to start with the Mad or Angry young Captain Kong Lê, and, as the account grows too involved, to keep reverting to him, for he is one of the least and at the same time one of the most complicated of the lot.

Captain Kong Lê, the author of a coup which jarred the world in 1960, sometimes seems like the architect of chaos in the anomaly which, in these days of nationalist mythology, passes for the constitutional monarchy of Laos. He is in fact typical of the decent, responsible, intelligent, far-above-average little man of Southeast Asia to whom the Communist formula sometimes offers hope in an all but hopeless dilemma. Along with his 750 paratroopers, the elite and virtually the only fighting force in the reputedly 25,000-man Royal Lao Army, he was always being casually dropped, unpaid, on forlorn jungle missions to eliminate evanescent guerrillas who shot at him while he dangled in the air but seldom lingered to be shot at in turn, on the ground. The politicians, meanwhile, seemed intent upon extending their futile control outside the shambles they had made of Vientiane, Luang Prabang, and Savannakhet.

Captain Kong Lê could not understand why Lao should endlessly be killing Lao, why the "imperialists" should apparently be abetting while the Communists were apparently restraining the slaughter, or why politicians should grow fat on American money while the people were deceived with empty talk of progress. The Communist proposition of universal peace, neutrality, coexistence, friendship, and cooperation—this, he thought, might possibly work.

Captain Kong Lê decided to rebel. In the lunacy which is Laos, he and his 750 paratroopers, plus a few agitators and the swarms of demonstrators who quickly rallied round them, on August 9, 1960, toppled the government. The politicians happened at the moment, to be sure, to be junketing off to Luang Prabang to attend to some urgent and festive rites in connection with the cremation of the late king. The revolutionaries indulged themselves in a frenzy of demonstrations in which Captain Kong Lê proved himself an aimless organizer but a stirring orator. Students, priests, and incidental riffraff roared revolutionary slogans and prevailed upon Prince Souvanna Phouma, when he came back from Luang Prabang, to form a government which was possibly no worse than its predecessors. The United States suspended its aid and military subsidies. The Russians established an emergency airlift of food, clothing, gasoline, and arms. The international world braced itself for yet one more brink, shuddered and counseled caution.

Then the Strong General Phoumi, refinanced and re-equipped by the United States, marched on Vientiane. He successively seized and lost the city in two brief scuffles in early September, tried again after an artillery barrage, and in the one real battle (December 13–16) of the whole dreary ten-year Laos emergency, drove Kong Lê's forces out into the countryside.

Captain Kong Lê retired to the Plaine des Jarres, where the Russians, the Viet-Minh, and the Pathet Lao's Red Prince Souphanouvong inundated him in a tide of personnel, matériel, and friendship. The Pathet Lao "Communists," the Kong Lê "neutralists," and the Russian and North Vietnamese "technicians" and "volunteers" began swiftly to extend their effective control over the major part of Laos. Meanwhile, the Jolly Prince General Boun Oum, as Prime Minister, set up a fragile new government in Vientiane. The Pink Prince Souvanna Phouma, who had made his getaway to Cambodia, sulked, gardened, and consorted with Prince Sihanouk, who had all along been demanding that Laos be "neutralized" and now thought it would be a good idea to neutralize Cambodia too.

At this point the United States, the Soviet Union, Communist China, and eleven other nations convened another Geneva Conference (May 16, 1961–July 23, 1962). Their varied degrees of interest and uninterest in this tediously recrudescent Laos crisis had by this time become almost impossible for themselves or for anyone else to analyze. The United States, accordingly, put pressure upon the Anti-Communist Prince Boum Oum to be less anti-Communist by once again cutting off aid. The Soviet Union and Communist China put mysterious pressures upon one another and upon the Red Prince Souphanouvong. The Pink Prince Souvanna Phouma, whom no one was pressuring, traveled from Cambodia to the Plaine des Jarres to Geneva, explaining his formula of "la neutralité dans le neutralisme."

Laos is now neutralized as of July 23, 1962. The Red and the Pink Princes have had another brief and hopeless go at coexistent government. The United States has withdrawn all of its 750 "military advisors"; the Communists have withdrawn an undisclosed number of their 7,500 "technicians." The White General has been restrained. The royal, the Pathet Lao, the Kong Lê territories, military forces, and administrations are all resisting the Geneva formula that they be "reunified" and "reunited" under the eyes of an International Control Commission, consisting of an Indian, a Pole, and a Canadian. No one, of course, ever thought that the 1962 Geneva settlement would work, the earlier and similar 1954 Geneva Agreement having failed under circumstances somewhat less prejudicial to its implementation.

Captain Kong Lê, for all the square mileage of news coverage he has had since his sudden emergence to prominence on August 9, 1960, is not much better known as an individual today than he was the day before his coup. He is thirty-one years of age—or perhaps forty-one, for the records are inconclusive and his appearance of bright-eyed, firm-muscled youth may be deceptive. He is just barely five feet tall—or perhaps five feet four—for the statistics are not official and the estimate varies according to whether he is seen standing alongside the Russian or the Chinese ambassador. In either case he looks minute. Both compact and wiry in build, he is endowed with the smooth brown skin and the brilliant white teeth which are the Laotian male's particular claim to handsomeness. Although he seems animated and indeed electric when he smiles or when he orates, he suffers, nevertheless, from a nervous tic, and he generally seems as tense as though he were spring-wound and about to jump.

By birth Captain Kong Lê is a Kha, that is, a mountain tribesman rather than a lowland Lao. Just which particular one of the nation's many tribal groups he belongs to, no one seems to know, although during his revolt the loyalists produced a woman of the Tchepone area who, they claimed, was his mother, pleading with him to come home. In education he reached secondary-school level. Although he himself speaks of "several" years in a French *lycée,* he does not say where; presumably it was the Lycée Pavie in Vientiane, after a French *collège* in Savannakhet. He speaks excellent French and passable English, the latter with a slight Filipino accent, for he learned most of it or at least improved it during a course of military instruction near Manila. He received his basic military training presumably from the French, and according to some reports, he served as a noncommissioned officer in the French colonial forces. Joining the Royal Lao Army in 1952, he soon afterwards entered officer training school and attained the rank of lieutenant. In 1957 he was sent to the Philippines for a year's training with the Philippines Scout Rangers. There he impressed his Filipino acquaintances as being extraordinarily alert, adept, and self-effacing.

On his return to Laos, Captain Kong Lê quickly earned for himself the reputation of being one of the most competent officers in the Royal Lao Army. Soon he was made commander of the crack Second Parachute Battalion, to which were assigned some ten American technical advisers, none of whom seem to have known him very well. By being indefatigably attentive to the personal welfare of his men, he gained their unquestioning loyalty. The army Commander-in-Chief, General Phoumi Nosavan, trusted him so implicitly that the headquarters files and intelligence, such as they were, regarding both royal and guerrilla forces, were completely at his disposal. Like other Lao army officers, Kong Lê made the rounds of American agencies in Vientiane, ready and eager, it would seem, to gain some sort of special American assistance for his unit. Some of the Americans who met him during this period, however, have difficulty even remembering what he looked like, let alone what he came for. They are much clearer but still not particularly precise about the Captain Kong Lê they later saw jeeping about Vientiane, flying the device "Chef du Coup d'État," guarded by Lance Corporal Katub (who was said to be magically immune to bullets, as, indeed, many people thought Captain Kong Lê himself was), both of them shouting such slogans as "Yankee, Go, Go, Go."

To fill out the Kong Lê dossier, one must have frequent resort to rumor, speculation, or mere oddments of fact. He is rumored, for instance, to have had at least six wives and quite a few mistresses. His first publicly acknowledged wife was a young lady named Kham Phiou, a niece of General Ouane, his former commanding officer. The marriage seems to have been arranged for him with no particular show of enthusiasm on his part, and it ended in divorce soon after his coup. He now seems to have one wife in Vientiane and another at the Plaine des Jarres. The latter is young and pretty and apparently rugged as well, for she has made an extremely simple frontier home for him, where she attracts favorable but distant notice from some of the visting newspapermen.

Captain Kong Lê's preferred quarters in Vientiane before and during the coup were the paratroop barracks on the airport road. There he was known to sleep on the bare floor in a dormitory room on a pad no thicker than those provided for his men. His acquaintances in the Vientiane foreign enclave were few, but he got on well with the rather sizable Filipino community at Operation Brotherhood offices and elsewhere. On occasion he would sing, dance, and joke with them, but never for long. Unless he was so unobtrusive as to escape the notice of the regular clientele, he did not frequent the squalid Vientiane night clubs where Thai and Chinese hostesses, regularly imported and fitfully deported, provided dim red-light diversion. He did not move with the Lao playboys who crowded these spots, the political set which had recently exchanged bicycle for Mercedes-Benz and gathered political and social speed accordingly. As a matter of fact, both after and before the coup, he himself drove a jeep, not one of his own but an army jeep. Unless he was only betraying a most un-Lao-like reluctance toward ostentation, his taste in vehicles identified him at once as a man of slender means. Apparently he was not one of the sharp operators who bought U.S. dollars officially at thirty-five *kip,* sold them unofficially at 100 to 130, and played the cycle with counterpoint embellishments of import-export licenses just as long as the American-aid administrators put up with the racket.

If Captain Kong Lê did not move with the operators, neither, according to all of the available evidence, did he move with the conspirators, the intellectuals, or the reformers. Up until the time of the coup at least, he was not a known frequenter of Quinim's "library," i.e., bookstore-gunshop-residence-political cell. He was not a member of or an agent of the Communist-affiliated Pathet Lao (Free Lao) faction with whose political party, the crypto-

Communist Neo Lao Hak Xat, and with whose leader, the Red Prince Souphanouvong, he seems to have had little direct contact prior to his coup. Nor was he one of the "Young Ones," the reform-minded military officers and civil servants who sought, beginning in mid-1958, to assume political control and did in fact achieve considerable control, reform, and also complication.

Difficult as it is to believe, Captain Kong Lê was probably a loner, at least until power suddenly fell into his hands. Then he attracted to himself a clique of activists and extremists, including a couple of especially fuzzy newspaper editors who churned out for him an unending flow of slogans, speeches, leaflets, and radio broadcasts. By adhering to the scripts which they handed him, he won over almost the total student population of Vientiane, some 150 of whom followed him into the jungle and then traveled on to Hanoi. But even at that, he was still dependent upon the professional politicians, primarily the sinister "librarian," but also the Pink Prince Souvanna Phouma, to whom, within hours of staging his coup, he applied for advice about how to run it. All the while, he billed himself as the "Chef du Coup d'État," surrounded himself with a "Coup d'État Party" of soldiers, priests, and students. He regarded a coup as a political system in itself, a kind of demonstrocracy, one into which a few of the old politicians might be admitted, however, as visiting technical advisors.

Captain Kong Lê is the average above-average little man of Laos. He yearned for the good of his battalion and his nation, abhorred the antics of the politicians, distrusted the Americans, and welcomed the Russians. He trapped himself and his country into a dilemma worse than the one he sought to escape. Probably he himself could have given no more coherent an account than could many an outsider of the course of events which led up to this tragic denouement. For Laos is not a nation but a quite accidental montage of virtually inaccessible mountain and jungle settlements. The river valleys are inhabited by dreamy and medieval-minded Lao farmers and fishermen, while the rather more vigorous but mutually indifferent tribal groups stratify themselves about the mountain peaks. The composite is ornamented by spectacular Mekong River scenery and by the ancient Buddhist temples and cultures of the three cities, Luang Prabang, Vientiane, and Savannakhet. Laotian history, especially in recent time, seems as inconsecutively episodic as a performance of the Chinese classic, *The Three Kingdoms,* in which motivations and characterizations rival each other in obscurity. It proves, nevertheless, such undeniably good theater that the plot should be summarized even at risk, however slight, of imposing clarity and pattern where none exist.

Much of what is now Laos constituted back in the fourteenth century a flourishing lot of little kingdoms, the greatest of them modestly rivaling Siam and Cambodia in the splendor of their courts, the strength of their armies, the wealth of their Buddhist cultures, and the hedonism of their general outlook on life. The rare Westerners who ultimately made their way up the Mekong to what is now Laos, notably the members of a mid-seventeenth-century Dutch commercial mission from Batavia, reported arrogant rulers, avaricious for gifts; indifferent administrators, obstructive to travel, commerce, or learning; and an idle, happy population indulging itself in endless religious contemplation and in innumerable festivals, conspicuous among them some rather shocking bacchanalia. The Dutch reports were either too little or too much sensationalized to attract less hardy travelers.

Laos first really came to European attention when the French, empire-building in Indochina in the late nineteenth century, decided to scoop up the Laotian kingdoms before the Thais did. They dispatched Auguste Pavie, a humanistic, scholarly colonialist, who outwitted and outbluffed the Thais, snatched the King of Luang Prabang away from an invading northern Lao enemy, and in 1887 settled in to administer the area. Along with a miniature academy of French scientific and administrative colleagues, Pavie fell in love with the happy, handsome, feckless Lao people and tried to protect them from alien contamination. The French, who regarded Laos as a delightfully baffling sort of eighteenth-century philosophical preserve of the noble savage, successfully resisted any passing impulse to organize or to exploit, or even to modernize to any greater extent than was absolutely necessary for their own comfort. They did turn Vientiane into a little Blois-sur-Mekong; they got some schools and clinics going; and they encouraged a few of the princes to go to Hanoi or even to Paris to continue their education.

Most notable among them were Prince Souvanna Phouma and

Prince Souphanouvong, who speak, think, eat, drink, dress, act, and often react in French, each of course, in his highly individualistic manner. Prince Souvanna Phouma, the weakly intentioned intellectual liberal, and Prince Souphanouvong, the rigidly determined intellectual radical, used to be far more at home in the elegant drawing rooms of Paris than in the tacky palaces of Luang Prabang. Many French self-exiles, correspondingly, were far more at ease in their flame-tree-shaded Vientiane bungalows than in the faubourgs of metropolitan France. Neither side deplored the adaptations of the other.

The French, of course, lost their grip on Laos during the wartime years. The Japanese at first left the French colonial officials in nominal control, but then, after an attempted French coup on March 9, 1945, executed or jailed them. With the removal of the French and the subsequent collapse of the Japanese, the Laotians were left for a few months to run their own affairs pretty much as they wished, even though the Chinese occupation forces began filtering in from the north during the latter part of 1945 and the French from the east in early 1946. King Sisavang Vong, urged on by Viceroy Prince Phetsarath, on September 1, 1945, declared Laos independent, only to discover that the Viceroy viewed independence as an occasion for usurpation. The King therefore deposed the Viceroy, and the Viceroy deposed the King. Then, as the French began to reappear in some force, the King resumed the throne on April 20, 1946, and the various princes took up arms, Prince Souvanna Phouma having fallen in with the lead furnished by Prince Souphanouvong in backing Prince Phetsarath. The French swiftly prevailed, the rebellious princes and some 2,000-odd followers (the Lao Issara, or Free Lao) retreated across the Mekong to Thailand, the King reigned, and after a new agreement with France (May 10, 1947), he was presumed, albeit not very widely, to rule as king of an "independent" state within the "French Union."

The three princes—Phetsarath, Souphanouvong, and Souvanna Phouma—together with an enterprising commoner, Don Sasorith (Rabbit) Katay, a Laotian Tom Paine who could be equally fiery writing in French as "Arsène Lapin" or in English as "Peter Rabbit," fought, pamphleteered, and conspired, not infrequently against each other. They maintained a few rather aimless soldiers in Northern Thailand and in Laos and suffered a few casualties. They suffered mainly, however, from dissidence and defection among themselves and among their Thai supporters, who soon tired of Lao ineffectiveness and began tightening up on both cash and promises. When the French in July, 1949, somewhat fortified Lao "independence" by acknowledging "autonomy," most of the self-exiled patriots proved both ready and willing to return to Laos to be reunited with their countrymen and to swear allegiance to the King.

Prince Souvanna Phouma, together with his eloquent friend, Don Sasorith Katay, who could make compromise sound positively defiant, accepted French air transportation back to Vientiane. Most of their associates accepted the land and river transport to which their Thai friends were only too happy to stake them, provided they would go back across the Mekong whence they came. Prince Souphanouvong and Prince Phetsarath, however, held out until after the 1954 Geneva Agreement, whereby Laos really did seem to them to become, if not in fact independent, at least not absolutely intolerant of their personal aspirations.

Prince Phetsarath stood for monarchy, with himself on the throne; he stood fast in Bangkok for ten years after the others deserted him, and by the time he did return to Laos not long before his death, he constituted no real threat to a king already much feebler even than himself. Prince Souphanouvong stood for armed revolution, and even while he was half collaborating with his half-brothers and with the Thais, he was seeking rapport with Ho Chi Minh, who introduced and recommended him to Mao Tse-tung. When Prince Souphanouvong found Bangkok growing too hot for him even before his brothers found it too cool, he organized in northern Laos the Communist-affiliated Pathet Lao government-in-exile and the Pathet Lao army-in-hiding. Prince Souphanouvong commuted from Laos to Hanoi to Peking, back and forth and round and about. For the next four years nobody much cared, or at least nobody much seemed to care what he was up to. Laos seemed to be making a happy transition from colonialism to independence. Or if it was not, neither the Laotians nor the French said so, at least not very audibly. As for anyone else, Laos was not yet easily accessible by air, and few were adventurous enough to make the long, arduous journey up the Mekong. The

American official presence for a time added up to about ten—a minister and some aid personnel packed into one house and a tent. Dien Bien Phu brought some changes, however, in Laos as elsewhere in Indochina. Viet-Minh troops, flushed with victory, overflowed from Vietnam into Laos, and Prince Souphanouvong was with them. Then came the Geneva Conference of 1954, and the Red Prince showed up there too. He demanded the right to participate as the Pathet Lao Resistance delegate, seated opposite Prince Souvanna Phouma, who represented the royal Lao government. Out of the Geneva settlement Prince Souphanouvong won acknowledgment of *de facto* Pathet Lao military control of the two strategic border provinces of Phong Saly and Sam Neua. He gained also pious agreement that the Pathet Lao forces and provinces would be integrated presently into the rest of the country, with himself presumably playing a key role. He did, but not in the manner which the more innocent of the Geneva conferees envisioned.

Most innocent of all the Geneva conferees appeared to be the United States, which saw or professed to see in the post-Geneva situation in Laos an opportunity to build up free-world strength. Here was a dangerous power vacuum. The United States would fill it. The Department of State and the Pentagon jointly devised a policy of such consummate simplemindedness that neither could have conceived it alone. At the cost of $50 million annually and loss of innocence, they attempted to implement it. The United States, it was decided, would underwrite *in toto* the recruiting, training, and equipping of a 25,000-man Laotian army, whose supervision would be in the hands of the French. It would finance any necessary or desirable or indeed, as it worked out, any feasible imports to Laos, from the sale of which would be realized enough state revenue to pay the army and the civil service, both of which would be indoctrinated in democratic principles, with import, sale, and indoctrination in the hands of the Laotians. Meanwhile it would provide adequate technical and financial assistance for a total program of national development to move Laos quickly out of the sixteenth into the twentieth century. This program was to be supervised by American technical experts who would swiftly be made comfortable, happy, and efficient on an

American standard of living some 1,000 winding miles up the Mekong.

Nobody had to predict to Prince Souphanouvong or even to Prince Souvanna Phouma what was likely to happen and did. The 25,000-man Lao Army, expensively mechanized, consisted for the most part of pacifist payroll padders, and lacked even the initiative to get itself bogged down in the swampy jungle. The aid money poured into and out of the pockets of the politicians and all their relatives and friends, including some Americans. The national development program resulted mainly in the frontier-boom-town expansion of Vientiane where Lao princes and politicians, Thai wetbacks, Chinese businessmen, international free loaders, and Thai and Vietnamese cabaret girls had never had it so good. As for democratic free-world principles, the state had a Constitution, a National Assembly, a series of elections, and it also had about as fancy a political imbroglio as has yet been seen outside of Latin America.

To all this Captain Kong Lê, except during his absence in the Philippines, where scandal, anomaly, venality, and "American influences" made the newspaper headlines daily, was an increasingly unhappy witness. In it Prince Souvanna Phouma, save for a happy two-year interval in Paris as Ambassador to France (1958–60) and also, of course, time for visits to the United States, the Soviet Union, and various midpoints, was a busy and increasingly affluent but not an especially effectual participant. As Prime Minister (1951–53), Minister of Defense (1953–55), and again as Prime Minister (1955–58), he was always a member of the cast. Prince Souphanouvong was sometimes a collaborator or a negotiator, sometimes a fugitive or a jailbird.

After spending the years 1950–57 mainly in the jungle or commuting to Hanoi and Peking, Prince Souphanouvong returned to Vientiane in late 1957 to cash in on the bonanza. As Minister of Planning and Economic Development (November, 1957–September, 1958), he gained control over the outlay of the American millions. The Red Prince's cooperative era began with his 1957 "reconciliation" with the Pink Prince and a concurrent new plan to "integrate" the Pathet Lao with the royal Lao government. It ended in 1959 when the "Young Ones," the junior military and civilian reformers of the Committee in Defense of the National

Interests (CDNI), gained the ascendency. The "Young Ones" presently provoked the Pathet Lao into a small fighting rebellion and then jailed the Red Prince (July 28, 1959). Reconciliation and integration, naturally, were off again for the time being and crisis began to gather momentum.

The penultimate crisis occurred just prior to the Kong Lê insurrection. Prince Souphanouvong, presumably with the knowledge if not with the consent of Prince Souvanna Phouma, made his escape from jail on May 24, 1960. He took fifteen of his lieutenants and a considerable number of his jailers off into the jungle with him to prepare for the inevitable moment of opportunity. To everybody's surprise, not the Red Prince but the Mad Captain seized it. In the meanwhile, little civil bush fires had developed several times into international smoke smudges. Until the moment that the smudges burst into open flame on August 9, 1960, the story is mainly Souvanna Phouma's and Souphanouvong's.

Prince Souvanna Phouma (b. 1901) and Prince Souphanouvong (b. 1912), to begin with the begats, are the sons by different mothers of the Viceroy Prince Ouphat Bounhong (1885–1920). Prince Bounhong was himself the son of the viceroy prince who was killed by Northern Lao invaders on the historic day, June 7, 1887, when King Oun Kham, grandfather of the present king, was spirited over the palace wall in Luang Prabang and across the Mekong to the sanctuary of the new French residency. Auguste Pavie then played the role of protector, benefactor, and friend, as he was presently to play the role of man-behind-the-restored-throne. The royal and the viceregal lines continued parallel through the next few decades, mutually accommodating and mutually suspicious, the viceroy ready and willing to displace the king should the French give the signal. The revolutionary hero, Prince Phetsarath, elder full brother of Prince Souvanna Phouma, was the last of the family to hold viceregal rank but not the last to entertain regal aspirations. Prince Phetsarath, whose antennae were attuned to various international wave lengths, gave his own signal in 1945 and announced the deposition of the king but did not quite risk proclaiming himself monarch.

King Savang Vatthana, whose sense of the historic past is keener than his perception of the confused present and in any event has but one wife and no very impressive male heir, eyes both the Pink and the Red Princes as impatient would-be heirs apparent. The Red Prince himself, ideology notwithstanding, creates the impression in the minds of many observers that he regards himself as more royal than plebeian. Certainly his conduct is imperious, and he demands something akin to obeisance from his subordinates. He has been heard to express envy—but not admiration—for Cambodia's Prince Sihanouk, who rules though he does not reign.

Prince Souvanna Phouma and Prince Souphanouvong were both born in Luang Prabang (two of five half-brothers), but with eleven years' difference in age they grew up practically in different generations of the royal family. They consorted with the offspring of dozens of other princes, most of them men of most extraordinarily polygamous attainment. They romped about freely in the sprawling riverside bungalow which passes as a royal palace. There Good Old King Sisavang Vong, who had at least eleven wives and 100 children of his own, scarcely noticed a few dozen children more or less, save on one tragic occasion when a whole canoeload of his own sons were drowned in the course of one of Luang Prabang's frequent river festivals.

Prince Souvanna Phouma's mother was a royal princess; Prince Souphanouvong's was a commoner (his father's eleventh wife, incidentally), a fact which may or may not account for his vigor and aggressiveness. Both princes left Luang Prabang at an early age to continue their studies in Hanoi. After graduation from the Lycée Albert Sarraut in Hanoi, they proceeded to Paris. Both were keen students and both took degrees in civil engineering, Prince Souvanna Phouma adding a degree in electrical engineering at Grenoble after finishing his earlier studies in Paris. Both returned to Indochina to enter the French civil service, Prince Souvanna Phouma in 1931, and Prince Souphanouvong in 1938.

Prince Souphanouvong was assigned by the French to northern Vietnam but was transferred during the Japanese occupation to Vientiane. Prince Souvanna Phouma served mainly in Vientiane, where he became Director of Public Works. His most important project was the restoration of the once splendid temple, the Wat Phakeo, now an unfortunate pile, its modern form-molded plaster ornamentation being a dubious improvement over its former dilapidation. One of Prince Souvanna Phouma's postwar accomplishments, according to rather untrustworthy rumor, was the sale of the city electric power plant to the Thais just across the river in order to raise money for the revolution. The fact that during his self-imposed exile the prince worked as a salaried employee in Bangkok of the Thai Electricity Company may be the slender basis for the rumor.

Neither of the princes, according to their later statements, liked working for or with the French, who treated them less like royalty than like menials. Both felt that however great might be the need for engineers, the need for political leaders was even greater. As a strict matter of fact, in the prewar years, neither of them had his heart either in politics or in engineering. Prince Souvanna Phouma's heart went, rather, to an extraordinarily beautiful and stylish young French-Lao girl, Mlle. Aline-Claire Allard, the daughter of a French civil servant. He married her in 1933. Prince Souphanouvong's heart went to an equally beautiful and stylish young Vietnamese girl, whom he married shortly after his return to Indochina.

Prince Souvanna Phouma's wife, to leap ahead a bit in the narrative, is now the mother of four children, the eldest of them a beautiful and brilliant daughter. Princess Souvanna Phouma and the children live in Paris, where the children are being educated, and return only occasionally to Vientiane. Prince Souphanouvong's wife was a member of the far left intellectual group of Vietnam when he married her and has moved progressively farther to the left ever since. For a couple of years Princess Souphanouvong was a highly stimulating and ornamental fixture of the Vientiane social circuit, but she prefers today to live in Hanoi. Her seven children are distributed among schools in Hanoi, Peking, and Moscow.

Both princes, when living in Vientiane, used to occupy big old French colonial bungalows. Prince Souphanouvong made quite a show of cultivating a few cabbages and papayas, not much of a garden but still enough to lend the common touch. Prince Souvanna Phouma preferred and still prefers the life of the gentleman farmer at his country place near Xieng Khouang, a few miles up the Mekong.

Prince Souvanna Phouma is by every instinct closely allied to the antebellum southern gentleman. His modest riverside country mansion, an inheritance, incidentally, from his father-in-law, could be set down in any unpainted, unweeded town in Mississippi and scarcely be noticed. On the estate, tenant farmers grow a few desultory bananas and shoot or net a few tired birds and pay rent, if at all, in kind. The Prince also owns a country villa in France. By his own account it is not much different from his place at Xieng Khouang, but he likes it better, France being rather better governed than Laos ever was. At his villa he is indeed lord of the manor, surrounded by loyal villagers for whom his occasional visits—which he would like to make far less infrequent and brief—constitute a major event. The Prince's present town house in Vientiane, a government property and not his own, is one of the biggest, bleakest, and busiest of the city's new stucco and air-conditioned villas, smack on the airport road. It is no place for a man given, as is the Prince, to contemplation.

Prince Souvanna Phouma has the reputation of being a great deal less tough in mind and body than Prince Souphanouvong. Prince Souphanouvong, according to his leftist friends, once worked as a day laborer on the docks of Bordeaux and learned enough about real life and real Frenchmen that on his return to Indochina he was never deceived by the colonialist version. He has also taken part in active combat. Once, when the French shot up a river convoy in 1946, he was so seriously injured that he required prolonged hospitalization, which he was given gratis in Thailand. He later marched with General Giap and the Viet-Minh forces during the period of the Battle of Dien Bien Phu and after the battle entered Laos with a column of Viet-Minh infiltrators. He can and does withstand the rigors of living in the jungle and trekking across untracked mountains. Prince Souvanna Phouma, in contrast, is a better musician than campaigner. He is an authority on traditional Lao songs and instruments and a connoisseur of Western classical music as well. He also excels at cultivating gladioli, as he did in Phnom-Penh during his self-imposed exile in Cambodia.

Both princes have a nice sense of discrimination in wines, tobaccos, and food. Prince Souphanouvong, when he entertains his brother at a jungle rendezvous, enlists Viet-Minh porters or Russian airlift assistance in order to emulate the French field officers in setting a table. The results would probably please even Ho Chi Minh, who was himself once a French chef's assistant in London. Both princes, furthermore, are finicky about their tailoring. Prince Souphanouvong is a tweedy, leather-jacket outdoor type, but there is no comradely nonsense about careless fitting. Prince Souvanna Phouma favors pin-stripe lounge suits. Both prefer the beret for the common touch and a walking stick for a bit of swagger. Both, naturally, speak exquisite French. Prince Souphanouvong likes also to practice his English, but Prince Souvanna Phouma lacks confidence. Neither approves, incidentally, of the rather rarefied French mannerisms of King Savang Vatthana, who became so completely gallicized during his stay in France, which started at the age of ten and continued until he took his university diploma, that on his return to his home country he could not even speak his own language. The King, a kindly man with a winning smile which suddenly lightens a very tired-looking face, prefers still to discourse in French, preferably not about the course of current local events but rather about nineteenth-century French literature and philosophy. He sometimes theorizes about the place of monarchy in a democratic society, but he seems unaware of the proletarian revolution close at hand.

According to common report in 1957, Prince Souphanouvong had both slowed and aged in recent years. During his imprisonment in Vientiane, the theory ran, he had forfeited the leadership of the Pathet Lao to younger, even tougher men. During his incumbency as Minister of Planning, to be sure, he had shown himself notably vigorous and decisive, and indeed, even by standards other than those of Laos, positively efficient. In the recurrent periods of Souphanouvong-Souvanna Phouma negotiations, furthermore, there had never been any doubt who was the quicker, the sharper, or the more determined as to what he wanted—and got. But Prince Souphanouvong, the argument went, was at once a feudal aristocrat and a Westernized intellectual and hence doubly suspect to the extremists. As he himself went to some pains to point out, although not quite in so many words, if indeed he were a Marxist, he was of the left-wing Socialist rather than the doctrinaire Communist variety. To the increasingly rigid Viet-Minh Communists, who were his allies, this spelled deviationism. Besides, did not his half-brother vouch for him that he was in fact no Communist but a nationalist, a patriot, even a monarchist? Such an endorsement, quite possibly by calculation, did him no good with the comrades.

Prince Souphanouvong, many usually well-informed observers concluded, had become a figurehead. If so, immediately after his escape he converted himself into a particularly animated figurehead. In contrast with Prince Souvanna Phouma, who often seems rather plumpishly and pompously phlegmatic, given to both physical and mental indisposition, Prince Souphanouvong seems generally fit and buoyant.

The two princes, despite major differences of personality and of politics, seems to entertain a genuine affection for each other. This is the one small fact which makes the bewildering Laotian developments of recent years just slightly more comprehensible. Neither brother seems disposed deliberately to betray the other, although, on the other hand, neither seems inhibited about taking advantage of the other whenever and however he can. Both seem, in fact, rather to enjoy the exercise of matching wits. The farce they acted out a few years ago, while seeming to comply with the expectations of the Geneva conferees that they would reduce and merge their armies, gives the clue that possibly they do not expect anyone else to take their posturings more seriously than they do themselves. Prince Souphanouvong then demobilized the more indisciplinary elements of his guerrilla troops, only to re-enlist them presently in the royal Laotian army at a base pay of $130 per year—munificent, by Laotian standards, plus quarters, rations, uniforms, guns, and opportunity for subversion.

Prince Souvanna Phouma meanwhile pulled a few fast *ipso post facto* changes about the rank he had agreed to confer upon the officers and men who did openly merge. Prince Souphanouvong, as it turned out, retained the trumps. He kept his elite troops, some 1,500 of them, in strategically located provincial camps where, said the Vientiane dandies, they looked and acted like Gypsies. Later when the Royal Lao Army tried to surround them, like Gypsies they quietly melted away only to regroup, attack, and batter the royal army troops themselves.

The royal brothers, like Captain Kong Lê, were visible only in the wings during the latter half of 1959 while the pressures were building up toward the 1960 explosion. Prince Souvanna

Phouma was in Paris, Prince Souphanouvong was in jail, and Kong Lê was as yet unknown. In late July, 1959, just at the beginning of the rainy season, when neither guerrilla foot soldiers nor mechanized royal troops could move through the jungles, there occurred something described by the Vientiane government as a "full-scale Viet-Minh invasion" of the border provinces. "Thousands of refugees" were suddenly sighted milling about the town and airfield of remote little Sam Neua and the headquarters of tough "fight-to-the-finish" General Amkha Soukhavong. Royal Laotian military intelligence put loaded questions to the refugees, also to some royal Laotian soldiers who happened to be fleeing past. From the answers they extrapolated an "invasion force" of 10,000 heavily armed North Vietnamese.

The invasion force, so far as anyone else could determine, moved only across the pin-studded outline maps at army headquarters. Foreign newspapermen dispatched stories of mysteriously evanescent invaders whom nobody could ever quite see, meet, or identify. A United Nations subcommittee, which arrived in response to a panicky Laotian government request for military aid, found evidence of virtually nothing except excitement, and even that, in sleepy little Sam Neua, of a flickering variety.

The Sam Neua "invasion," which the international world feared might trigger World War III, triggered in fact only a coup in Vientiane. General Phoumi decided to hold a rigged election, and the winning party, the CDNI, decided to make sure of retaining power. General Phoumi and the CDNI, therefore, staged a military coup (December, 1959) by which they overthrew Prime Minister Phoui. The King, pressured by Western ambassadors who feared disorders, appointed not the Strong General Phoumi but gentle, aged, inactivist Kou Abhay as Prime Minister. Both of them now disgusted, Phoui and Phoumi collaborated to rig the subsequent April 24, 1960, elections, after which the King, yielding once again to Western pressure, appointed neither Phoui nor Phoumi as Prime Minister but the "pleasant" Tiao Somsanith.

At this point ex-Prime Minister Phoui conceded the field to anyone who wanted it and departed for a rest cure in France. General Phoumi, in anticipation of the next ploy, tightened up discipline in the armed services. The CDNI, meanwhile, got tough about loyalty in the ministries, most of which it controlled.

For reasons which escaped the outside observer, Prince Souvanna Phouma decided that this was the propitious moment to return from France and assume the post of Foreign Minister. For equally mysterious reasons, Prince Souphanouvong chose this as the moment to escape from prison and vanish into the night, together with his jailers. The general population of Vientiane, although it was little moved by the other excitements, was stirred momentarily by the Red Prince's Count of Monte Cristo exploit of May 24. It soon relapsed, however, into its more accustomed state, one which even the Laotians, seeking French-wise the *mot juste,* described as euphoria.

While Prince Souphanouvong and Prince Souvanna Phouma, newly returned to their accustomed elements, were presumably maneuvering to have another go at their particular variety of disintegration, suddenly Captain Kong Lê anticipated them and staged his coup on August 9. The Mad Captain set himself up as Chef du Coup d'État. The White General set himself up in Savannakhet in the South as Chef du Comité du Contre-Coup d'État. Captain Kong Lê called upon the Pink Prince to be his Prime Minister and rejected a compromise coalition government headed by the Jolly Prince Boun Oum, which the Pink Prince and the White General tried to splice together in Luang Prabang. So Captain Kong Lê went on managing his coup as though it were a cabinet. The Pink Prince, to be sure, graciously accepted titular position as Prime Minister. The sinister "librarian," by name Quinim Pholsena, became Information Minister. The real business of the coup, however, was entrusted to the soldiers, students, and priests, who served as rioters, and to the Russians who served presently as logisticians. The coup went whirling along until the Jolly Prince and the White General, backed by the United States, mounted a successful attack from Savannakhet. The Pink Prince then flew off to Cambodia, commandeering the entire small commercial fleet of Royal Air Laos planes to transport himself, five of his ministers, and enough of his chattels and retainers to tide him over for a few months. Kong Lê withdrew to the Plaine des Jarres. General Phoumi occupied Vientiane. The international world set itself to devising a new Geneva Agreement whereby the Red Prince, the Pink Prince, the White Prince, the

Mad Captain and everyone else could happily reunite in a government from which the White General could virtually retire.

It is advisable perhaps, to pause to introduce some of the newcomers to the scenario. The Jolly Prince Boun Oum, to begin with, has acquired even among the Lao the reputation for being rather an unusually exuberant and boisterous *bon vivant*. Technically, he is heir to the Southern Laotian kingdom of Champasak, whose throne he renounced, however, when King Sisavang Vong was declared monarch of a united Laos and he himself became "Inspector General of the Realm." He renounced the throne but few if any of its perquisites. As a matter of fact, reigning as king might have interfered with his true avocation, which, in all senses of the word, is the chase.

Prince Boun Oum's addiction to the chase—also his professional level skill at boxing in the rough-and-ready Thai fashion—form the basis for an enduring friendship with one of his Champasak subjects, General Phoumi Nosavan. Prince Boun Oum shares also with General Phoumi a record of leadership during and after the Japanese occupation of the Lao Youth Organization, i.e., the nationalist movement. The prince, incidentally, holds the most impressive collection of decorations in all of Laos save only that of the king. Among them are the Ordre de Mérite Civique, the Croix de Guerre, the Ordre du Regne, Chevalier du Million d'Éléphants, Officier du Million d'Éléphants, and the Commandeur du Million d' Éléphants.

Prince Boun Oum and General Phoumi, despite their sporting pursuits, had little use for the sinister "gunsmith," Quinim Pholsena, who seemed, in fact, to almost all of the other leaders except Souphanouvong and Kong Lê to be rather a boorish upstart. Quinim Pholsena, whose father was Chinese, was accepted at an early age as a foster son by the mother of Prince Souphanouvong. He made an outstanding record in traditional studies for the mandarinate and rose fast in the French colonial administration. Later he was elected vice-president of the National Assembly of the independent nation. Quinim Pholsena, who ran the only bookstore in Vientiane which stocked very many English-language books, mostly paperbacks, was closely associated with trade. A good part of the aristocracy, at least until it got into the American-aid-financed trade itself, very firmly put him in his place.

Their concerted snub may be a factor which helped account for what was generally regarded as his embittered, quarrelsome disposition.

After the latest Geneva settlement, the Red, Pink, and White gentry reassembled in Vientiane to attempt a troika, although a tandem had already stripped its gears. The King, accompanied by almost everybody else, including Quinim Pholsena, soon headed off on a bout of good-will visits to thank the international world for setting up the neutralized government which almost nobody was actually left at home to run, but many to sabotage. Captain Kong Lê, now a general, consorted happily on the Plaine des Jarres with the Viet-Minh. There were in fact, however, three armed services in the field—the Red, the White, and the Pink (the Pink being Kong Lê's "neutralist" supporters of Prince Souvanna Phouma).

Before long the travelers returned and the Red and the Pink troops began to gun for each other. General Kong Lê's right-hand-man was murdered by the Reds. Quinim Pholsena, then Foreign Minister, was murdered by the Pinks. Kong Lê's troops were subjected repeatedly to artillery barrage by the Viet-Minh. The U. N. Control Commission (still Polish, Indian, and Canadian in composition) was deadlocked over almost all really significant issues. The Indian chairman, however, proved more neutral this time in favor of the Pinks than of the Reds, especially after some U.N. helicopters were shot up and some Indian personnel killed by the Reds, events which synchronized with the Chinese-Indian border dispute. Prince Souphanouvong departed Vientiane presently to take up residence on the Plaine des Jarres, where Prince Souvanna Phouma frequently dined with him. Prince Souphanouvong, naturally, began to make new demands, refusing to negotiate and threatening to fight. The Laos crisis, in other words, in 1963 resumed its accustomed aspect of explosive opacity.

Probably the best political consultant for anyone wishing a forecast of Laotian developments would be an experienced astrologer of the sort who is to be found, generally, in the cool, quiet compound of the *wat,* where all of the leading characters in the Laotian national drama are likely to pay him visits. Of the visitors, one of the most assiduous in the past, not for purposes of having his horoscope cast, however, but rather to bring the horoscope-casters themselves up to date on the mood and will of the people, has been Prince Souphanouvong. Another has been Captain Kong Lê. Prince Souvanna Phouma has showed up mainly to get the priestly blessing for each of his new governments and King Savang Vatthana to invoke divine guidance for his reign. Prince Souphanouvong and Captain Kong Lê have managed, in the recent past, to stir the drowsing priests to burst out of their cells to yell and sing in demonstrations.

In Laos, the Land of the White Parasol (symbolizing the Lord Buddha) and of the Million Elephants (symbolizing the crown), the elephants these days seem outmoded and outnumbered, but the white parasol may perhaps soon be dyed and retailored into a red flag. The Red Prince and the Mad Captain conduct themselves on that assumption. Neither the Pink Prince nor the White General, each a sporting gentleman, would be likely to give odds that they are wrong.

From *Thakin* to
Bo to Chairman

Burma's revolutionary dictator, General Ne Win, lives with the knowledge that in 1946 some of the Burmese revolutionaries violently eliminated the nation's first great nationalist leader, General Aung San, and that in 1962 some others—of whom he was one— "gently" jailed its second, Prime Minister U Nu. In now seeking to combine Aung San's verve and U Nu's vision, both of which seemed to many outsiders to be a bit overrated and in any event basically incompatible, General Ne Win seeks also to achieve for himself, his revolutionary followers, and his dreamily turbulent nation, a harmonious adjustment between the extremes of gentleness and violence which seem peculiarly characteristic of Burma, past and present. The gentleness makes for the ethereal Burmese personality, which can contemplate the golden Swedagon Pagoda and ignore the filthy slums nearby. The violence makes for the Burmese dacoit predilection which leads many a peasant to abandon his plough and pick up a gun in order to loot the gold he may offer next day at the pagoda.

General Ne Win himself seems neither as vigorous nor as sagacious today as he used to be, and he seems more and more to favor compulsion over persuasion. Having caused himself to be declared heir to the mantles of both Aung San and U Nu, he has the extremely delicate job of retailoring the garments to fit his rather less supple person. The Burmese nation, meanwhile, is living with the memory or the actuality of three highly diverse national heroes: Aung San the dynamic, U Nu the serene, Ne Win the irascible. All of them were intimately known to each other and at one time or another they tried deliberately and none too successfully to compensate for each other's weaknesses. Many of the leading Burmese seem less given to emulation of any one particular example than to contemplation of who and what may come next.

To the normally observant outsider, General Ne Win, U Nu, and General Aung San, for all their conflicting temperaments, have seemed sometimes rather like Burmese triplets, and their careers have been so inextricably interwoven that it is difficult to determine who first thought, did, or said exactly what. General Ne Win today, for instance, after displacing U Nu largely because he thought U Nu was becoming too mistily religious-minded to head the state, is beginning to inject massive dosages of U Nu's Buddhist philosophy into the Marxist political economics which trace to Aung San. General Ne Win's speeches today, furthermore, are interlarded not only with the religious and political pieties of U Nu but with his coexistentialist dogma as well, albeit in far less polished prose, just as they are loaded also with the revolutionary theory of Aung San, albeit without Aung San's homely awareness of practicality. General Ne Win is quite capable one day of demanding or implementing such dramatic revolutionary policy as foreclosure on private enterprise, especially the foreign owned, and next day of deploring worldwide lack of confidence and security. "It is regrettable to note," he has said and has many times elaborated with detached disenchantment upon more or less the same theme, "that at the present time, such cardinal virtues as mutual trust, magnanimity and the spirit of cooperation are almost nonexistent."

Pronouncements like the above help to account for a most unmilitary sort of elusiveness about the person and the personality of General Ne Win. In enacting the role of Burma's savior, he seems sometimes mysteriously to have absented himself from the stage just at the time that the scenery was being arranged. Even when physically present, he seems to be not exactly the trim, decisive, commanding military figure of his photographs. It is as though General Aung San, too, were hovering nearby, in his dirty, smelly old khakis, urging the people to awaken and to act, and as though U Nu were meditating in the wings, radiating somnolence and resignation. General Ne Win, not unnaturally, seems a bit distracted by the ectoplasmic interference.

So the story of General Ne Win, unavoidably—and happily, since the other two are more winning and hence more characteristically Burmese types—introduces as a supporting cast both U Nu and Aung San and others of somewhat less speculative past or future than the general himself.

General Ne Win was born on May 14, 1911, in the hamlet of Paungdede in the town of Paungde in the District of Prome in Central Burma. His father, U (Mr.) Po Hka, came from a provincial family of modest circumstances and held the job of government revenue surveyor for the Paungde area. U Po Hka's job was classified in the lower level of the civil service scale, so he drew a monthly salary of about forty rupees ($12.50). Unlike most civil servants, he actually did get out and work with his hands, carrying a chain measure to determine the amount of land on which the people had to pay their taxes. U Po Hka's wife, Daw (Mrs.) Mi Lay, managed to keep the household going on her husband's minute salary. Like most Burmese housewives, she was content with living facilities which meant little more than a roof, four walls, and a cooking pot. She was able by shrewd bargaining and occasional minor dealings on her own in market produce to make budgetary ends more or less meet.

U Po Hka and Daw Mi Lay, each retaining in the Burmese style their personal names, which reveal nothing of family or matrimonial affiliations, named their son Shu Maung. Since the "Shu" is not distinctively Burmese, the name suggests that there was probably a Chinese strain on one side of the family. Young Shu Maung grew up as an ordinary Burmese village boy, undistinguished for industry, athletic prowess, or academic proficiency. He was distinguished, if for anything, in that, unlike most village boys, he was unable to swim and was only mildly interested in the *nats,* the capricious and ubiquitous spirits of Burmese folklore. His father did assure him of much better than ordinary prospects, however, by sending him off to Prome for English-language secondary education in a government school. Shu Maung, his devout Buddhist family no doubt assumed, would fulfill his *karma;* as he went on to newer things, for better or for worse, he would possibly decide to change his name—as indeed he later did—in order to signify a fresh start and to gain propitious spiritual vibrations. It never seems to have crossed anyone's mind, certainly not his teachers', that Shu Maung was headed for the top.

Shu Maung proceeded from Paungde to Rangoon in 1931 to enroll in the University College. He signed up for the literary course, which was regarded as the easiest the institution had to offer. At the end of the first year, however, he failed his examinations and was firmly advised to withdraw. Shu Maung's mistake—or perhaps it was his *karma*—was that as an agreeable and handsome country boy he had fallen in with fast company. He had been bedazzled by Rangoon's rather dim city lights and gratified by the quick and easy acceptance he gained into a set of young-men-about-town who mistook Sule Pagoda Circus for Piccadilly. He had made the heady discovery that he had an attraction for women, a capacity for wine, and a gift for song. He had discovered, furthermore, that he had a natural gift which could be parlayed into profit. Athletics, soldiering, and politics were all to come later. This was a flair for spotting winners at the races.

Shu Maung became an habitué of the Rangoon Turf Club, a pivotal feature of British colonial society. The Turf Club was also the resort of most Burmese who were Anglicized enough to like sport or who could afford the price of admission in order to gamble—two categories which included just about everyone who counted. Shu Maung's flutters on the races earned him a nice but not altogether reliable little income. They also gave him entree to more serious university types, those who preferred, rather than distract themselves from academic study in order to analyze the racing forms, to plunge with him in his betting pools. Shu Maung's university career, consequently, was far from being the complete failure it seemed, for he became well and favorably known to some of the academic and society leaders who were soon to become politicians.

During the next few years, nevertheless, Shu Maung went through an extremely unhappy period. His academic hopes had been blighted. His romantic life led him into a youthful marriage with a young woman who was a frugal housekeeper, as she needed to be under the circumstances, a good mother to the two children who were born in quick succession, but not the educated, sophisticated wife who could move in the circles which Shu

Maung himself preferred. He had been forced to take a steady job to support himself and his family, and he had made the unhappy discovery that with his limited educational qualifications he could rate only the lower level of the civil service. It never seems to have occurred to him, as it seems rarely to have occurred to any other tolerably well educated young Burmese, to look for employment outside of government. He settled for a clerical job in the Churchill Street Post Office in Rangoon at a monthly pay of about seventy-five to eighty-five rupees ($25–28). Nobody seems to remember whether he was a good or an indifferent postal clerk, but he was certainly a discontented one.

Shu Maung's growing dissatisfaction with his status was shared by a great many young Burmese of his period. Some, like him, were working at jobs which they regarded as far beneath their competence or their dignity. Others were still university students but were anticipating difficulties yet to come. Almost without exception, they identified British colonialism as the source of their own and their nation's troubles. The more forceful and articulate of these young men in 1930 formed an amorphous sort of discussion society called the Dobama Asiayone (We Burmans). Partly in derogation of the British, partly as a display of self-confidence, they addressed each other as Thakin (Master), a term heretofore reserved for the Europeans. They were asserting, they said, their own equality with the British and their determination to achieve an egalitarian Burmese society. The activists among them, particularly the university student leaders, began to stir up student and labor demonstrations such as have been a lively feature of Burmese life ever since.

Shu Maung, naturally, soon became Thakin Shu Maung, a distant but not yet an intimate associate of the two most famous Thakins of all, Thakin Aung San and Thakin Nu. Thakin Nu was known for having transformed himself at the age of fifteen from an extraordinarily precocious tippler and idler into the aspirant G. B. Shaw of Burma. He was also a devout young man who often took time before starting his academic and literary day to join the pilgrims in sweeping the platform of the Swedagon Pagoda. Thakin Aung San was known for his uncharacteristically Burmese antipathy to bathing, changing his clothes, exchanging normal conversational courtesies, or speaking slowly enough or

correctly enough (in English) that he could be readily understood. He was known also for being almost oblivious to hunger,
bedbugs, or flattery, for practicing before a mirror the mannerisms
of a commanding general, and for practicing upon anyone who
would listen a torrent of oratory about all aspects of Burmese
politics, economics and society, especially the colonial.

Thakin Aung San, as editor of the student newspaper *Oway*
(Cry of the Peacock) suffered the martyrdom of expulsion for
publishing an article entitled "Hell Hound At Large," in which
he attacked the university administration. Thakin Nu, who had
recently failed to provoke the British to arrest him when he
burned the Union Jack in front of the high court or to expel him
when he condemned "slave education," now managed by fiery
speeches to rally the whole university student body to the Thakin
cause. With Thakin Aung San and Thakin Nu strategizing the
campaign, 700 students provisioned themselves with sardines,
marched into downtown Rangoon, and squatted at the Swedagon, there to parley and pray and put out protests as fast as
they could compose them. Thakin Shu Maung was a spectator,
not a participant in these stirring events, but when the next
round started he was in the ring.

The Thakins decided they needed outside help. They made
overtures, therefore, to the Chinese and to the Japanese, both of
whose consular representatives had exhibited an interest in
Burmese nationalist protest. Their own problems—and those of
the Chinese and the Japanese in replying to their advances—were
not simplified by the fact that various of the Thakins were going
through soul-searching phases. Some were autointoxicated with
Marxism—Aung San, for instance, had organized the Burmese
Communist Party; some were disillusioned with militarism—the
Japanese campaign in China seemed to many of them imperialist
aggression; some were skeptical about Asian democracy—Chiang
Kai-shek's implementation of Sun Yat-sen's teachings gave rise
to doubts.

The Chinese were noncommittal. So were the Japanese, who, it
seemed, according to Thakin Aung San's later report, regarded
them as a pack of Bolsheviks. The British precipitated matters,
however, when they put out a warrant for Thakin Aung San's
arrest on charges of sedition and offered a five-rupee (U.S. $1.75)

reward for information as to his whereabouts—a calculated insult, said the Thakins, who felt that a 5,000-rupee reward would have been more tactful. Thakin Aung San, accompanied by one Thakin Hla Myaing (now a Communist), on August 6, 1940, slipped out of Rangoon on a Chinese freighter, the pair of them disguised as Chinese sailors. In Amoy, the two émigrés, now Tan Luang Shuang and his companion, awaited overtures from anyone who cared to make them. The Japanese nibbled first, and they proceeded by air to Tokyo. There they were met by a certain Mr. Minami, who turned out presently to be a certain Colonel Suzuki, an agent whom the Japanese Army rather unenthusiastically staked to a mild gamble on these rather seedy-looking prospects. Colonel Suzuki invited the two Thakins to a modest country inn to talk things over. His hospitality included an offer of girls, which the Thakins shyly declined, although Aung San later was to become lyrical about Japanese women. Presently he offered military training for a whole group of young Burmese if the Thakins could assemble them and deliver them to Taiwan.

In March, 1941, a rather peculiar-looking Omoda Monji San, purser on a Japanese freighter, went ashore at Bassein, hired a rickshaw which delivered him to the wrong address—the house of a well-known pimp. Presently, however, he found the man he was really looking for, and when he had removed kimono, geta, and false teeth, there was Thakin Aung San, back to recruit the now famous "Thirty Companions." As soon as the word spread, the Thakins began volunteering. Some were teachers or students, some were petty officials, one was a mendicant who traveled with a monkey. Thakin U Nu was not among them; he was in a British prison, where he remained until the outbreak of the Pacific War, but then, as he himself admitted, he was an unlikely candidate for the army. Thakin Shu Maung was one of the first to make himself free to travel.

The Thirty Companions smuggled themselves out of Burma in mid-1941, traveling on Japanese freighters disguised as Japanese crew members, and presently they reassembled on Taiwan. There the "Thakins" became "Bos," the traditional Burmese term for military officers now being adopted both as title and familiar form of address. Bo Shu Maung adapted with rather less difficulty than did most of the others to the extremely arduous six-month-long regime which the Japanese laid out for them. Accommodations were Spartan, food was both bad and unfamiliar, discipline was rigorous, and the training was so rugged that many at times fainted from exhaustion. Two of the thirty, disgusted both with the routine and the Japanese, defected from the group. Bo Shu Maung, however, seemed to thrive. He acquired physical strength and vigor such as had never characterized him earlier, and he rated with his Japanese mentors as perhaps third or fourth best in the outfit.

Bo Aung San, who was promoted informally by his companions to Bogyoke (Generalissimo) Aung San, rated first. He was physically slight and always looked both undernourished and underwashed, but he had nerves and muscles of steel and he was sustained through the roughest going by an inner fire. Bo Let Ya, Bo Aung San's closest associate and Bo Shu Maung's closest friend —until in later years Bo Let Ya chose to go into business and become a rich capitalist—probably rated second. All were thoroughly toughened by the time they finished the course on Taiwan, the continuation on Hainan, and a short postgraduate course for which the Japanese shipped them off to the fighting zone in China, in order, as Colonel Suzuki described it, "to blood them up in combat."

The Thirty Companions (in fact there were now only 28) were ready and willing when Japan precipitated the war in the Pacific. They accompanied the Japanese forces into Thailand and in Bangkok laid their plans for a Burma campaign. There they recruited a few hundred Burmese and Burmese-Thai volunteers, intending with this small force as the nucleus of a new Burma Independence Army (BIA) to march on Rangoon, recruiting more and more volunteers as they went. They believed they could thus preclude the need for any major Japanese army operation or a full-scale Japanese occupation. The Japanese, of course, had other plans, but the Thirty Companions, on the eve of battle, envisioned themselves as the liberators and rulers of Burma.

At the suggestion of Bogyoke Aung San, they decided to take new names in order to signal this bright new departure in their own lives and that of the nation. Bogyoke Aung San chose the name Te Za (meaning "powerful") but soon reverted to Aung San. Bo Shu Maung chose the name Ne Win ("brilliant as the sun"), and since he had no particular desire to remind anyone of the former Shu Maung, he retained it thereafter. Colonel Suzuki, incidentally, became Bo Mo-gyo ("thunderbolt") and began to act very, very Burmese, favoring the *longyi,* the Burmese sarong, for leisure-time wear and the Burmese language for ordinary conversation, much to the amusement of his now highly Japanized companions.

The Bos did not always seem heroic to each other, even during their most histrionic phases. The Burmese sense of the ludicrous prevailed over self-importance. Bo Yan Aung (Thakin Hla Myaing) thus can reminisce today about Bo Aung San: "Aung San would often be wrapped in thought. . . . Once Aung San was late for a staff meeting, and Min Gaung had to hurry him on. On the way to the meeting, Min Gaung had to fix the buttons that the general had done wrong, buckle the sword that dragged, and finally, stop Aung San, who complained that his boots were pinching him and take the boots off and put the right one on the right foot."

Bo Ne Win, along with several of the others, actually preceded the Japanese forces into Burma, crossing the border even before Japan had declared war on the British. Colonel Suzuki dispatched them, it seems, on his own authority, perhaps in disobedience to his own superiors. At any rate, he explained to the Bos that the Japanese military command would disapprove but he would say the Bos had escaped and thus the BIA plan of operations would go into effect. On signal from Bangkok, Bo Ne Win and his companions began marching on Rangoon, collecting volunteers as they went, all in accordance with the plan except that the main Japanese forces marched too, and so far as the military campaign was concerned, the Japanese conducted it.

The Burma Independence Army, possibly because it did practically no fighting, mushroomed into an unwieldy, unorganized, untrained, undisciplined force of some 50,000. Even in the opinion of many of the Bos, it was a "rabble army," for it attracted not only students and teachers, who were often motivated by patriotism, but a footloose riffraff who were motivated by practically anything else, mainly by the Burmese dacoit tradition of ruffians and brigands. To whatever BIA unit cared to accept it, the Japanese delegated responsibility for military government. The BIA thereupon staged an orgy of rape, loot, and murder, the memory of which still creates trouble today between the new Burmese national army and the villagers. At the end of the war the returning British compiled frightful evidence of BIA atrocities. They even prepared—but did not pursue—a case against Bogyoke Aung San, who was personally implicated, they said, in some of the excesses of the BIA kangaroo courts. Bogyoke Aung San, of course, had been first in command of the BIA; Bo Let Ya was his Chief of Staff; Bo Ne Win shared with one Bo Zeya (now a Communist guerrilla) the command in the field.

Once they had consolidated their hold upon Burma, the Japanese made an effort to restore order to the countryside and among the BIA troops. They dissolved the BIA as such and from some of the least unpromising of its remnants organized three battalions which became known as the Burma Defense Army. When Bogyoke (presently Major General) Aung San became Defense Minister in the new "independent" Burmese government, Bo (presently Colonel) Ne Win became Commander-in-Chief. Colonel Ne Win, having few troops to command, devoted himself mainly to intrigue. The others of the Thirty Companions were in a mutinous mood, and Colonel Ne Win's office became their conspiratorial cell. They were angry with the Japanese for having deceived them all along the line. They found ready allies among the civil officials—Thakin Nu, for instance, now the Foreign Minister, whose official function was so exclusively the dispatch of congratulatory messages to the chiefs of the Axis states on each anniversary or victory that he himself referred to the Foreign Ministry as "the Telegraph Office."

Bogyoke Aung San, Bo Ne Win, and Thakin Nu could not accomplish much while the Japanese were strong, but as Japanese defeat became a certainty, they devised the strategy which put the Burmese nationalists more or less on the side of the victorious Allies, more or less in time to avoid reprisals. Bogyoke Aung San, with Japanese consent, ordered the Burma Defense Army into the Irrawaddy Delta to resist the re-entry of the British. Once his troops were in the field, Bo Ne Win announced that they would fight against the Japanese and cooperate with the British. Bo Ne Win himself participated in a few of the sharp encounters which occurred between Japanese and Burmese troops before the Japanese army collapsed in the face of the Allies.

Restoration of British military and civil authority in Burma resulted in even worse chaos than had its collapse four years earlier. The British proposed to rehabilitate the country first, to talk politics later. The Burmese demanded firm assurances of independence before they would cooperate. General Aung San, whom the British, after long indecision, decided to treat as a patriot rather than to try as a traitor, eventually won the Burmese point. Thakin Nu, meanwhile, had gone into virtual retirement, from which he emerged only at Aung San's insistence. Colonel Ne Win had the job of converting the old Burma Defense Army into the new Burma Forces, which the British expected to be subject to their control and the Burmese nationalists expected to remain subject to theirs. About the Burma Defense Army were rallying certain new forces, one of them the paramilitary branch of the newly organized nationalist political party, the Anti-Fascist Peoples' Freedom League, or AFPFL; another was the People's Volunteer Army, which was virtually indistinguishable from a Communist organization.

These and other armed and semi-armed conglomerates were all too unhappily reminiscent of the lawless Burma Independence Army of 1945. Among Colonel Ne Win's Thirty Companions were Communists, crypto-Communists, and extreme nationalists who were eager to assume control of any or all of these forces, recruit still more, and fight the British and each other. Colonel Ne Win had to work fast to retain even the loyalty of the troops most immediately under his own command. His onetime colleague, Colonel (Bo) Soe, was plying them not only with inflammatory Communist propaganda but with little extras which he was able for a time to persuade the British to fly in to him— nylons, for instance, and lipsticks for the camp followers.

British capitulation (January 27, 1947) to Burmese demands for independence seemed for a time to ease the situation. But six months later (July 19, 1947) General Aung San was assassinated by gunmen in the hire of U Saw, a brilliant but unstable prewar Prime Minister implicated in wartime treason, who was infuriated by the thought that a man whom he regarded as a barbarian was assuming national leadership. Thakin Nu was called on to complete the negotiations with the British and then to become Prime Minister of a new nation which almost nobody thought could survive. Colonel Ne Win was called on to restore order in a capital city where guerrilla warfare went on in the streets and even schoolboys went armed and were virtually indistinguishable, in any event, from the youthful cabinet ministers. In the countryside three major armed forces were fighting the government and each other. The distant border states, which remembered the BIA, were about to go into active insurrection. Colonel Ne Win at this point had perhaps 5,000 poorly trained troops who would accept his command; the rest had defected to the various feuding guerrilla forces.

As a matter of strict chronological fact, Colonel Ne Win was not yet actually in command. General Aung San, whose relations with Ne Win had become somewhat strained for reasons which were even then obscure, had named Let Ya as his choice for the command of the new Burma army. But Let Ya, whose own relations with Ne Win also became strained during this period, for reasons of his own preferred to go into politics and then into business. The government named Lieutenant General Smith-Dun as new Commanding Officer. His Chief of Staff was Brigadier Shi Sho. His Chief of Operations was Brigadier Kya Doe. Colonel Ne Win was Deputy Chief of Staff. The general and the two brigadiers, however, were British-trained Karen State nationals and hence doubly suspect to the Rangoon nationalists, who feared British influence and anticipated Karen State insurrection. The insurrection quickly materialized; the general and the two brigadiers retired; Colonel Ne Win was named Commander in Chief, said his critics both then and later, either by reason of his political reliability or sheer chance, not because of his military accomplishments.

Prime Minister Nu and General Ne Win brought off the job which only a very few outsiders thought they ever had much chance of accomplishing. Gradually, between 1948 and 1952, they established a reasonable degree of order and security—not enough, to be sure, to enable Burma to make any very significant progress, but enough to save it from outright collapse into anarchy.

Thakin—now once again by preference U (Mr.) Nu, or sometimes Ko (Elder Brother) Nu—emerged as the "serene statesman." He epitomized those virtues of piety, charity, and sincerity which the Burmese manage to talk about and to espouse without appearing to be sanctimonious. U Nu seemed personally irradiated by an inner fluorescence. His eyes glowed with kindness and wisdom. His voice inspired delight by the melodic precision of his diction. His philosophic aura remained undimmed even when he enunciated at formidable length with pedantic elaboration of sentitious irrelevancies the eight foundations of Buddhist socialism, or the five principles of neutralist coexistence and internationalism, or the five labors of civic love.

U Nu, wearing the sandals, *longyi* jacket, and pointed headdress of an office clerk; refraining from meat, drink, tobacco, or sexual intercourse; retiring to a monastery to let the flame within him smoulder whenever it threatened either to blaze up or to burn out—U Nu seemed so good, so gentle, so joyous that it was almost vulgar to inquire where, other than into a Buddhist socialist nirvana, he was in fact leading the nation. To those who thought their eyes were wide open, he seemed to be leading it rather dreamily through the thickets of national self-determination, or, as it seemed to a great many others, of alternating self-abnegation and self-despoliation. He led the international world into despairing acceptance of the thesis that nothing much could be done in, by, or about Burma, but that perhaps it did not much matter. He led his political associates and opponents eventually into a fury of bafflement which many of them, including in the end General Ne Win, decided was in fact deliberate. It took two more than usually diffuse crises and one well organized interregnum, however, to bring to an end the curious U Nu-Ne Win partnership, one of mutual disassociation.

U Nu wanted nothing to do with the army, and Ne Win wanted nothing to do with politics, and for ten years they enjoyed each other's confidence on that *ad hoc* basis. Ne Win wanted to organize, discipline, train, equip, and command an army which would be an efficient fighting force capable of establishing and maintaining order. He had had his fill of a rabble army dabbling violently in everybody's business when it was not more actively engaged in subversion. Ne Win, finding his forces automatically purged by reason of the defection of most of the dissident elements, explained to his officers, his men, the politicians, and the general public his simple aspiration to form a competent army, free from political influences. U Nu agreed enthusiastically, especially since Ne Win was content to forego badly needed foreign military assistance—save for a British military mission and officer training in Commonwealth countries—in order to avoid the international complications of nonneutralism.

By international standards, Ne Win's 50,000–100,000-man army is not very well trained and not very well equipped, nor a particularly impressive fighting force. By Southeast Asian standards, however, it is relatively honest, loyal, and politically detached. The officer corps, for the most part, has not acquired, or at least it has not conspicuously displayed, an insatiable taste for big houses, cars and privileges. The troops do not normally make a spectacle of themselves by swaggering, bullying, or just taking their ease, although deplorable lapses into rowdyism and brigandage do occur. As a result of Burma's dedication to the practice of state socialism without making any provision for trained state socialists, the army years ago inherited as much by default as by design the control of major segments of the nation's economic life, including the critical export of rice and the import and distribution of manufactured goods. Along with control came corruption, but again, by Southeast Asian standards, the Burmese army itself has been until recently, at least, relatively poor and honest.

While General Ne Win was building up a military force capable of taking if not necessarily of exercising control, U Nu was building up a series of political crises which eventually proved beyond his capacity to resolve by counsels of philosophy or maneuvers of politics. His AFPFL split apart. His own right-wing segment sought alliance with the non-AFPFL leftists, including near-Communists. The leftist section sought alliance with the non-AFPFL rightists, including secessionists. U Nu suddenly sought rapport with Ne Win, and on October 28, 1958, turned the government over to him—with the approval of the Parliament—on a temporary caretaker basis pending new elections. U Nu himself turned to monastic contemplation, interrupted only for electioneering.

General Ne Win called in his colonels and gave the orders. After some little delay the colonels devised and carried out crash programs to achieve certain relatively clear and limited objectives. They launched a campaign to bring some of the more corrupt of the political and economic operators to justice. They undertook to put down the guerrillas who still ravaged great areas of the countryside and to prepare for democratic elections. They undertook also to unplug the bureaucratic bottlenecks, the installation of which had consumed the major part of the U Nu government's time and energy, and to take a few of the obvious actions which U Nu had avoided for years, such as destroying a hundred thousand starving, mangy Rangoon street dogs, despite the Burmese Buddhist aversion to the taking of other than human life.

The achievements of the Ne Win government were both showy and reassuring. The army actually carried out a campaign to "cleanse with sweat" the filthy city of Rangoon. Under an astonishingly agile 300-pound military mayor, it recruited troops, civil servants, and mere civilians and bystanders as well to sweep, shovel, and cart away much of the accumulated litter of two decades. It removed 100,000 squatters from the squalid street-side hovels, razed the hovels, helped the squatters build two new and respectable satellite towns, and provided fast, cheap bus and interurban service to shuttle them back and forth to work in Rangoon. It even brought the guerrilla terrorists almost under control.

The defects of the army's program did not show as clearly on the surface as did the achievements. The military suspended and disrupted many of the long-range development programs which the bureaucrats, after contriving ingenious obstructions, had at last allowed to get under way. They infiltrated all political and economic activities so thoroughly that it became difficult for them really to withdraw even if they wanted to. When it came to formulating not quick-action projects, but long-range programs, they developed critical internal feuds. Then they turned the government back, lock, stock, and empty barrel to U Nu, whose "clean" AFPFL had swept the February, 1960, elections. They served warning, as they did so, that if the politicians reverted to mere politics, as inevitably they would, the military would resort to arms. U Nu, on his return to power, started promising more local autonomy for the secessionist-minded, more state religion for the devout Buddhist, more nationalized enterprise for the

Marxists, more of everything for everybody except those who wanted only modest, visible, tangible beginnings of progress.

General Ne Win himself was more the autocrat than the architect of the original clean-up policy. He called upon Brigadiers Maung Maung, Aung Gyi and Tin Pe as his chief assistants and left the job to them. In view of the special circumstances, the triumvirate looked like a good working combination, and from all external indications it constituted a fairly harmonious little clique. All three of the brigadiers hailed from General Ne Win's home region and all three had been associated closely with him and with each other over a long period of years. For Ne Win, his brigadiers, and the Burmese public in general, loyalty to old friends and native place seemed at least as inspiring a set of motivations as loyalty to country. The three brigadiers, sharing a common background and presumably a common outlook, represented nevertheless the main shadings of Burmese political-economic thought from the relatively pro-Western (Maung Maung), through relatively pro-Chinese (Aung Gyi) to neutralist with pro-Russian leanings (Tin Pe), none of their outlooks, naturally, being quite that clear-cut.

Brigadier Maung Maung was free and easy in his contacts with Westerners, a man of lively wit and intelligence. He was to be the first of the inner clique to lose out in the internal maneuverings for influence. He was assigned abroad as ambassador to Israel just before the 1962 coup. Brigadier Tin Pe was the man of mystery, cold, aloof, and for that matter ill, having undergone one serious operation and being about to face another. Brigadier Tin Pe was generally ruled out as a potential survivor in any major power shuffle, but today he stands next to Ne Win.

Brigadier Aung Gyi was relaxed and friendly—but with the Chinese rather than with the Westerners. He is a man of real intellectual attainment, an omnivorous reader, a good talker, an appealing public figure. Endowed with great physical energy, he drives himself hard. A man also of simple, almost austere tastes, he is known for preferring fatigue to dress uniform, street-stall to restaurant food, and the less ostentatious models of house and car. During and after the original Ne Win regime, he was responsible for building up the Burma Economic Development Corporation, a vast, army-run import-export, wholesale-retail organization which displaced much private business. The BEDC seemed, in comparison with other state enterprises at least, reasonably efficient in operation, albeit unrealistic in price-cost relationships since it bought dear and sold cheap. Brigadier Aung Gyi was commonly regarded as Ne Win's heir apparent until, in February 1963, he suddenly got the sack. After brief retirement to the provinces, where he was actively encouraged to remain, Aung Gyi returned to Rangoon and began busying himself in religious circles, which are second only to the military in power and second to none in influence.

The record, at this point, is rather extensively anticipated, but some of the more salient facts still need to be sorted out. General Ne Win and the brigadiers, then, deposed U Nu on March 2, 1962, and constituted themselves a Revolutionary Council responsible for the Revolutionary Government of Burma. They promulgated a Marxist-sounding program called "The Burmese Way to Socialism." Then, instead of staging a campaign of fast action such as they had carried out back in 1958, they turned in a year-long performance which rivaled in irresolution even that of the U Nu regime.

In February 1963, however, things began to happen again. The first noteworthy event was the dismissal ("resignation") of Brigadier Aung Gyi—because, to itemize some of the conflicting speculations, he advocated policies too moderate for General Ne Win's tastes, such as toleration of private enterprise; or because he advocated policies too leftist, such as greater cooperation with Communist China; or because the Revolutionary Council needed a scapegoat; or because he was about to stage his own power coup. Shortly afterward, General Ne Win himself announced new restrictions on foreign traders, nationalization of the banks, nationalization of the Burma Oil Company, and later the nationalization of all import-export activities, in fact virtually anything susceptible to nationalization. He began promoting greater fraternal accord between the military and the peasants and workers.

The prospects of the Ne Win regime led to much speculation at home and abroad during 1963 that Burma, as had so often been predicted before, was making not just a swift but a decisive swing to the far, far left. But events in Burma are rarely if ever either swift or decisive, and events of the recent past have been even more bewildering than the norm. The first Ne Win government had been basically military and pragmatic. It had aimed at getting the long-stalled Burmese government machinery cranked up and into motion, but not at determining what direction the nation would take. The second Ne Win government set the course for Burmese socialism, which, presumably, had been the course all along. It immediately became involved, however, in an imbroglio not only with the politicians and public but within the military revolutionary clique itself.

The coup of March 2, 1962, was a model operation upon which the nearby Thai army, for all its experience, could scarcely have improved. In preparation for the coup General Ne Win had called into Rangoon the Fourth Burma Rifles, Burma's crack military outfit, the one with which he himself and Brigadier Aung Gyi had been most closely associated. His intelligence officers mapped the accustomed movements of the politicians, including those of some fifty *sawbaws* (Shan State chieftains) whose presence in town to lobby for autonomy actually precipitated the coup. The military knew, therefore, exactly where at 2:00 A.M.—in the home of which wife, for instance, in the case of the polygamous, or of which good friend, in the case of the amorous—to lay their hands on each of the gentlemen it took into custody. They miscalculated only twice. In one case they had to pounce several successive nights in several places to catch their man. In the other, when they raided the home of Sao Shwe Thaike, the former President of Burma, they encountered spirited resistance on the part of his young son, whom they shot dead in the scuffle. But by six o'clock on the morning of March 2, when Rangoon's citizens were setting out on their way to work, city traffic was moving in its normal rather unhurried pace and the Rangoon radio was carrying General Ne Win's assurances that the coup was a success, that all was well, and that as Chairman of a Revolutionary Council he would give Burma a revolutionary government appropriate to its needs.

All was not half as well as Chairman Ne Win and much of Rangoon originally seemed to think. The early and widespread assumption was that notwithstanding ominous references to a Revolutionary Council operating a revolutionary government without benefit of Parliament, elections, ordinary courts, or other familiar fixtures, this was going to be a repetition of the 1958 clean-up, speed-up campaign of which Burma was once again badly in need. But Chairman Ne Win and the Revolutionary Council, as it developed, were really serious about a revolutionary government and a revolutionary new solution to Burma's ills. They proposed this time to tackle the big difficult problems rather than just the little easy ones, as before. In slow succession, the delay causing conjecture whether the Revolutionary Council had indeed any clear idea what kind of revolution it wanted, Ne Win promulgated a new state philosophy which nobody could understand, inaugurated a new party which nobody joined, and announced the achievement of benefits which nobody could see.

The philosophy was a badly drafted document, entitled "The Burmese Way to Socialism," which seemed to emphasize nationalization of virtually all enterprises. As publicly reinterpreted by one of its chief authors, Brigadier Aung Gyi, it seemed to allow private enterprise practically the same scope as before, notwithstanding the intimation that eventual nationalization was even more inevitable than it had been all along. "The Burmese Way to Socialism" had to be redrafted a year later as "The Philosophy of the Socialist Programme Party," in order to "clarify" the objective, namely, to "correlate man and his environment, deviating neither to right nor to left." In this second document, superimposed over the original elements of political and economic mysticism, were major elements of the religious.

The vehicle of Burmese socialism was to be the Burmese Socialist Programme Party, whose constitution provided for rigid selection, discipline, and training of party members. The colonels failed, however, to set forth workable conditions of recruitment until almost a year later, when they began to appoint army personnel as party cadres. The quick achievements of the new regime, as publicly announced, included miracles of new army management, which converted long-stagnant state enterprises into profit-making concerns, at least until the Revolutionary Council recalled that it disapproved of the profit motive, and then the emphasis shifted to happy management-employee relations. Major attention was devoted to reforms in agriculture so that at last, it was stated, the peasant was to get an immediate and fair cash payment for his rice, easy government loans, and plentiful new equipment, including tractors.

The difficulty was that the Burmese had heard a very great deal of this a very great many times before. The first Ne Win government, while it had antagonized many bureaucrats, had actually brought quick and visible improvements. The second brought instead quick and visible curtailment of democratic processes, of which the empty Parliament building in downtown Rangoon was just one symbol. Improvement, of course, might follow, but first came the coup and then came talk, and in the opinion of many Burmese the politicians had been better talkers.

General Ne Win, his brigadiers and his colonels became aware that a considerable proportion of the Burmese intellectuals were criticizing them for being either unparliamentarian or unproletarian and, in either event, un-Burmese. They became aware also that the Rangoon student population, never slow to constitute itself the protesting public, was spoiling for a showdown. The students, who harbored political suspects (including Communists) in their dormitories, defied government curfew regulations, and felt strongly about such unpopular academic practices as the administration of examinations and the collection of fees. Finally they provoked the military beyond endurance by barricading themselves into the Student Union building and defying the military to enter. The army launched an attack (July 7, 1962), and the students launched a counterattack of invective and insult in the course of which General Ne Win's name was loudly mentioned. General Ne Win himself gave the orders to shoot. When the immediate crisis subsided next day, sixteen students were dead, forty-six were wounded, the Student Union had been bulldozed, and all of Burma that was shockable had been shocked into awareness that the Ne Win regime was in real trouble.

General—and Chairman—Ne Win's reaction to trouble in the case of the students was that of a military man caught in a nonmilitary situation which he does not like and cannot understand and yet is forced to cope with. During the first year of his new regime, Chairman Ne Win showed little indication that he liked or understood the general situation in Burma any better than the student situation, that he had any more of a soberly thought out plan of action, or that he himself reacted other than in annoyance.

He found himself in the anomalous position of the general whose troops are deployed but whose tactics and strategy remain to be worked out, or of the chairman whose committee is assembled before an agenda has been drawn up. Fortunately, the enemy was not at hand, or at least it was not identified, and action seemed no more imperative than in years past, and little more likely. But there were onlookers about, and some of them, like the students, were derisive. General Ne Win had given orders that a program was to be devised, implemented, and applauded, but Chairman Ne Win had neglected to devise the necessary mechanism. He reacted, on the whole, rather as though he wished he had not got himself involved, but was not about to let anyone criticize or displace him.

The second year of the new regime, like the first, seemed to most outside observers to be marked by far more frustrations than accomplishments, and General Ne Win himself, who appeared increasingly irascible, could scarcely have felt otherwise. The domestic situation was bad enough, but as the year 1963 opened, General Ne Win was also contemplating the China-India border crisis, the repercussions of which could easily be heard on his own frontier, which was within earshot of the shooting; as it closed he was contemplating the new Vietnamese, Cambodian, and Laotian crises nearby, and the Indonesian-Malaysian crisis not far removed, as well as the minor crisis in Thailand resulting from the death of Prime Minister Sarit. In the China-India border dispute, he achieved new heights of neutralism which antagonized even some of his more neutralistic compatriots; and in the late 1963 Southeast Asian crises his performance was even less positive than that of most other statesmen in that he scarcely even dared mention the dangers.

It was becoming increasingly obvious that the accident of geography and the recurrent accidents of history were much more decisive in Burmese affairs than the policies of the Revolutionary Council, which seemed always to lead to inconclusive or contradictory developments. Chairman Ne Win had resorted to apparently drastic economic measures during the year 1963, ordering wave after wave of nationalizations. The Burmese economy, according to everybody's predictions and reports except those of the Revolutionary Council, continued its leisurely and visible deterioration, and even the more energetic businessmen seemed reconciled merely to accepting defeat.

In November, General Ne Win made strenuous efforts to negotiate with the wildly assorted lot of Communist and minority-group guerrillas who kept rekindling armed insurrection. The negotiations led neither to any working agreement such as might have resulted in participation of outright Communists in government nor to any effectively renewed military drive against them. The Revolutionary Council accused the guerrilla representatives of treachery; it broke off the talks; and it arrested some 500–1,000 "leftists," about 50 per cent of whom appeared to be mere critics of the regime, of leftist sympathies no greater than the Burmese norm.

The Ne Win government, throughout the year, had been rounding up and jailing prominent representatives of the disaffected intellectual elite, and the continuing series of arrests of politicians, businessmen, journalists, and trade unionists of many descriptions precipitated the sort of major student protest demonstration and riots which had broken out in 1962. This time (mid-December, 1963), the disorders occurred not at Rangoon University but at the new Technical Institute built and staffed by the Russians. The year 1963, then, in immediate retrospect, looked dreary for Burma and for the Ne Win regime, and no one was predicting brighter prospects for 1964.

For better or for worse, Chairman Ne Win does not look as yet like a great revolutionary leader conscious or capable of his role. He lacks most of the characteristics which might make him either the prophet or the demagogue. He is not a profound thinker, a smooth talker, a canny plotter, an astute planner, or a flamboyant actor. He has many sterling qualities and at least as many human weaknesses, but none of them is very dramatic. He is handsome and dignified in public, and animated in private when he chooses to be; but he is obviously balding, sagging, and aging. He gives the distinct impression of preferring not to make much more effort than is absolutely required of him in a public appearance, of excluding from responsibility anyone who was not already a member of the inner circle, and of much preferring, on the whole, the role of the man who has already once saved the nation than that of the man who is about to save it again. In other words, to put it in Madison Avenue terminology, he lacks not only the ability but the will to project an image, and indeed he seems not to have decided exactly what image he wishes to project. To put it in terms of the political analyst, he does not quite "identify" with the nation nor the nation with him. In five words: he is short on charisma.

The "real" Ne Win, to be sure, may have as yet to reveal himself, but the fact is that after fifteen years of national prominence, several of those years having been spent in the spotlight, Ne Win remains today, so far as the general public is concerned, a man of ill-defined capability and personality. He avoids public contacts and personal publicity, and since he is far from being as popular or even as approachable as he was in 1958, reports about him are conflicting. Nevertheless, some few salient facts stand out and are worth assembling.

General Ne Win lives today in a luxurious new government villa built on the shore of Rangoon's Inya Lake, the posh residential area ever since the British decided to install a scenic reservoir, now more posh than ever since it is favored by the diplomatic corps and is the site of Rangoon's new Russian-gift luxury hotel. The home is heavily guarded both at the land and the lake approaches. The general's public appearances in Rangoon are infrequent, save for the inescapable ceremonial chore of meeting, greeting, and speeding Rangoon's heavy traffic of VIP's. He shows a marked disinclination to appear in any confined space close to any considerable number of people, and when he travels by road he moves in an armed convoy. Generally he appears smart and fit, and until recently played tennis and golf, but his health is not in fact very good. He is beset by long-standing complaints which are sometimes described as "sinus trouble," sometimes as "kidney trouble," sometimes as nervous disorders involving semiparalysis of one hand, and occasionally call for long periods of treatment and recuperation abroad. Shortly after his assumption of office as Chairman of the Revolutionary Council, for instance, he spent three months out of the country (July 13–October 13, 1962), and he is recurrently rumored to be contemplating further travels. His last trip included pleasure visits to England, Switzerland, and elsewhere, as well as a medical visit to Vienna.

General Ne Win's travels bring up the matter of state visits which, in Burma, as elsewhere in Southeast Asia, consume an appalling amount of time, money, and energy, and produce an appalling output of words. Since his first venture abroad under Japanese auspices in 1941, General Ne Win has feted and felicitated virtually every national leader whose country can raise or borrow the price of a chartered plane. He has himself visited the United Sates (1952), Indonesia (1953), China (1955), Israel (1959), the UAR (1959), and China again (1960). This does not by any means exhaust the list and does not, as a matter of fact, put him in a class with U Nu as a globe-trotter. His travels, nevertheless, and the necessity for toasts, speeches, joint communiqués, and the like, have given him an unerring choice of platitudes which, conceivably, conditions some of his thinking on domestic and foreign policy. General Ne Win's pronouncements these days, many of them in English, read rather more predictably than most official communications. Even in Burma, they are rather less attended to. Unlike U Nu's prose, the general's is both tedious and pedestrian. This, to be sure, may be the fault of his aides, but when General Ne Win speaks or writes impromptu, the words and the rhythms seem the same. Revolutions, fortunately perhaps, are rarely made on stuff like this.

One partial explanation for General Ne Win's lackluster rhetoric in public and his brittle temper in private is that he feels constrained to speak in circumlocutions and to avoid the issue. The general believes himself trapped, indeed he believes that Burma is trapped, by the whim of geopolitics which gave him common borders with neutralist India, Communist China, SEATO-allied Thailand and Pakistan, and enigmatic Laos. Whatever he says or does in the area of international affairs, even if it is completely innocuous, seems quite certain to land him in trouble. On the China-India border dispute, for instance, his agile neutralist attempts to avoid assuming an identifiable stance other than that of benevolent onlooker very much annoyed the equally accomplished Indian neutralists.

General Ne Win is not just a neutralist but a particularly exposed, vulnerable and therefore edgy neutralist, hypersensitive to any action that seems to compromise his position. He is still indignant, therefore, about some thousands of stray Nationalist Chinese troops who lived for years as armed squatters in Burma with logistic support from Taiwan and indirectly from the United States. He is even more incensed about American aid to Burma. During his first period as head of government he made the decision to accept substantial aid, thus, he felt, compromising himself with Communist China. Furthermore, the United States grew evasive about his top-priority project. General Ne Win wants to build a modern highway leading from Rangoon northward toward the China border. Considerations of economic utility, engineering feasibility, and military strategy deter American officials from becoming enthusiastic about actually starting construction on this road, even though for political reasons the money has been made available. General Ne Win, consequently, is highly skeptical of American good faith.

Ne Win, as a strict matter of fact, is unhappy about Burmese-American relations in general, for the great postwar extension of American influences, taken in combination with the British, seems to him and to a great many other Burmese to tie Burma all too closely to the Western bloc. He has given the orders, accordingly, for termination of American foundation activities in Burma, curtailment of all programs of educational exchange with the Western world, and extreme caution about renewing any old or entering into any new commitments. He is almost equally queasy, however, about Burmese-Chinese and Burmese-Russian contacts, even though he feels compelled to build them up via aid programs and diplomatic exchanges in order to counterbalance the long-established influence of the Western world. General Ne Win finds himself, therefore, in the melancholy dilemma of the hypochondriac who goes on self-prescribed medication for what he thinks is his ailment only to discover that he has a violent allergy to all the available antibiotics.

General Ne Win's home life is more of a preoccupation with him than his public life. He has long since divorced his first wife, by whom he had two children, one of them a son recently trained in aviation in Scotland, now a pilot for Burma Airways. The general remarried after the Pacific war, this time to the daughter of Burma's most prominent surgeon, a young lady who had been trained as a nurse and had married and divorced a prominent Burmese physician. Daw Khin May Than, as she is now called, rather to the surprise of many old friends who used to know her as "Kitty," is an extremely attractive and animated young woman who is devoted to literature, the theater and dancing, both ballet and twist. A Burmese Bohemian, she holds a salon for a cosmopolitan set of bright young people who might hail from Mayfair, a circle to which the general seems half attracted, half indifferent. Daw Khin May Than shares the general's attraction to the races, although the general himself has now sold off his stable and abandoned the sport—indeed, the Revolutionary Council has ordered the closure of the track, and after some little wavering, has reaffirmed its position that horse racing does not befit a socialist state and must go. Daw Khin May Than, according to common report, has other interests which one might not expect so close to a Revolutionary Council—a discriminating taste in jewels, for instance, and an instinct for private real estate ventures.

This, say some of the general's many critics, is scarcely the model first family of a military revolutionary, marching hand in hand with the people down the Burmese Way to Socialism. Quite possibly the fact that it is not and that the leading Burmese know that it is not may keep that Way more Burmese than socialist. The Burmese resistance to becoming doctrinaire in anything more specific than Buddhist sincerity, piety, and charity may just possibly rule out any very quick acceptance of the revolutionary cadre system which General Ne Win himself seems to dislike, although he can think of nothing better.

Monarch *de l'État du Coup*

His Majesty King Bhumibol Adulyadej of Thailand was born in Cambridge, Massachusetts, and educated in Lausanne. He is so thoroughly Occidentalized that notwithstanding intensive re-orientation in Bangkok, he seems today somewhat alien to the lighter-hearted Thais who are his subjects, a contradiction to the belief that among the Thais frivolity prevails. The King, whose name, according to rather more phonetic but less official systems of spelling, sometimes appears as Pumiphon Aduldet and Phumi-phon Adundet, seems so irreproachable a monarch and citizen, husband and father, traditionalist and innovator as to invite polite incredulity. The crowning touch is that he is married to Queen Sirikit, who is even more beautiful than her photographs and as self-possessed as she is photogenic.

King Bhumibol and Queen Sirikit are condemned to live in, with, and for their "images" as the all but perfect rulers. They are subject to such exacting standards of public and even private deportment that the king often seems frozen and the queen glazed. An attempt to break through the *niello* curtain which screens palace from public generally results in the conviction that they are indeed almost as Olympian as they seem. The only way to humanize them may be to resort to banalities.

The King, then, in his off-duty hours, is not just a dilettante in jazz and weight lifting, but an accomplished musician and ath-lete. The Queen is not just a model of beauty and fashion but a model palace-keeper. The King and the Queen are genuinely de-voted to each other, their four children, their country, their people, even—perhaps this is stretching it a bit too far—to the international audience which follows the royal calendar of receptions, investitures, and state visits. It helps to report, as is true, that they themselves deplore the "image" but know they are stuck with it. Candid reply to the question, "What are they really like?" serves, then, merely to introduce another, best phrased perhaps in the composite idiom of the two commonest types of inquirer, the gusher and the pundit: "Can a royal couple, regal in the most exemplary sense of the word, keep the Thai monarchy viable in a revolutionary Southeast Asia?" The quickest answer is to report that in Bangkok, where *coups d'état* seem to occur at the rate of a dozen a decade, there is some speculation, reinforced for the moment at least by the peaceful transfer of authority on the death of Prime Minister Sarit (December 8, 1963), that the next coup may take the form of an evolutionary monarchial restoration.

While modern Thailand has retained its king as a state figure, it has also experimented with a military dictatorial style of quasi-democracy in which many people now have their eyes on the "people's democracy" model. They may settle eventually for a democratic constitutional monarchy of a benevolently autocratic variety. Such a development might vindicate yet once again King Bhumibol's great-grandfather, King Mongkut, who studied systematically the British, French, and American systems and set about making his own country as distinctive in the East as each of these three powers was in the West. Since the Chakri Dynasty has a most remarkable history of successful experimentation, it may in fact be able to bring off the feat of finding for Thailand that genuine "national identity" for which every Southeast Asian nation is groping. This happy denouement, of course, is multiply contingent, but even the contingency is justification for examining further the lives and personalities of a couple who seem the more improbable the more factual one becomes about them.

The story of King Bhumibol begins quite a long time before the day, December 5, 1927, when he was born in Cambridge, where his father, Prince Mahidol, was then a medical student and his mother had been a student nurse. To a greater extent even than for most royalty, the story depends upon the royal antecedents. Most significant among them was the great King Mongkut (reigned 1851–1868), who placed Thailand (which was then

called Siam) on a firm footing of equality with the Western nations, thus sparing both the Thais and the international world
another traumatic colonial relationship. By making the deliberate
decision to modernize his country, King Mongkut put Thailand
far out ahead even of Japan as an Asian nation voluntarily and,
what is more, peacefully transforming itself. Although the major
changes were left to his successors, the volition, the precedent,
and the momentum were King Mongkut's. So was the self-
assured conviction (in contrast to the prevailing xenophobia elsewhere in Southeast Asia) not only that the Siamese were just as
good as the foreigners, but that foreigners were just as good as—
or no worse than—the Siamese.

King Mongkut corresponded, accordingly, with his "Dear
Sister" Queen Victoria, sending her a crown and receiving in return a locomotive; with "His Respected and Distinguished Presidency Buchnan [*sic*] Esquire" (although it was President Lincoln who actually received the letter), volunteering to supply
breed elephants—which Lincoln declined—with which to stock
the "American jungles." He did not feel impelled, unfortunately,
to transmit to Washington the results of his researches into a
subject which should be of profound interest in any bureaucratic
jungle, namely, the distinguishing characteristics of the genuine
white elephant, most conclusively identifiable to the connoisseurs,
he decided, not so much by its yellow eyes, white hair, white toe-
nails, and pink skin as by its "beautiful snore." Copies did drift
to Washington and around the world of the voluminous output
of his new palace printing press, for which he composed in his
own despotically designed English idiom, treatises on topics both
more and less significant than "the absolute monarch's advice
against the inelegant practice of throwing dead animals into the
water-ways."

King Mongkut found time also to re-edit the Siamese religious
classics and in between séances of astrology to make precise
astronomical calculations which enabled him, for instance, to pin-
point accurately for visiting scientists the best spot in Siam from
which to view a solar eclipse. An English gentlewoman, Anna
Leonowens, employed as governess to the royal children, presumed to publish her rather gaudy memoirs of Mongkut's court;
an American missionary lady further to fictionalize them; Broad-

way and Hollywood to apply overlays of embellishment; and the historians are just now beginning to work back to the real Mongkut, who out-Leonowened Leonowens.

King Chulalongkorn, King Mongkut's son and successor (reigned 1868–1910), ruled, wrote, and lived with less verve than did his father, but his record all the same was an impressive one. In his private life he made provision for ninety-two wives, and in his public life—whether or not as a result of the influence of Anna, whom the Thais disparage—he introduced massive dosages of Western administrative, legal, and social concepts. After extensive travels abroad, he tried even to improve upon Siamese architecture, which needed no change, and upon Siamese city planning, which did. The Thai-Italianate pink Chakri Palace was his idea; so was Rasadamnoen Avenue, Bangkok's composite Mall, Champs Élysées, Pennsylvania and Madison Avenues. King Chulalongkorn inherited along with the crown British and French rivalry to carve Siam into spheres of influence, but by relinquishing minor bits and pieces of his domain, he managed to preserve the whole almost intact. He found Siam strong and left it stronger, but with his own son and successor, King Vajiravudh it looked as though the true genius had died out of the Chakri line and as if the constellations were failing the nation.

King Vajiravudh (reigned 1910–1925), who studied at Christ College, Oxford, then entered Sandhurst, and meanwhile rode to hounds and played cricket, was not the best possible testimonial to a Western education for an Eastern prince. As king, he had little time for administration and little patience with those who warned him of growing nepotism, incompetence, corruption, and extravagance. He devoted himself to the arts and to the artists, also to the political intellectuals, among them incipient revolutionaries. He himself translated Shakespeare and Voltaire into Siamese and authored plays of his own, some of which, much to the dismay of the traditionalists, he himself produced and acted in, the rest of the cast including persons commonly regarded as shady. A tweedy outdoor type as well as a dilettante, King Vajiravudh popularized golf and soccer among his subjects. He affronted the princes and princesses, however, by exhibiting a marked preference for the society of a clique of racy young commoners. He indiscreetly organized his youthful companions into a "Wild

Tiger Corps," which gradually expanded into an obnoxious little palace army. Regular army generals, after trying first to infiltrate the corps by enlisting as privates, decided presently that violence was a better device and planned but did not quite dare to execute what would have been Thailand's first modern coup. Only toward the end of his reign did King Vajiravudh become seriously concerned about the throne and about the succession. After declining for many years even to contemplate matrimony, he began marrying wives by relays. At the time of his death, however, he was still without male issue. The succession, according to a new law of the Royal Household, which he promulgated in 1924 at almost the last possible moment before his death, passed to his youngest brother, seventy-sixth child and last son of King Chulalongkorn.

Until the 1924 act of succession was promulgated, King Prajadhipok (reigned 1925–35) had had little or no reason to think that he would ever sit upon the throne or even, since he had an aversion both to administration and to ceremony, much reason to want to. He soon had good reason to give it up, for along with the throne he inherited the whirlwind which King Vajiravudh had sown. Young military and civilian officials, mainly Western educated, had constituted themselves a People's Party and were demanding reforms. They engineered Thailand's first modern *coup d'état*, the peaceful "1932 revolution," which resulted in drastic curtailment of royal prerogative and in proclamation of a constitutional parliamentary democracy. Quite aside from his difficulties with the People's Party, the King had his personal troubles: for one thing, he was swiftly going blind. In 1935 he abdicated the throne and retired to quiet country life in England.

The succession passed to the line of one of his brothers, Prince Mahidol, who had died in 1929 leaving two infant sons who were to become successively the late and the present king. As a "celestial prince" (i.e., the child of a wife who had been named a queen), Prince Mahidol himself had enjoyed both the prerogatives and the penalties of his rarefied rank. More perhaps than any of his thirty-one half-brothers, he had attended seriously to his father, King Chulalongkorn, who had admonished his progeny to take advantage of their opportunities, to economize in their expenditures, and to prepare themselves to serve their country.

Prince Mahidol studied diligently at Harrow, later submitted himself to stern discipline in the Imperial German Naval Academy, and conscientiously improved his mind while he widened his experience by extensive travels throughout Europe, guarding his purse and his person against any who sought to impose upon him as a possibly wayward princeling.

Among his peers, Prince Mahidol acquired the reputation of being a bit of an eccentric. For one thing, they said, he was extraordinarily close with his money. He stayed in cheap London lodgings rather than in the luxury hotel suites which they themselves favored, and he eschewed even the minor extravagances of the pubs and the race courses. He was also, they thought, rather tediously insistent about making patriotic use of his qualifications once he had acquired them. He had a perfectly good, safe commission in the Imperial German Navy, but he resigned it to return to Thailand, prudently doing so, to be sure, shortly before King Vajiravudh declared war on Germany. He then volunteered for active sea duty with the rudimentary Royal Thai Navy, even though he was clearly given to understand that he was much too exalted a personage to be risked afloat, especially on the leaky torpedo boat which he aspired to command.

Prince Mahidol's successive attempts at adjustments between the idealities of King Chulalongkorn's Polonius-like precepts to his sons and the realities of daily life at court never quite came off to anyone's satisfaction, especially his own. He tired of petitioning for sea duty and attached himself to the Royal Thai Cavalry, which, for a celestial prince, proved little more earthy than the navy. His full-dress navy uniform brought him much attention in parades but no combat duty and not even much chance to display his horsemanship.

Prince Mahidol decided upon a complete switch of careers. In 1920, therefore, he traveled to the United States, where he enrolled in Harvard University, first undertaking to study public health, later shifting to medicine. Soon after his arrival in Boston he met and fell in love with a pretty young Thai commoner, a nursing student named Sangwalya Chukramol. Prince Mahidol interrupted his studies to take his intended bride back to Bangkok and there, after receiving the consent of his family, the young couple was married. For a time thereafter, Prince Mahidol served in the Thai Department of Public Health, but feeling himself once again frustrated by formalities, he decided to resume his foreign travel and studies. Prince Mahidol's next academic itinerary took him successively to England, Germany, and then back to the United States. He stayed long enough in each country to take some university courses and for his wife to bear him a child. Princess Galyani was born in 1923 in London, Prince Ananta Mahidol in 1925 in Heidelberg, and Prince Bhumibol Adulyadej in 1927 in Cambridge. In 1929, after completing his medical studies at Harvard, Prince Mahidol returned once more to Siam, but this time he steered clear of government. Leaving his wife and children in Bangkok, he himself went to Chiengmai, where he became an interne in the McCormick Hospital of the American Presbyterian Mission and took up residence in the home of a certain Dr. Cort, the American head of the hospital.

Prince Mahidol, it seemed, had at last found his calling. According to the 1924 law of succession, he was now the Heir Apparent, but he took much less interest in his distant dynastic prospects than in various professional projects. One was a Mission Leper Colony in Chiengmai. Another was the selecting and financing for medical study abroad of a few especially promising young men. Yet another was the attracting of international philanthropic interest, especially that of the Rockefeller Foundation, to Siamese medical institutions. Prince Mahidol had barely started in his new career, however, when in 1929 at the age of 37 he died.

Princess Sangwalya found herself in the difficult position of being the widowed mother of two infant princes who were by law the leading candidates for the succession. Scores of other royal princes and princesses were jockeying in more or less refined fashion to prejudice the coming decision of the Royal Council with regard to a throne which was now very shaky. The princess made a stateswomanlike decision. She hustled her whole family off to Switzerland. When King Prajadhipok abdicated in 1935, young Prince Ananta Mahidol was named his successor, but the family stayed on in Switzerland all the same, where the princes were enrolled in school. Throughout World War II the Princess Mother and her three children remained safely and quietly at their handsome villa in Lausanne, where they rarely rated even casual mention in the newspapers.

When the war was over and the young King was approaching his twenty-first birthday, the Princess and her family returned to Bangkok (1946). They arrived at a time when the Thai politicians, for all their virtuosity in maneuvering, seemed for once to be taxing even their own capacities. The government had just carried off the ambivalent wartime policy of being officially pro-Axis and unofficially pro-Allied, and the postwar feat of declaring the Declaration of War on the side of Japan retroactively null and void. It had been an involuntary but territory-sharing partner in Japan's militant East Asia Co-Prosperity Sphere (acquiring provinces of Cambodia and Malaya), and a voluntary leader in the Southeast Asian anti-Japanese underground.

The Prime Minister, Pibul, had been a Japanese collaborator; the Regent, Pridi, had been an Allied agent; the Minister to Washington, Seni Pramoj, had formed a Free Thai Movement; while the King had been an innocent schoolboy in neutral Switzerland. The Thai people themselves had been relaxed about the whole affair until economic austerity caught up with them and politics threatened to become serious. In the immediate postwar period, the wartime Prime Minister was named the national villain; the Minister to Washington became a democratic monarchist; the King came home; the people were mildly enthusiastic. The situation, obviously, was fluid. Then politics became truly serious and tragedy struck: on June 9, 1946, the young King was mysteriously assassinated.

At this point in the narrative, before ushering the former King off or the present King onto the stage, it is necessary to introduce the supporting actors who have been until 1964 in fact the leads. The featured billing is shared by four very distinguished gentlemen whose careers repeatedly overlapped and collided: Pridi, Pibul, Phao, and Sarit.

Nai Pridi Panomyong, the first of the quartet to achieve prominence, was a Paris-educated (Doctor of Law; University of Paris), Marxist-oriented, personally corrupt statesman, conspirator, and sometime patriot. As one of the prime movers in the 1932 revolution and in the governments which followed, he excelled in almost everything save getting along with his colleagues. The first truly memorable breakup occurred when he took his party's revolutionary platform rather too seriously, and in conformity with it authored a radical new economic program. He called for the government to nationalize the land, hire the peasants, pay them in script negotiable only in government stores, and thus to achieve agricultural "progress." His military colleagues, like the King, regarded Pridi's proposal as Bolshevistic. They urged upon him the desirability of continuing his foreign travel and study. A year later they invited him back again to use his most recently acquired knowledge to help formulate a domestic and foreign policy which the political worriers regarded as fascist.

Pridi soon became Foreign Minister, but when the Thai government rearranged itself for the wartime period, he became Regent. In effect, he assumed for himself the prerogatives of royalty, and when royalty returned home after the war, Pridi naturally was reluctant to relinquish his pretensions. During the war he established himself as the center of liaison between the anti-Japanese underground and the anti-Japanese loyalists abroad. In 1944, when the pro-Japanese Thai government lost face and, what was almost more important, solvency, he managed on July 17, 1944, to engineer the overthrow of the Prime Minister, Pibul. After the war, Pridi caused Pibul to be arrested and charged as a war criminal, and he himself later assumed the post of Prime Minister.

Pibul, naturally, conspired to reverse the coup. Since Pridi was arrogant, corrupt, and careless, Pibul experienced no great difficulty in building up an anti-Pridi movement. When suddenly the young King was murdered, there were whispers which climaxed in open charges that Pridi was implicated in the regicide. Pridi abandoned the Prime Ministership on November 8, 1947, and departed Bangkok precipitately for Singapore. Not long afterwards he moved on to Peking. There he organized a Free Thai movement, masterminded at long range a couple of abortive Bangkok coups, broadcast a few calls for revolution, and then mysteriously subsided.

Exit Pridi. Re-enter Pibul.

An opportunist and a pragmatist, who had received advanced military training in France, Pibul Songgram was coconspirator with Pridi in the 1932 coup and coarchitect of the subsequent prewar governments. First as Commander of the Bangkok Area, then as Minister of Defense, then as Prime Minister, Pibul was Der Leiter in Thailand's prewar and wartime fascist phase. As Prime Minister he tried to stay in favor both with the Japanese and with the anti-Japanese underground, but succeeded better in the former than in the latter undertaking. In 1944 he was maneuvered out of office by Pridi; in 1947 he himself maneuvered Pridi out; and from 1948 to 1957 he was the real power before the throne in Thailand. Almost monotonously, he survived plot after plot, attempted coup after attempted coup.

Field Marshal Pibul concentrated into one lifetime rather more than the normal amount of excitement to be expected even by a Thai politician. His way of life becomes clear, for instance, from Prince Chula Chakrabongse's matter-of-fact reminiscences in *Lords of Life* * about what seem to have been viewed as fairly routine events:

> . . . while dressing to go out to an evening party, he [Pibul] found his valet beginning to shoot at him. It was awkward for Pibul, who had his half-Wellington boots on already, yet had not done up his trousers, but he managed to evade the bullets, and the man was arrested and charged. . . . News came of another attempt on Pibul's life, this time by poisoning. His wife was also stricken, and when seen by the present author . . . they both looked seriously ill. It was not surprising that after their recovery they would not eat or drink anything outside their home for some time.

On a later occasion, Pibul was kidnapped by Thai naval officers from a dredge which he had just a few minutes earlier accepted as a gift from the United States. He was hustled over to a nearby Thai naval vessel which the Thai Air Force promptly bombed. It was awkward for Pibul, as Prince Chula might have remarked, but he managed to dive into the swift, muddy river and swim safely to shore. It was not surprising that Pibul felt the need of some really tough assistants. He relied upon a pair of his cronies, who proved in the end to be his undoing.

Pibul's chosen colleagues were General (later Field Marshal) Sarit Dhanarat, the Commander of the Bangkok Area, and Gen-

---

* Taplinger Publishing Co., Inc., New York, 1961.

eral Phao Sriyanonda, the Chief of Police. Beginning in 1948 the Pibul-Sarit-Phao triumvirate ran the city and the nation. General Sarit Dhanarat (the name is also romanized as Srisdi Dhanarajata) was a man of obscure and presumably, therefore, humble origin. His father, reportedly, was an army officer; he himself first attended traditional Thai-style religious school in the Wat Maharn in Bangkok, then entered the Prha Chula Chom Kla (Military Academy), from which he graduated in 1929. The young Sarit got ahead by sheer personal drive, managing to rise rapidly in the army and to attend several advanced army schools but never traveling outside Thailand until after his achievement of national prominence. General Phao Sriyanonda was almost an identical twin to Sarit and *alter ego* to Pibul.

Despite personal and physical traits which made them fairly easy to distinguish in a crowd, Pibul, Phao, and Sarit were in effect Siamese triplets. Although Pibul seemed mild and quiet, all three were in fact rough, tough, bluff, jovial men, handsome, corrupt and convivial. Exuberant Renaissance *bon vivant* and ruler types translated to the modern tropical Orient, they knew that wealth, power, and pleasure could readily be seized by anyone who would take the gamble, and they never hesitated. They made and obeyed the rules of the Bangkok political arena, which were approximately those of Thai boxing. Any blow landed on a rival was a fair one, whether a blow of hand or foot, knee or elbow, above or below the belt. All contestants—or at least all survivors—were so fit and alert as to be able to look out for themselves and to admire and even applaud the dexterity of their opponents. All three of them lived hard, drank hard, worked hard, played hard, and seemed to enjoy life enormously regardless of the enemies they made, the scandals which piled up about them, or the trouble they created for each other. They carved out for themselves financial empires which matched their military and political pretensions. Pibul managed for more years than almost anyone, including perhaps Pibul himself had ever expected, to maintain the extremely delicate balance of power and antipathy among them.

At last, as was inevitable, Pibul miscalculated. The balance seesawed, a coup was clearly called for, and Sarit beat Phao to the draw. Pibul vanished but was soon discovered to have proceeded by private car under punctilious military escort as far as the Cambodian border. Presently he settled into well-heeled retirement in Japan, where he now likes to reminisce about more exciting days. General Phao simply drove out to the airport, where the officials courteously expedited his movements through the departure formalities, and friends waved him off to Ceylon. Phao, it appeared, had experienced a sudden urge to enter a monastery. After a brief monastic interlude, he retired to Switzerland, where on November 21, 1960, he died of a heart attack.

General Sarit remained in control in Bangkok for more than six years, as vigorous, confident, and happy—save for intervals of hospitalization—as he could possibly be when he had only one kidney, retained a taste for fancy food, drink, and houses, and kept hearing the remark that it was an extraordinarily long time since Thailand's last coup. General Sarit, people thought, seemed extraordinarily relaxed about the possibility of a coup, even when people began to mention specific names, like that, for instance, of Lieutenant General Prapas Jarusathien, Minister of the Interior, and a notably articulate, active, and ambitious man. Pridi, of course, was the only survivor among his great rivals, and Pridi was apparently quiescent in Peking. General Sarit, it almost seemed, might be grooming the young King eventually not just to reign but to rule. The evidence was in fact beginning to build up that the king was being transformed from schoolboy into statesman—a development best traced, perhaps, in his relationships with the durable trio, Pridi, Pibul, and Sarit.

Nai Pridi was still regent when Prince Bhumibol and his brother, King Ananta Mahidol, returned in 1946 to a nation which was in a mood to celebrate—whether a royal restoration or deposition was not quite clear. Nai Pridi, conflictingly motivated by his own demi-royalist aspirations to rule Thailand himself as an aristocratic dictator and by his Marxist antipathy to the very institution of monarchy, was determined, it was thought, to destroy the royal family. He treated the two young princes in a manner which indicated either that he regarded them as juvenile delinquents or that he sought to make them so. Invoking the need for security, he surrounded them with informers and troublemakers and placed almost intolerable restrictions upon their freedom of movement even within the palace grounds. He acted at times the role of petty tyrant, once even going to the extreme of making off with young Prince Bhumibol's piano in order to deny to him a source of private satisfaction. He attempted to play one member of the royal family off against another, and in a jealous court, where experienced conspirators sought diversion and advantage, there were many willing to cooperate.

The royal palace was already a wretchedly unhappy place when there occurred in the early morning hours of June 9, 1946, the tragedy which truly shocked the nation. From the King's bedroom came the sound of a gunshot. When the palace attendants entered they found the King already dead, shot through the head with a bullet from his own pistol. No outsiders were known to have been present in the palace at the time; only the royal family and the palace staff, which, to be sure, included a very large number of persons.

Reports of suicide, accident, and regicide spread as fast as did the report of the death, and explanations were as elaborate as the fertile Thai imagination could invent. The government investigated and made obscure and contradictory announcements. Suicide by accident seemed to be the favored official explanation at the time, even though nobody believed it. Years later, two palace pages were tried, condemned, and executed for regicide, but the details of the case against them were never made public. From the very first, Pridi was widely accused of complicity; but Pridi, curiously enough, even from the distant safety of Peking, seems never to have offered his own defense or to have given his own version of the mystery. The tragedy still continues to stir up speculation in Bangkok, and although it is no doubt best put out of mind, it did bring nineteen-year-old King Bhumibol to the throne. For him, since by all accounts he was deeply attached to his brother, it was undoubtedly a traumatic experience and one in which Pridi featured as a sinister figure.

Prince Bhumibol was named successor, but he was not actually crowned until four years later, for as soon as possible after the elaborate ceremonies commemorating the demise of one king and the designation of another, the Princess Mother prudently removed herself and her son once again from the sultry climate and politics of Bangkok. The royal family returned to Switzerland, where Prince Bhumibol continued his education.

Unfortunately for his biographer, King Bhumibol's two Swiss interludes were marked by no dramatic achievements in scholarship, truancy, or other forms of personal assertiveness. They were marked, rather, by steady application to his studies, culminating at the university level, first in engineering, then in law. All along he was interested also in music, especially the piano, and in his extensive musical studies he exhibited both industry and talent. He had time also for a vigorous routine of sports, including swimming, skating, tennis, and mountaineering. He showed some partiality also for automobile racing, a sport particularly popular among other young Thai princes who were then studying in Europe. It was not in auto racing, however, as has often been reported, but in a routine highway accident that he experienced severe injuries. A car in which he was a passenger, not the driver, plowed into the back of a truck which had stopped one dark night in the roadway near Lausanne. The King's injuries left him blinded in one eye and with a compensating mannerism of facing rather stiffly straight forward.

Toward the end of his second stay in Switzerland, study, music, and sports were not King Bhumibol's exclusive interests. He found occasion also for romance. It was a romance so appropriate, so circumspect, and so unmarred by misunderstandings that save for the obvious facts—the King was manly, the Princess was beautiful, and the matchmakers were somewhat taken aback—it might have seemed contrived.

Mom Rajawongse Sirikit Kitiyakara first appeared on the scene when she accompanied her father, Prince Nakkhat, then Thai Minister to France, on a holiday to Switzerland. The next year, when her father was Ambassador to London, she returned and enrolled in school. It had been assumed all along, of course, that Prince Bhumibol would marry a Thai princess, and various princesses, among whom the standard of beauty and accomplishment is notably high, just happened to be routed through Switzerland on their busy international travels. Back in Bangkok there were several princely families with eligible daughters who felt that regardless of traffic right-of-way in Lausanne, their lines ranked near enough to the celestial to lead the competition. King Bhumibol, it seems, had no difficulty at all in making up his mind for himself.

The royal family returned to Bangkok in early 1950 to feature in three major ceremonies: a marriage, a cremation, and a coronation. Bangkok, as usual, was in a state of somewhat obscure political crisis, the economic situation left much to be desired, and international troubles loomed. The horoscopes, however, were propitious, and the city readied itself for three glorious affairs of state which quite eclipsed anything else of the kind which Southeast Asia had seen since the war. The royal court revived all of the dazzling ceremonial of the past which, against the flamboyant gilt and colored tile of the city's splendid temples and palaces, spelled spectacle too vast to be vulgar. Even King Mongkut would have been satisfied, especially with such innovations as press, radio, and camera coverage, and the attendance of foreign dignitaries jostling each other to get a better view.

The 195-year-old, forty-two-ton royal funeral carriage was hauled out of the National Museum, repaired and regilded so that its multitiered platforms looked like a piece of old Ayuthia made mobile. The late King's funeral urn, encased in a series of ancient gold and lacquer casques, was placed on the topmost pinnacle of the carriage under the nine-tiered royal white umbrella. From the Grand Palace, soldiers and sailors dragged the carriage to Pramone Ground, in front of what had once been the Second King's Palace (now the National Museum), where, in King Mongkut's day, there had lived a young nobleman rather unexpectedly named Prince George Washington. There the urn was placed atop the funeral pyre; the royal court performed its elaborate obeisances, and March 29 the new King lighted the flame. Before and after the cremation, Bangkok celebrated. Feasting, drinking, boxing, and theatricals converted Pramone Ground into a vast fair which far outdid the attractions of its regular Sunday market, where the visitor can gratify almost any wish, whether it is to have his horoscope cast or to eat fish charcoalbroiled on skewers or to buy a kite which, in the next windy season, he can fly from the same open field.

For all their splendor, the wedding on April 28 and the coronation on May 5 did not quite measure up to the cremation as public spectacles. But Bangkok enjoyed them all the same and set a precedent which has had quite uncalculated significance. In Bangkok, in contrast with various other capitals of Southeast Asia, the great public event is not the advent or exit of a cabinet or of a good-will mission or of a party of state guests. Rather, it is the traditional state ceremony in which royalty features—and now features more and more conspicuously. The vigorous and romantic young King, by his mere return, began to rebuild the traditional prestige of the Thai monarchy which in 1932 and again in 1946 had seemed quite unlikely ever to stage a real comeback. Young King Ananta Mahidol, of course, never had a chance to impress his personality upon the state, and reports conflict whether he did or did not display much of the hereditary Chakri vigor. King Bhumibol, by acquitting himself with dignity in the initial state ceremonies, was off to a far more auspicious start.

King Bhumibol was faced immediately, however, with the acute problem of determining his relationship with Thailand's politicians, most especially, of course, with Pibul. During the King's earlier stay in Bangkok, he had been caught in the middle of the Pridi-Pibul push-pull for power, with Pridi regarding him as a nuisance and Marshal Pibul assuming toward him something of the attitude of the tough drill sergeant eying a coddled young recruit. Pridi's precipitate departure after King Ananta Mahidol's murder had removed the real ogre from the scene, but it resulted in the installation of Pibul as a new martinet who might yet turn out to be a monster. The King, however, soon departed for Switzerland, where—on Pibul's suggestion—he shifted from engineering to law as a field of specialization; and on his return to Bangkok in 1950, whether by plan or by instinct, he played it safe. He did not create any issues, and neither did Pibul. In any event, everyone was preoccupied with the state ceremonies, which were the responsibility of the Buddhist clergy and the elders of the royal household. Once the ceremonies were over, the King devoted himself to learning his way around and through the intricacies of the royal court, while Pibul, together with Phao and Sarit, ran the government.

For a period of years King Bhumibol and Queen Sirikit were apparently content to lead a life of royal detachment, appearing in public on state occasions, but devoting themselves mainly to the palace and to their growing family of children. The mere problem of education for the children became a serious one, and the parents concerned themselves actively about it. Basically, they had to decide whether to rely upon palace tutors, or to send the children abroad, or to devise some other arrangement. Like King Mongkut before them, they decided to set up a palace school of their own. To it they invited not only children of the court, but children of commoners as well, including presently, Americans. The school stresses rigorous education in the Thai language in all standard subjects, the study of English and French as foreign languages, plus plenty of "field work." The field work includes trips to government offices and attendance at state occasions. The curriculum includes also plenty of dramatics, dance, and sport. The back quarters of the Chitraladda Palace—a big but rather bleak-looking villa built in the unfortunate "modernistic" style of the 1920's—have been converted into agreeable schoolrooms which serve also as the general area for family relaxation from the rigors of the formal drawing rooms. Near the schoolrooms has now been built a modest swimming pool—the King had re-sisted the idea of a swimming pool for the palace before the city of Bangkok itself was plentifully supplied with piped water. Near the school also are located the tennis courts, where the King and the Queen both play. The palace golf course, however, is now neglected, golf being one of the few sports which the King does not particularly enjoy. He does favor speed-boat racing and water skiing, in addition to the sports of his earlier years.

The King's interest in education extends well beyond the palace school. He goes far beyond the call of royal duty, for instance, in attending each university commencement, listening attentively to the speeches, and personally handing out diplomas to the graduates. He has continued his father's practice of financing promising young men to study medicine abroad. In memory of his father and his brother, he has established the Ananta Mahidol Foundation. Recipients of foundation grants, or other persons par-ticularly qualified in the field of medicine or medical education, gain easy audience with the King and find him eager to talk. Some of those who have returned from abroad are commonly presumed in Bangkok to be on terms of closer personal confidence with the King than are any of the politicians. The King's interest in public health is matched by the Queen's interest in the Red Cross, of which she is not merely the honorary but the active na-tional president. Both the King and the Queen have been prominent in Red Cross disaster-relief projects, as, for instance, during the unusually bad floods in southern Thailand in 1962.

Soon after his coronation, the King began seriously to study the affairs of his country, developing, for one thing, a more than amateurish interest in agriculture and crop diversification. He has converted part of the palace grounds into an experimental garden where, occasionally at least, he actually does work with his hands. He does so partly as a hobby, partly as an example to his subjects who may, he thinks, be impressed by talk about new agricultural techniques if they learn that the King is trying them out.

The King's interest in music seems more enduring and more professional than his gentleman farming. He maintains a palace orchestra which he rehearses regularly, and no foreign visitor to Thailand and to the palace has been more welcome than Benny Goodman, who has performed as guest soloist. A few years ago the King, who is also a composer, wrote songs good enough, with some little readjustment, to be featured in a Broadway show. Concerts by the King's own band are a regular feature of Thai radio broadcasts, and the King at times appears as guest artist with local orchestras during his travels abroad. To date, however, the decision has not been taken whether protocol would permit the King to take the show on the road in his own country.

During the relatively relaxed early years of his reign, the King took the opportunity to discharge the religious obligation, incumbent on the male Buddhist, to spend a few months in study and contemplation in a monastery. He shaved his head, put on the plain saffron robe, disowned all worldly properties, and for six months followed the prescribed rituals. He even went so far as to dispense with his bodyguard. He did not, however, venture out regularly at sun-up with the rest of the monastic community, to allow the public—which might in his case have proved overly importunate—to gain merit by ladling rice and vegetarian curries into the begging bowl.

Gradually the King began to break loose from the virtual confinement of the palace and to meet not only the court and the religious establishment but also the public. Pibul, who had eyed the King in previous years not exactly as a prisoner but more as a fixture of the palace, began gradually to unleash him. Pibul, it seems, decided to popularize the monarchy; not necessarily as a measure to convert the King into a national leader but rather as a measure to build up public support for the King's government, i.e., his own. He relaxed some of the security precautions which had served conveniently as impediments and started the King and the Queen off on a tour of the provinces. They were surrounded with bodyguards, of course, both in uniform and in mufti; their schedule of arrivals, meetings, greetings, and departures was so congested as to challenge human resiliency; frequently they were mounted on elephants high above the heads of the public, which no longer, however, had to avert its eyes as royalty passed.

The royal tour was a great success in stirring public enthusiasm, if to no very clear purpose, and other excursions followed. Once he had dismounted from his elephant, changed his clothes, and shaken his guards, the King sometimes slipped off quietly, not quite like Harun al-Rashid, to wander in the bazaars. Here for the first time he began to encounter his subjects face to face. The King's photograph being thoroughly well known, the subjects almost always recognized him. It is difficult to estimate whether in the early days subject or King was the more abashed by the encounter. Certainly neither proved very articulate. Nevertheless, if mainly by means of press, radio, and public ceremonial occasions, contact began to be established.

The King, then, was gaining both in confidence and in prestige, and Pibul, one can but assume, was led to wonder just what it might be that he had allowed to get started. The newly evolving relationship between the King and Pibul never really clarified itself. Pibul apparently could not quite make the King out. To him the King seemed much too correct and solemn to do anything so rash as to make a bid for power; yet certainly his importance was growing and had to be guarded against at the same time that it could be used. So Pibul continued mildly to encourage the King to humanize himself, and at the same time he took precautions that he should not seem too appealingly human, or, for that matter, too incomparably exalted. Accordingly, Pibul stage-managed events so that on political occasions it was more a matter of the King being also present than of the King presiding. This was a distinction exceedingly difficult to make in the minds of mere onlookers. It was more apparent to the others on the platform, for if Pibul did not exactly seat the King behind the flowers, neither did he seat him under a spotlight. The King, for his part, went along with Pibul's arrangements, but he took to dragging his feet a bit when he wished to emphasize a point. According to the Thai Constitution, the King's signature is necessary to convert any act of Parliament into law. When Marshal Pibul presented him with a paper to sign, the King not infrequently told him he would think it over, which he did sometimes at length, although in the end, of course, he signed.

Pibul was so preoccupied during this period with the latest manifestations of the Thai political crisis that he had, in fact, relatively little time or inclination to think much about the monarchy. He had returned from a trip to the United States and Great Britain fired with enthusiasm for liberal political processes. He suddenly decreed, therefore, that Thailand should have free political parties, a free press, and free speech. He deliberately invited criticism of his regime, especially, as soon became evident, criticism of the performances of General Phao and of General Sarit. Both of them, it seemed, were getting a bit out of hand and were crowding not only each other but also Pibul himself.

Bangkok accepted Pibul's invitation with its accustomed abandon. Pramone Ground became a little Hyde Park where orators made revelations which were little more sensational than the truth with regard to the public and private activities of top officials. The press, which had long entertained itself and its public by fabricating stories about the competition, now found the news itself almost racy enough for its tastes. Marshal Pibul obliged the press, furthermore, by lining his cabinet up in a row at a weekly press conference which sometimes operated according to the general procedure of a Siamese inquisition. When such sessions began to get too hot for Pibul's purposes, inspired newsmen would deliver long hortatory inquiries which left little to be explained and little time to explain it. Politicians began organizing new political parties. The generals began bidding competitively for press and party support. General Sarit—unsportingly, some thought—suddenly withdrew from the bidding, allowed a Pibul-Phao combine to buy reporters, candidates, and voters at marked-down prices, and then suddenly denounced the whole wicked business and much more besides.

Obviously the time had come for a coup, and Sarit staged it.

Rather, he staged two coups. The second was possibly a bit redundant, for Sarit was already in personal if indirect control, and had only to replace a fully complaisant Prime Minister of his own selection whom he had put into office so that he himself could proceed abroad for medical attention. Both coups went off with that practiced Thai efficiency which causes no disruption to city traffic or to office business. One really noteworthy but almost unnoticed feature of the second coup, possibly its *raison d'être,* was that Sarit cut the King in on it. Not that the King was invited to approve or to participate; merely, he was advised in advance what to expect, and was ready, therefore, when the coup came, to announce at once his confidence in the new government.

The King and Sarit, surprisingly, hit it off quite well, but then a great deal about the Sarit regime occasioned surprise. When he came into office as Prime Minister, Sarit had the reputation of being anti-American, possibly even anti-SEATO and anti-West. The reputation was based in large part upon the fact—or was it rumor?—that he was angered because the United States granted major financial support to General Phao's police for projects about which he, Sarit, was unenthusiastic, some of them projects which might give the police an edge over the army in available capital. Sarit turned out, however, to be no less and no more cooperative toward the United States than had been his predecessors.

During the Sarit regime there occurred rather more, perhaps, than the standard number of alarms over Thai-American misunderstandings. One series of crises developed over what Sarit regarded as weak-kneed American policy in Laos, the Thais being convinced that military intervention by SEATO was essential to maintenance of their own security. Other disagreements related to American provision of military assistance to Thailand's Castro—Cambodia's Prince Sihanouk. Notwithstanding his strong convictions about the folly of American policy in Laos and in Cambodia and his recurrent assertions that the United States gave greater aid and comfort to its enemies than to its friends, General Sarit appeared as a relatively reliable American ally in an area where American alliance was becoming increasingly unpopular.

General Sarit's six years as the leading figure in the Thai government came to an end on December 8, 1963, when a long-standing, much medicated and complicated case of cirrhosis of the liver finally caused his death. Had the general been a young, healthy man when he became Prime Minister, his exertions in office would still have seemed phenomenal. For a man with one kidney and a predilection for the bottle, he performed truly prodigious labors. His penchant for clean-up, speed-up, and build-up enabled him to condense about ten years' normal Thai progress into a mere five.

General Sarit's program involved major campaigns—with major American assistance—not only to build up Bangkok, which was already thriving, but to extend development programs into the provinces, where progress had long been stalled and unrest threatened. Under General Sarit, Bangkok suddenly and proudly exhibited wide new avenues, big new urban and suburban building projects, great increase in all public services, even promising little industrial developments. In the remote back country as well roads were being built, and on the newly opened lands excess urban workers were resettled as farmers while urban capitalists started up corn and cattle ranches.

For years the Thais had declined to be serious about land development, crop diversification, and small industries, but suddenly they began to become very serious indeed—quite a few of them becoming very rich in consequence, and nobody more serious or more wealthy than Sarit. According to the economic graphs and charts, Thailand was gathering momentum, and in the city homes and on the farms, where life had always been good by Southeast Asian standards, it was rapidly becoming even better, at least if the incidence of sardines, nylon, transistors, and motorcycles was any criterion. For all of its bustling progress, Thailand was preserving its leisure and its relaxation. Manifestations of popular enthusiasm were still directed chiefly toward temple ceremonies and fairs and sports, not political rallies or riots.

General Sarit's program included spasmodic attempts, with rather less continuity or success, to clean up Bangkok's night life, to deter bankrupts from committing arson in order to collect insurance, even to encourage people to obey sanitary and traffic regulations. The general himself gave the orders for some quick, severe object lessons to prove that he meant business about such small matters as ridding the streets of *samlars* (trishaws); also about such big things as arson and subversion, for which on certain memorable occasions he ordered immediate executions. He also gave the orders, which no doubt gave him peculiar satisfaction, for reform within what had been General Phao's police force, especially for suppression of the opium traffic which, for a series of very generous considerations, Phao's police had not only tolerated but encouraged.

On Sarit's explicit instruction, huge stocks of opium and opium-smoking equipment were collected and destroyed at Pramone Ground in a flaming pyre which rivaled the royal cremations. Opium dealers were closed out or had to resort to such ingenious devices as mobile dens on river boats or in trailer trucks. The international opium syndicate, which flew its product out of Laos into or over Thailand, discovered that Thailand really did mean business about shooting or forcing down its planes.

General Sarit made himself a more popular figure by far than any of his predecessors had been. He showed up indefatigably for fires, floods, and fetes, thereby becoming a mainstay of Thai television, which, when it is not carrying Grade D American westerns and even more deplorable local commercials, is now featuring the national news, much of which Sarit made. He had in fact only two serious rivals for television-viewer interest: the King and the Queen.

General Sarit seemed to have decided that a popular, indeed even a powerful king might be advantageous to the nation and to himself. He removed many of the remaining obstructions, therefore, to the King's freedom of movement, and the King, in turn, foreshortened his periods of study of measures which the government presented to him for signing. General Sarit, furthermore, made such significant gestures as designating the King's birthday a national holiday, focusing attention on the King whenever he appeared in public, and encouraging him to undertake not only more domestic but more international travels. The King and Queen, accordingly, paid state visits to Indonesia, the United States, Western Europe, Malaya, Australia, Japan, and elsewhere, a succession of triumphs in some thirty countries.

The King, whose public manner is still somewhat stiff, has proved in private to be able to impress upon his hosts the fact that he is a well informed and well organized young man, one who views the profession of kingship as an extremely demanding one whose duties he will not shirk. The Queen, who is subjected to sharp scrutiny of her beauty and elegance, manages also to come through as a human being able, like the King, to remember faces, names, and facts, and over all the banalities of protocol to maintain intelligibility—a feat which in itself bespeaks an intellectual capacity far beyond what is expected on state occasions.

Although their prestige shines the brighter at home for success abroad, it is not their social graces which will determine the future position of the King and Queen in their own nation, which, like other nations of Southeast Asia, is undergoing rapid change. It will be the ability to command public exertion more meaningful than mere applause. The King and Queen have still a long way to go before they become truly popular figures in the sense that they can talk directly or indirectly with ordinary people and that ordinary people can talk to them. Indeed, the question is still wide open whether they would or should go that far—if, indeed, it were clear that they could.

The barriers of Thai monarchial ceremony, for all of Anna's claim to have freed King Chulalongkorn from the royal compulsion to make his subjects grovel before him, are still enormously high, thick, and deep. The natural response of subject is still to abase himself, and the natural response of King to subject is still to condescend. The King, who is his own public-relations adviser, is acutely aware of the problem and is proceeding cautiously. The Queen, who needs no consultant, has only to smile. General Sarit seemed to be encouraging both of them to test themselves out, anticipating, possibly, that in the post-Sarit period they might play the critical role he preferred during his own lifetime to reserve for himself.

Thai royalty today, then, is not royalty in the guise of commonality (to use one of King Mongkut's favorite words) as in Sihanouk's Cambodia; nor is it royalty in the role of ornament, as it is in Malaya; nor is it a figurehead, as in Laos. It may just possibly be on the point of becoming royalty in the role which King Mongkut tried to bring up to date, royalty, that is, which actively takes a hand in establishing tradition as well as in maintaining it. Such a development would be an important new departure in Southeast Asia, where in most countries democracy has not worked out very well nor dictatorship any better, but where the monarchial infusion seems, on the basis of the evidence to date, perhaps to be an asset rather than a liability. Malaysia looks sound, Cambodia at least looks active, and Thailand has got on notably well. It seems almost reactionary on the part of any Occidental observer to hope or even to think that there is much chance, but barring too many coups—a massive proviso—King Bhumibol of Thailand may succeed in finding a distinctive new monarchical *modus vivendi* in the troubled Southeast Asian world.

Postscript: Excising the Occult from the Cult of Charisma

The man of charisma—the leader possessed of a mystical rapport with his nation and thus, it seems, with destiny—is the man of the century in the Asian tropics. In each new state, one single charismatic figure is the archetype and three or four others are the parallel prototypes, these human types deriving from and contributing to the emerging stereotype of the nation itself. The man of charisma, characteristically, is a public figure of compelling personality, capable of mesmerizing his followers by projecting a radiant public image on which the creeping corrosion is concealed by artfully arranged floodlights. He is likely also to be an oracular politician, propounding a message of nationalism, revolution, and independence to a nascent people which aspires to become a power. Although the components of charisma originally include major elements of nationalist inspiration, the ultimate manifestation is all too likely to be charlatanry and chauvinism. The twentieth-century messiah then becomes a demagogue; his idealistic apostles become cynical and corrupt; his once hopeful new state deteriorates into apathy or adopts the reckless devices of desperation. There are those, nevertheless, whom charisma genuinely becomes, as well as those whom it dangerously bemuses, the beneficial effects occurring in reverse ratio to the degree and the duration of autointoxication. The biographic sketches which make up this book constitute in fact comparative studies in charisma, which Webster defines as a "gift of the gods" without mentioning that it can readily become a curse.

This is the era, then, of President Sukarno, who has both

wrought and wrecked the irresponsibly emotional Indonesian colossus, and of Prince Sihanouk, who has aroused lethargic little Cambodia to a sustained if often feckless exhilaration. It is also, fortunately, an era which can put forward a Tengku Abdul Rahman, Malaysia's maverick, a gentleman too unaffected to be hypnotic, too reasonable—indeed, too indolent—to manufacture a mystique, one who wears the cloak of charisma flung rather carelessly over his tropical worsteds. Sukarno and Abdul Rahman represent respectively the feverish and the rational range on the scale of charismatic possession; their nations, correspondingly, represent the retrogressive and the progressive forces of Southeast Asia, although Sukarno, of course, vigorously argues the reverse of the proposition. The Sukarno-Rahman, Indonesia-Malaysia contrast suggests that by calibrating the exact degree of charismatic self-hypnosis on the part of the national leader, one can make a fairly safe prediction regarding the degree of progress and prosperity of his nation. In any event, whoever would know Indonesia must know Bung Karno, just as whoever would know Malaysia must know the Tengku. Ideally, the acquaintance should neither start nor end just there, but if it does, the misconceptions will be far less profound than if it should begin or end almost anywhere else.

The cult of charisma, then, both simplifies and complicates the problem of anyone who would seek to comprehend the charade of contemporary Southeast Asia, where history is not infrequently histrionics. The Tengku and the Bung and other leading figures are not only the archetypes but also the architects of their nations. Their personal histories, therefore, seem almost identical with national history. Their personal fortunes become national triumphs or disasters, although it may be difficult at times to distinguish exactly which. The late Ngo Dinh Diem's personal tragedy, for instance, seemed at the time to be South Vietnam's reprieve from destruction. The very mention of Ngo Dinh Diem, however, constitutes a caveat against the categorical. Ngo Dinh Diem once seemed to be Vietnam's male Cassandra, later its Jeanne d'Arc, ultimately its Pandora, and South Vietnam is not the only nation in Southeast Asia where fate is both vengeful and ironic, where reversals are themselves reversible, and definitive history, like biography, will be some little time in the writing.

Iconolatry being one consequence of charisma, these Men of Destiny are liable to being enshrined, while they still frequent the television screen more naturally than the history books, as sacred symbols of the national verity. Since iconolatry generally climaxes in iconoclasm and these particular national heroes are all too intimately known to their own immediate posterity, the plastic halo proves anything but shatterproof; but then, too, the cloven hoof is also at times exposed as a fake. The disparity between the aging, Dorian Gray-like Bung Karno of 1963 and his persisting image as the dynamic, magnetic Bung Karno of 1927 is one which cannot be ignored by anyone who wishes to understand, to sympathize, indeed to empathize with present-day Indonesia, which, thanks to Bung Karno, is in a state so wretched as to inspire pity, and along with pity, fear. The image of the volatile Prince Sihanouk, by contrast, gains validity with the passage of years, save that the Prince, who bills himself as a political saxophonist, contrives well in advance of the concert to collect his own admissions at scalpers' prices for what seems in fact like international light opera. Even Malaysia's Tengku Abdul Rahman, who is generally represented as being neither very bright nor very brash but just thoroughly honest—even the Tengku is not quite what he seems. So atypically "underdeveloped" that he regards a British colonialist as a good sport, so urbane that he considers a whiskey-soda a soft drink, the Tengku sometimes gets away with political mayhem by first blinding his victim with the floodlighted image of himself as the gullible innocent.

The founding fathers of the infant equatorial nations of Asia are no more saintly or scoundrelly a lot of national leaders than can be assembled on any other continent. Whatever their shortcomings, they are at least good theater. They are men of audacity if not always of judgment, some of them more given to idiosyncrasy than integrity, to ingenuity than to industry. Above all else, they are pragmatic politicians. They are no ignorant Lumumbas catapulted out of obscurity into oblivion through one brief flash of notoriety. For the most part they are men of considerable intellectual attainment, now middle-aged-to-aging after long years of national and international prominence. They simultaneously inspire and reflect the compulsive drive of their peoples right here and now to become great, rich, powerful, and therefore, it is assumed, both happy and free. Great expectations such as these inspire extraordinary devices. The sometimes foundering founding fathers are impelled, therefore, in building nations out of materials which would dismay persons of greater circumspection, to attempt at times to tranquilize with violence, at others to stimulate with sedatives.

The role of nation builder is infinitely more difficult in 1964 than it was in 1649, and the difficulties are not diminished by the fact that the new nation builders are indeed men of their age. For all their charismatic luster, they frequently seem, if seen or heard at all clearly, like men of mediocre stature, obscure principles, confused vision, and blemished achievement, and few of them seek the silent shadows. Our own founding fathers lived in ruder times, when oratory was mercifully muffled, not amplified, in intercontinental transmission and shots heard round the world carried no atomic fall-out. They were spared the state visit, the press conference, the simultaneous translation, the radio-TV coverage and similar twentieth-century ordeals. Such obligatory penance for prominence can magnify human frailty by taxing human endurance and diminish the appearance of greatness, let alone of grandeur. The new leaders of the newly emerging nations, then, face an omnipresent world audience whose demands are fantastically exacting. If they sometimes exhibit symptoms of megalomania, hypochondria or xenophobia, they are by no means incapacitated thereby from moving with their peers in either the Western or the Eastern world. They are the stuff that world politics is made on, also Italian opera, Shakespearean history, Greek tragedy, and Hollywood spectaculars. As men of charisma determined speedily to remodel the century in which they live, they may be working from a design which has not yet been revealed even to themselves, and their labors may seem chaotic, but the ultimate effect may nevertheless prove to be heroic.

Selected Bibliography

In preparation of this book, the author has consulted virtually all of the significant books on Southeast Asia written in the past two decades and a very large body of periodical literature as well. The following have proved particularly helpful for biographic purposes—a highly select list of books and articles written for the most part by Southeast Asians themselves or by Westerners who are personally well acquainted with the men about whom they are writing.

Abdul Aziz bin Ishak, Wan King Cheong, and Tan Kah Jee. *The Architect of Merdeka: Tengku Abdul Rahman.* Singapore: Tan Kan Jee, 1957.

L'Action de S.M. Norodom Sihanouk pour l'Indépendence du Cambodge, 1941–1955. Preface by S. E. Samdech Penn Nouth. Phnom-Penh, n.d.

Alamsjah, St. Rais. *Bung Karno Dihukum 4 Tahun.* Bandung: E. M. Dachlan, 1954.

Alamsjah, St. Rais. *10 Orang Indonesia Terbesar Sekrang.* Djakarta: Mutiara, 1952.

Berrigan, Darrell. "Thailand: New Cast, Same Play," *The Reporter,* XVII (Nov. 28, 1957), 12–14.

Biographie de S.A.R. Le Prince Norodom Sihanouk, Chef d'Etat du Cambodge. Phnom-Penh: Royaume de Cambodge, n.d.

Chakrabongse, Prince Chula. *Lords of Life: The Paternal Monarchy of Bangkok, 1782–1932.* New York: Taplinger Publishing Company, 1960.

Champassak, Sisouk Na. *Storm Over Laos: A Contemporary History,* New York: Praeger, 1961.

Conférence de Samdech Preah Norodom Sihanouk Upayuvareach Président du conseil des Ministres. Faite à La Fondation du Cambodge à Paris, le 17 Mai, 1959. Phnom-Penh: Imprimerie du Ministère de l'Information, n.d.

Facts on His Majesty the King. His Majesty's Private Secretariat, Bangkok, August 17, 1961.

Gwekoh, Sol H. *Diosdado Macapagal: Triumph Over Poverty.* Manila: G. & G. Enterprises, 1962.

Herz, Mertin Florian. *A Short History of Cambodia from the Days of Angkor to the Present.* London: Stevens, 1958.

Is Trust Vindicated? A Chronicle of the Various Accomplishments of the Government Headed by General Ne Win During the Period of Tenure from November 1958 to February 6, 1960. Rangoon: Department of Broadcasting, 1960.

Macapagal, Diosdado. *The Common Man: Speeches by Vice-President Diosdado Macapagal.* Compiled by Vincente G. Martinez. Manila, n.d. (Includes an excellent biography by Leon O. Ty, reprinted from the *Philippines Free Press.*)

Maung Maung, ed. *Aung San of Burma.* Introduction by Harry J. Benda. The Hague: Published for Yale University Southeast Asia Studies by M. Nijhoff, 1962.

Miller, Harry. *Prince and Premier.* London: George G. Harrap and Co., 1959.

Nasution, M. Yunan. *Riwajat Ringkas Penghidupan dan Perdjuangan "Ir. Sukarno."* Djakarta: Pustaka "Aida," 1951.

Norodom Sihanouk. *Le Cambodge et Ses Relations avec Ses Voisins.* Edité par le Ministère de l'Information. Phnom-Penh, n.d.

Nu, U. *Burma Under the Japanese: Pictures and Portraits.* Edited and translated with introduction by J. S. Furnivall. London: Macmillan, 1954.

President Ngo Dinh Diem. Saigon: Presidency of the Republic of Vietnam, August 1957.

President Ngo Dinh Diem on Democracy: Addresses Relative to the Constitution. Saigon: Presidency of the Republic of Vietnam, February 1958.

Quijano de Manila. "The Man and the Myths," *Philippines Free Press,* LVI, No. 1 (Jan. 5, 1963), 3 ff. (Other Quijano de Manila articles on Macapagal in the *Philippines Free Press* are also excellent.)

Shaplen, Robert. "Reporter in Vietnam," *New Yorker,* XXXVIII (Sept. 22, 1962), 103–104 ff.

Sukarno. *Toward Freedom and the Dignity of Man: A Collection of Five Speeches.* Djakarta: Department of Foreign Affairs, 1961.

Tinker, Hugh. "Nu, the Serene Statesman," *Pacific Affairs,* XXX (June, 1957), 130–137.

Tunku Abdul Rahman Putra Al-Haj: Prime Minister, Federation of Malaya. Kuala Lumpur: Department of Information, 1963.

Index